"This is the story of a journey that took seven years and the loss of everything I had. What I learned along the way is that maybe the answer to grief, or to feeling lost, is to give recklessly and passionately. It is in those acts of giving that you become open to receive life's most tremendous blessings."

ACCLAIM FOR

JANTSEN'S GIFT

"[A] skillfully written account of finding hope after grief."
—*Kirkus Reviews*

"Inspiring...beautifully told...It's a powerful story, and I defy anyone to read it without shedding a few tears."
—*Buffalo News*

"Relevant, moving, and thoroughly engaging...This ground-breaking book is destined to change many hearts and minds around the world."
—*Arkansas Democrat Gazette*

"A profound reminder of what a difference one person can make in the world."
—*Washington Parent*

"A wonderful story of a woman whose personal tragedy gave birth to a gift and how she fulfilled that legacy to make the world a better place."
—*Publishers Weekly*

Jantsen's Gift

Jantsen's Gift

Jantsen's Gift

A True Story of Grief, Rescue, and Grace

Pam Cope

with Aimee Molloy

GRAND CENTRAL
PUBLISHING

NEW YORK   •   BOSTON

Copyright © 2009 by Pam Cope
Afterword Copyright © 2011 by Pam Cope
Reading Group Guide Copyright © 2011 by Hachette Book Group

Grand Central Publishing
Hachette Book Group
1290 Avenue of the Americas,
New York, NY 10104

www.HachetteBookGroup.com

Printed in the United States of America

Originally published in hardcover by Grand Central Publishing.

First Trade Edition: August 2011

10 9 8 7 6 5 4 3 2

Grand Central Publishing is a division of Hachette Book Group, Inc.
The Grand Central Publishing name and logo is a trademark of
Hachette Book Group, Inc.

The Library of Congress has cataloged the hardcover edition as follows:

Cope, Pam.
    Jantsen's gift: a true story of grief, rescue, and grace / Pam Cope
with Aimee Molloy.—1st ed.
        p. cm.
    ISBN 978-0-446-19969-8
    1. Cope, Pam. 2. Child welfare workers—Biography. 3. Child
welfare—Case studies. 4. Social work with children. I. Molloy,
Aimee. II. Title.
    HV713.C667 2009
    362.7092—dc22
    [B]

                                              2008035511

ISBN 978-0-446-19970-4 (pbk.)

To the boy we left behind in Atigangome Kope,
and the hundreds of thousands of other children like him,
whose names we've not yet learned.

Acknowledgments

Writing a book is truly a collective effort. I will never take credit for writing this book. Without Aimee Molloy's collaborative spirit and creative mind, this book would not be half of what it became. Not only was I blessed with an amazing writer but there's no one else with whom I would rather have shared this journey, from the streets of Saigon to the back roads of West Africa.

Jamie Raab, thank you for wanting to publish my story and also for editing the manuscript. With your gifts and talents it was fine-tuned and you were able to push us all to make this book something I will always be proud of. Thank you, Dennis, for sharing your wife during a crisis in your personal life. Jamie you are a great example of courage and endurance.

Thank you to Heather Schroeder at ICM for acting on your gut instinct while reading *The New York Times* on the train one morning. You made this happen and fought for this book you believed in.

My hat goes off to *New York Times* reporters Sharon LaFraniere and João Silva for doing their job. Thank you for climbing into that carved-out canoe on Lake Volta and standing in the gap for these children who do not have a voice. Your journalism and photography will forever change the lives of children in Ghana and around the world.

Thank you George Achibra and Fred Asare, who love their country and believe in Ghana. These two men believe in education and have laid their lives down for the least among us day after day by opening their homes to orphaned children and leading by example of how we should serve children in crisis.

I'd like to thank Dana and Marilyn Daniels, whose monthly support in the beginning provided the shot of encouragement we needed to keep going.

I cannot go without thanking my wonderful husband Randy. Without you I would not be the half-sane woman I am today. I love you most because you have such a Daddy's heart and have loved each one of your children to the very core of their being. Thank you for not giving up on me.

Last, and most importantly, I want to thank my creator and Heavenly Father. Thank you, God, for sustaining me and encouraging me to put one foot in front of the other when my life was so dark and hopeless.

—Pam Cope

Any writer would fail to find the words sufficient to express how grateful I am to Pam, for sharing this story with me, and everything else she's given to me during this process. And thanks to Randy, for sharing his wife, his insights, his support, and his amazing sense of humor.

Thanks to Jamie Raab for making a great story into a great book and to Sara Weiss and Laura Jorstad for their dedication and hard work. Special thanks to Kris Dahl at ICM for suggesting this project to me, and for all her support.

And thanks to Patrick, Abby, Ryan, Brigid, Mary, Kevin,

and Caite, for reminding me why it's so important to tell stories like this; to Mark and Megan, for their support during this process, in more ways than one; to Bob and, especially, to Moira, for traveling to the far ends of the world to share this journey with me; and, of course, to my mom and dad, who've taught me the real meaning of what it means to come home. And, now, most of all, to my husband, Mark, for being the best addition to this part of the book, and the best thing that's happened to me.

—Aimee Molloy

Jantsen's Gift

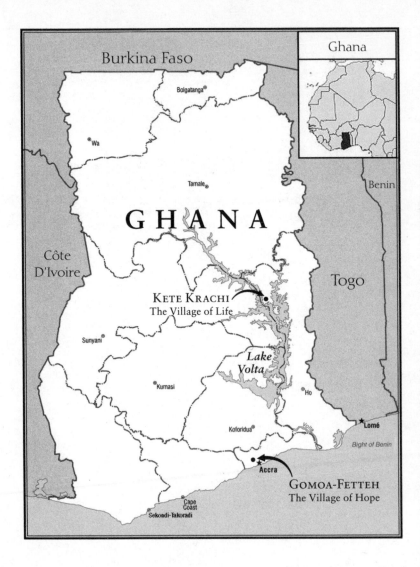

Burkina Faso

Ghana

Bolgatanga

Wa

Benin

Tamale

GHANA

Côte
D'Ivoire

Togo

KETE KRACHI
The Village of Life

Sunyani

Lake
Volta

Kumasi

Ho

Koforidua

Lomé

Bight of Benin

Accra

GOMOA-FETTEH
The Village of Hope

Cape
Coast

Sekondi-Takoradi

Introduction

I n late October 2006, I was sitting on a bed in a Hilton Hotel room, high above Times Square. My husband, Randy, and I had decided to take a last-minute vacation to New York City to see *Mamma Mia!* with our friends, and it had been a great weekend filled with long meals, lazy naps, and one annoying show tune that I just could not get out of my head. That Sunday morning, Randy had gone out for a walk, and as I rested my book on my lap and watched the cream form volcano clouds in my coffee, I drank in the stillness of the room. With two eight-year-old children at home, quiet, undisturbed moments like this were far too rare. But the tranquility I felt at that moment was about to be shattered as Randy rushed through the door, holding a copy of *The New York Times*.

"Put that book down," he said, "you've got to read this." As I took the paper from him, I saw the photograph on the front page: a tiny African boy, standing in the shadows of what looked like a mud hut. He wore an adult-size T-shirt printed with an image of the Little Mermaid. The shirt swallowed him whole: The collar was so worn and stretched, it hung down near his navel, revealing the bones in his chest and scars on his skin. Its hem nearly touched the floor, making it appear as if he were wearing a dress. But it was the haunted look in his eyes that truly seized me.

I took my time and read the article slowly. When I finished, I got up from the bed and walked to the window, which glowed orange and pink from the lights off Times Square. A soft rain was falling outside, and I watched the thousands of people milling about under dark umbrellas dozens of stories below me.

Mark Kwadwo, the boy in the photograph, was a six-year-old slave. He lived in Ghana, West Africa, and his parents had sold him to a man who fished Lake Volta, the country's largest lake. He was forced to work on the lake fourteen hours a day, seven days a week, beside hundreds of other boys like him. His typical day began around 5 AM, when the man he called Master woke him by hitting him with a branch torn from a nearby tree. Then, wrapped in a thin bedsheet to keep warm, he hiked barefoot in the darkness to the cold waters of the lake, climbed into a canoe, and helped paddle to the nets that had been laid the previous evening. The older slave children on his boat, stripped naked to make their work easier, dove in to pull up the catch while Mark used a sawed-off cooking container to scoop out the water that slowly pooled on the floor of the leaky canoe. He did it not only because it was his job, and he'd be beaten for failing or refusing, but also because he was afraid. He had never been taught to swim, and if the boat sank, he'd likely end up like other boys he'd seen—the ones who descended into the black waters, got trapped in the nets, and never resurfaced.

Mark's master had paid Mark's parents the equivalent of about twenty dollars a year for this work, and he was one of five children they had sold into servitude. Two of his siblings worked in the same village: His eleven-year-old brother Kofi fished with him, and his nine-year-old sister Hagar was a domestic servant, helping to raise the master's children and clean the fish for market. The last time Mark saw his mother was the day she told him a man was coming to take him to visit his father. Instead he'd been brought to this village and showed what was to be his new home for the next several years: a dark six-foot-square hut with a single tiny window. He would share it with four other boys.

I slipped the newspaper into my carry-on bag. Randy and I had to get ready to go. We had to gather our things to head downstairs to meet our friends for breakfast before checking out of the hotel, but I had trouble getting myself together. At breakfast, I could barely eat. Making circles in my yogurt, I could not stop thinking about Mark. He was not much younger than Van and Tatum, my two youngest children, and the idea of them having to endure such a life . . . it was unthinkable. I asked the others if they knew exactly where Ghana was, but nobody did.

Later that evening, after Randy and I had arrived home and put Van and Tatum to bed, I read the article again. The photographer, João Silva, had captured something extraordinary. It wasn't only the details of Mark's surroundings, or his Little Mermaid T-shirt, or his bony frame; it was the question in his eyes. They seemed to ask: *Now that you know about me, and what I'm made to do, what are you going to do? Just turn and walk away?*

I put the paper down and went downstairs to the little office I had set up around the toys and laundry, and I got on the Internet. I didn't know Africa at all. As I looked at a map of the continent, I imagined the conversation of someone trying to describe to me where Ghana fell geographically.

It's west of Togo.

Really? Where's that?

Next to Benin.

Where's that?

South of Burkina Faso.

There's a country called Burkina Faso?

Here's how the location of Ghana should be described: It's on the western stump of Africa, sort of where the armpit would be if you pictured the continent as the torso of a one-armed man with no legs and no head. Which, at nearly midnight that night, was sort of how it looked to me.

The country is no bigger than Oregon, and compared with many West African nations it is relatively well off. Lake Volta, which covers nearly three thousand square miles, is one of the largest human-made lakes in the world; it was created in 1965 in order to generate hydroelectric power for the nation. I studied the layout of the country, looking for Aboadzi, the town where Mark's parents lived, and tried to measure how far it was from Lake Volta. And then I started to read about child trafficking in Ghana.

According to the United Nations, of the nearly 1.2 million children worldwide sold into servitude each year, Africa's children make up nearly one-sixth. It's estimated that one of every four children in Ghana has been sold into slavery, a majority of whom work in the fishing industry. Like Mark, the children sold to a fisherman are made to work long hours under severe and hazardous conditions, and are deprived of an education. Many of the fishermen were once child slaves themselves and have endured what they now bestow: backbreaking work, severe beatings, and a life of fear. Parents who sell their children reportedly believe that doing so is the best chance their child has at a better life, and while they are sorry for what their children are made to suffer, they cannot survive without the money the fishermen pay; the fishermen, in turn, cannot survive without the children's help. Though young kids like Mark are not the ideal sort of worker—too small to do the bigger jobs, unable to swim, always afraid—they are cheaper than older boys and therefore often chosen first.

Just a year earlier, in December 2005, the Ghanaian government had passed the Human Trafficking Act, making these activities illegal. But without adequate resources to enforce the law, it was considered completely ineffective. In fact, in the year since the law had been passed, not one arrest had been made.

Back in bed, I couldn't get the image of Mark out of my head. Thousands of people had to have read that article, I thought, and surely somebody would step in and try to help him. Now, there was certainly a time in my life when I would have easily decided that that someone could not be *me*. No, courageous acts were reserved only for certain people: the rich, the educated, the type who knew where Ghana was without having to consult a map. After all, I was just a forty-four-year-old mother of four, a homemaker, a former hairdresser in Neosho, Missouri, who'd never been to college. Help a child like Mark Kwadwo, a stranger who lived in what seemed like one of the most remote places on earth? No way.

Nine weeks later, I was on a plane to Ghana.

———

It was, however, a journey that took seven years, and the loss of everything I once had, that gave me the courage to go.

Chapter One

When I was younger, I never would have believed anyone who told me that I'd one day be rescuing child slaves in West Africa—or for that matter, take into my care more than two hundred former street children in Vietnam, or travel to a remote jungle area to find a legless baby whose parents had tried to kill her in a family suicide pact, or visit a brothel for teenage prostitutes in Phnom Penh, Cambodia. For most of my adult life, my idea of "travel" typically entailed the drive to Target or to visit my parents, who lived a good five minutes away, in the house where I grew up in Neosho.

When I arrived in Ghana, I loved it immediately. I had no idea what to expect, but I found a beautiful country and people whose idea of hospitality would put Martha Stewart to shame, and who fiercely revered the idea of hard work. The thing I was most surprised to find, however, was something I never expected: a greater understanding of myself. There's one Ghanaian tradition that I particularly love. Whenever any two people meet for the first time, they share two things: *This is where I've been, and this is my mission moving forward.* While I do not believe that this story is about me as much as it is about the people—the children especially—I've met, and who helped lead me out of a depression as dark as death, in keeping with the Ghanaian tradition I suppose there are a few things you should know about me before we get to them.

My parents met in Bangor, Maine, where my mom grew up and my dad was stationed with the US Air Force. They got married a few months after my mom graduated from high school, and the first time my father brought my mother home to Missouri to meet her future in-laws, Grandma VanDorn was in the chicken coop, beheading that evening's dinner.

By the time my mom was twenty-five years old, she had five kids under the age of five: Cheryl, Ralph, Kim, and my twin sister Tam and me (yes, we were really twins named Pam and Tam). After I became a parent, I was amazed at how easy my mother had always made everything seem. Every day, while my dad was at work at his job as an aircraft mechanic, she would fix us breakfast, load us into the brown Plymouth, and cart us to the grocery store, or the town pool, or the hairdresser, where we flipped through our picture books and tried to catch the more juicy snippets of conversation from the next room, where the woman cut our mother's thick black hair into the latest style. As we got older, our house became the place where the neighborhood kids gathered, and my mom always made them feel welcome. Maybe she was trying to create for us what she had always wanted herself as a child. Her dad, Grandpa Durant, had a serious love affair with alcohol of all kinds and worked the night shift on the railroad, which meant he slept during the day. My mom and her four siblings were never allowed to bring their friends home. They had to spend their afternoons tiptoeing around so as not to wake him—and possibly send him into a rage that could quickly erupt into violence, sometimes against his own wife. Grammy Durant made up for Grandpa with her love and kindness.

My house growing up was nothing like that. It was one of the safest places I'd ever know. My siblings and I were instilled with my father's Midwestern sense of family and hard work, and my mother's Northeastern grit and humor. On most Sundays, we'd go out to my grandparents' farm on several acres of rolling pastureland cut in two by a gentle creek. There, with my father's eight siblings and their kids, we'd each be given a job, though it rarely felt like one: picking potatoes from the huge garden for our grandmother; brushing Topper, my grandfather's horse; baling hay, which left itchy scratches on our hands and arms. My favorite time was Butcher Day, when my dad and uncles would slaughter the pigs they spent all year plumping up. They'd divide up the meat for each family, wrapping it in thick white paper. When they were done, my cousins and I would scramble up the tractor and lie down on the packages, spreading our arms and legs to keep them from falling off.

When I was a sophomore in high school, just sixteen years old, I met my first—and last—boyfriend. Randy Cope was a year older than me. He was the guy the other boys wanted on their team, and the girls wanted to date. The first time I met him, he was dating my best friend Rhonda Crumbliss. For some reason, I found myself accompanying them on a date to the movies one evening. Sitting behind them—thinking that would give them some privacy, I suppose—I could barely see the screen, obstructed as it was by the two of them kissing. In the beginning, I didn't see what all the fuss was about, but eventually, after they broke up, I started to pay more attention to Randy. I'd notice him driving to school in his orange jeep, or see him down at the creek on Saturday nights, where my friends and I gathered to drink Boone's Farm wine and smoke cigarettes. He had such an easy, natural way with people, which I admired, and it didn't hurt that he wore the coolest silk shirts (this was, after all, the era of *Saturday Night Fever*). Eventually I decided that my friends were right: He *was* better looking than John Travolta. During my sophomore year, we had classes near each other, and I began to carefully position myself in the hallway just when I saw him coming. I'd walk a few steps ahead of him, hoping he was lusting after me from behind. It worked. A few weeks later, he asked me on a date.

The first time Randy invited me to his house for dinner, and to meet his parents, I was absolutely panic-stricken. The Copes were a prominent local family—his dad owned the local newspaper—and while I adored my own family and always felt pride in them, I wasn't sure I could measure up here. I was just some young punk girl with a smart mouth who played sports like a boy and, I'm sure they thought, was the party responsible for the empty bottle of wine discovered under the front seat of his mom's car the previous weekend. That evening, driving up the winding driveway toward their big house with the sprawling, manicured lawn, I had to steel myself. Over dinner, I tried to make small talk and pretended I knew exactly how to eat the fondue his mother served, despite the fact that I had never seen anything like it before. (Seriously, meat and cheese *on sticks?*) Randy and I passed awkward glances to each other all evening. When the meal was over and his parents ushered me toward the door, all I felt was an enormous sense of relief for not blowing it.

If fondue wasn't daunting enough, imagine how I felt a few months later when Randy suggested that I come to church with his family. They were very serious members of a local Christian church. My family, on the other hand, did not go to church— something that in southwest Missouri often felt as outrageous as admitting we didn't wear clothes in our home, or were planning on joining the circus. But now that Randy and I were becoming more serious, it was important to his parents that I become more church-like. I agreed. That first Sunday, wearing the nicest dress I could find in my sister's closet, I walked through the big wooden doors and into their world. It was a large church—with a capacity of about five hundred—and about half full. Settling in next to Randy, I looked around with a forced smile on my face, nodding hello to people as if I had been doing this same exact thing every Sunday for my whole life. I wasn't here because my boyfriend went to this church, my smile conveyed, I *belonged* here.

Of course, I knew that wasn't true, and as the minister preached and the people around me prayed with such conviction, I figured everyone else there knew it, too. I was not one of them: a holy, good, Lord-fearing person. No, I was just another sixteen-year-old girl who had come along merely because she was pathetically in love with her boyfriend.

Either way, I succeeded at winning them all over, and the summer before his senior year in college, Randy and I got married in a ceremony in his parents' front yard. I was twenty years old and had recently graduated from cosmetology school, having decided long ago that I was not college material. Even if I had considered myself "smart"—which I certainly didn't—my parents never could have afforded the tuition, and I decided to make a living out of what had been a hobby in high school: cutting my friends' hair into Farrah Fawcett wings and layers and, when Rave perms became popular, lovingly wrapping their burning scalps in plastic.

Our wedding ceremony was very beautiful, though by today's standards probably a little cheesy. We were broke at the time, and everyone I knew pitched in to help. Randy's brother Mike, who had recently become a minister, married us, and my sister Cheryl's new husband, Mark, played Henry Mancini on the trumpet. We'd borrowed chairs from the town recreation center, and as I walked down the driveway on my father's arm, all I could see were the words NEOSHO REC DEPT written over and over in sloppy black marker. Afterward, we had punch and cake by the pool. My friends from cosmetology school were the servers. I had chosen little white aprons with black trim for them, thinking they would look like classy waitresses. What they looked like were pole dancers.

But I loved everything about that day. We soon settled into a small house in Neosho and, with Randy still in college, lived largely on love. Two years after we were married, our son Jantsen was born. I enjoyed being pregnant, if for no other reason than the excuse it offered to eat whatever I wanted, and as much of it as I could. The delivery, however, was an excruciating experience that nearly killed both of us. As soon as the doctor pulled him from me, after a last-minute emergency C-section, it was evident that something was very wrong. Jantsen's skin was blue, and he was having trouble breathing. As the doctor and nurses worked to keep him alive, Randy heard one of them whisper, "This baby looks like he's been overdosed." Maybe it's better that I didn't hear this myself, as I'm sure the last thing anyone needed at the moment was me screaming like a madwoman. Instead, I was focused on the searing pain I felt running down my arm, before the room went black. When I finally woke up (the doctors didn't know what exactly had happened to me, but my blood pressure had plummeted), Randy was standing beside me with a look of horror in his eyes. Jantsen was in intensive care, still unable to breathe on his own. The nurse wheeled me into the ICU, and when I saw him there, tied up in tubes in a hospital's white bassinet, I thought my heart was going to break. Later that night, after having to leave him there alone, Randy and I pushed around food we could barely eat and talked about it: No matter what, even if he was brain-damaged or had any sort of medical problems, we were going to make sure he got home, where we'd take care of him and love him to the bone.

Everything turned out fine, at least this time. Eleven days later, he made a full recovery, and other than suffering from asthma he was a healthy, spunky, and easy child. Being his mom brought me great joy. Two of my sisters had children around the same time, my nephew Darius and my niece Gregan, both of them C-sections like mine. As soon as my mom got one of us home and on our feet, she was back at the hospital, doing it again. Every day, we'd get together to swim or go to the park and then grill dinner in one of our backyards. Jantsen, Darius, and Gregan spent so much time together, they seemed more like siblings than cousins.

It wasn't long before we were ready for another child. Our doctor had advised us that because of the problems we'd experienced with Jantsen's birth, it was too risky to try another delivery, and Randy and I began to discuss adopting. The idea was equal parts scary and exciting. Randy's parents had adopted his younger sister Brenda, and while everyone loved her to pieces, she had been severely abused until she was two, before the Copes brought her home, and had suffered a lot because of it. Randy knew far too well the difficulties a whole family can face in a situation like that.

I was plagued by questions of my own. Can you love someone else's child as much as one you gave birth to? Would I prefer Jantsen to this child, screwing her up completely? It made me extremely nervous to think there was a social worker somewhere who was going to choose a baby for us, quite randomly: *Okay, this one is yours. Good luck!*

We talked about it for a long time, and in the end we realized what we had known all along: A family is about much more than biology and genetics. In 1987, when Jantsen was three, we filed our papers with an adoption agency in St. Louis.

Anyone who has ever tried to adopt a child knows how challenging it can be. The paperwork seems endless. The interviews force you to consider who you are not only as a parent, but as a person. Were we open to an interracial child? What about one with medical problems? I knew, most of all, that I wanted a newborn girl, and that was what we applied for, but I felt guilty about it at the time, like I was special-ordering a child from a catalog.

I'd like the jersey sheets, the white dinner plates, and a newborn girl. Something exotic looking if you have it.

Afterward, the only thing left to do was wait. And wait. Finally, a little more than a year later, we heard from the adoption agency. It was ten o'clock on a Thursday night, and the caseworker called to tell us our little girl, who was eight weeks old, was waiting for us; we needed to be in St. Louis, which was a five-hour drive away, the next morning. I spent hours on the phone with our family and friends while throwing our clothes and Jantsen's toys into a large duffel bag. In the morning, after Randy got home from passing out cigars to everyone we knew, we went to get our daughter.

Her birth mother was in the military and had gotten pregnant at twenty-one by a man she had known only a few months. They had split up, and she doubted her ability to raise a child on her military salary. Having grown up herself a child of divorce, she wanted her daughter to be raised by two parents, in a stable, loving home. We were sitting in the waiting room with Jantsen, who worked on a coloring book at our feet, when the caseworker brought her in. She was the tiniest little thing, with a full head of jet-black hair sticking straight up in every direction. She was wearing a one-piece velour pink jumper and looking around quietly, so cute and divine . . .

Until they handed her to me.

As soon as I took her, Crista Marie Cope made clear what

would be the dynamic of our relationship through the years: Of the two of us, *she'd* be the one calling the shots. She started screaming bloody murder and I could not believe the lungs on this child. I walked her around the room. I tried rocking her. I sang softly in her ear. She would not stop screaming.

I looked at Randy. "Do you think they gave us the wrong one?" I whispered.

Taking her out of that building was such a bizarre experience. I couldn't believe that they were going to allow us to bring this baby home with us and be in charge, like, *forever*. That night in the hotel room, Jantsen stayed near Crista's side until he fell asleep. He stared at her, and kept rubbing her head, saying to us: "Her hair is kinda wumpy lumpy."

As Randy and I sat on the bed watching the two of them try to figure each other out, I felt awed by this gift we had been given and knew that they were feeling exactly what we were: This baby was meant for our family. She was perfect.

If we had been friends during those years when my children were young, I probably would have had you convinced that I was one of those people who had it all. You know the type—the woman with the nice house and the right clothes, the well-behaved children and the loving husband. I worked hard to put forth that image, maybe because I had been taught that being a wife and a mother was the most important, meaningful thing I could do. When I was a young girl, I didn't dream about being a doctor or a teacher or an astronaut. I dreamed of being a wife and mother. And that's not to say that I wasn't happy in these respects. While I did, of course, have my fair share of annoying, way-too-frazzled moments, I loved being a mom. Randy's job as the publisher of the *Neosho Daily News* allowed me to stay home with Jantsen and Crista when they were little, and I found them to be amazing, funny, well-adjusted kids. After they started school, my sister Tam and I opened a small hair salon in town—A Cut Above!—which we decorated in deep mauves and floral wallpaper. I worked there a few days a week for extra spending money. And my marriage just got better each year. Even after eleven years together, whenever we weren't busy hating each other, Randy and I really were in love.

In 1995, Randy took a job with a publishing company in Fayetteville, Arkansas, and I was excited about the idea of moving out of Neosho for the first time in my life. The new job was quite a step up for him, and we were able to buy a nice house and a new car. I spent weeks decorating our new home, searching for the perfect school for the kids, and getting us settled. We made friends quickly, and on weekends we'd go hiking or go to watch a football game. We also joined a new church, and every time we walked into a service, with Crista's hair in a bow and Jantsen in a starched shirt and crisp jeans, I saw that everyone was looking at us the way that I hoped they would: the perfect Christian couple, such a nice family, such *good people*. In fact, whenever I got together with friends or family, I saw how much people approved of the life we had built for ourselves—how they even envied the things we had.

I have to say, I put on a hell of a performance. For a long time, I even had myself convinced of how good and right everything was in my life. At times, I flaunted it a little, assuming the role of Super Mom. Nothing in my house ever out of place, my hair and makeup always perfect. More than that, though, I never said no to anyone. Entire villages could have been fueled by the energy I expended trying to please people. Even when all I wanted to do was stay home and read a book, if someone wanted me to cut their hair, or needed help decorating their kitchen, or wanted to go out to lunch, I was there. I mean, risk someone *not liking me*? No way.

Even my kids became props in this game. They always had to look and act as perfect as I did. They had to excel at sports, and at school, and it was very important to me that they were popular. Holidays were the worst. I'd kill myself making sure ours was the best-decorated house on the block at Christmas, and I would never have thought of buying a costume at the store for Halloween. I was Super Mom, and Super Moms don't do that. Instead I stayed up all night making costumes so intricate, there was no way they weren't going to win Best Costume at school again that year. One year I dressed Crista in a sunflower costume I had borrowed from a friend for Jantsen's Halloween party at school. Crista could not have cared less about her costume; she just wanted to get to the party before the good candy was gone. But at the last minute, as I dabbed her cheeks with blush, I decided that I could have done better. Before I knew it, I was in the garage cutting wire to thread through her hair and turn her into Pippi Longstocking, a decidedly cuter choice. She stood there looking miserable as I peeled the yellow sweater off her, pulled on a red-checkered pinafore dress that didn't fit her, and made her step into the funky striped tights I'd bought on clearance, just in case.

But when Crista and I finally walked into the classroom at South School and everyone commented on how adorable she looked, I didn't feel proud like I was supposed to. All I felt was exhausted. It was the same way I felt when I was cutting friends' hair or decorating their kitchens. Yeah, I did it, but it didn't make me happy. Instead, I'd spend my whole time there wishing I was somewhere else, and then resent the person for putting me in that position.

For years, this sense of weariness stayed mostly in the background. There were times when an annoying little voice popped up, reminding me that despite everything I projected on the outside, something important was missing from my life. Well, it wasn't that *something* was missing, because I certainly had a lot of stuff. It was more like *I* was missing. While I may have seemed secure and happy, I was nothing like the person I presented to the world. In fact, I didn't feel any differently than I had when I was sixteen years old and sitting in Randy's church, pretending I belonged. But now it wasn't being a member of a church that I was faking; it was my entire life.

I ignored the voice and chose instead to believe that my *real* self—my content self—was just on the other side of a few important *if onlys*. I'll feel a lot more at peace with who I am if only I can finally lose ten pounds. Or if only I get better highlights in my hair. If only we get the Chrysler Town and Country minivan I had seen advertised on television. But even if I did make the changes I wanted, there was always another list of *musts* that kept me from feeling whole.

Realizing that this inner voice spoke the loudest to me in the moments I was silent and undistracted, I noisied things up a bit. I kept the radio on when I drove, the television on while I cooked. Any moments alone, I called a friend to talk, or ran out to the mall to see what was new there. For a time, I became obsessed with redecorating my house, telling myself that what I *really* needed was more knickknacks: colorful glass bottles and big, chunky candlestick holders. And then it was picture frames, or paint, a new color each month for another room. It became a joke in my family that ours was the only house in which you could fall asleep in a blue bedroom and wake up in a yellow one. Finally, it was pillows. I think I spent more time hunting for pillows than some people spend choosing a husband, and the whole thing was starting to drive Randy crazy. One evening, he could barely make room for himself on the sofa.

"Pam," he said, throwing my favorite pillows on the floor. "I think the pillows in our house are giving birth. Please stop buying them. Nobody needs this many pillows."

I knew that he was right, of course. But rather than pay attention to the voice that was telling me the pillows, and the candles, and the jeweled frames were a misguided attempt to fill the void I felt, and maybe I was chasing the wrong things, I convinced myself that this was part of my journey toward meaning. Really, I thought, you can't have a truly meaningful life if you're not *cozy.*

And this is when I began to go where so many of us go in times of spiritual and emotional crisis: the Self-Help section of Barnes & Noble. Its aisles became my new church, and convinced I could find the answers somewhere among the pages of those aisles, I loaded myself down with every type of book I could find: *Making Things Right When Things Go Wrong. On the Anvil. Getting the Life You Want!* I'd go home and read every word. Then I'd put the book down, and although I was learning a hundred new ways of expressing the word *empowered,* I still felt nothing inside except a sense that I was on the wrong side of a wall I could not climb over.

I was finally forced to truly confront my nagging sense of discontent during, of all places, a trip to Disney World in 1998. I had seen that commercial where Kathie Lee Gifford slipped down the slide of a Carnival cruise ship singing "Ain't We Got Fun," and I decided that was the answer—I needed to take a trip, and see the world, and be more like Kathie Lee. And so we went. First, Randy and I spent a few days on a Caribbean cruise—the ultimate couple's vacation—and afterward, we met Randy's brother Mike and his family, and Jantsen and Crista, in Orlando. We spent a week at Disney World—the ultimate family vacation—and didn't scrimp on anything. We stayed in a beautiful room at the Polynesian Resort inside the Magic Kingdom, and we explored every inch of the park.

While I was sure this would be one of the happiest times I'd ever spent, it wasn't. There was always something a little off—it was too hot, the lines were too long, and all the money we were spending was stressing me out. But I was more disturbed by the idea that this vacation hadn't filled me with the sense of contentment I'd expected. Was I just impossible to please?

Weirdly, the best time I had during that vacation was on the way home, when, due to a storm in Florida, we were stuck at the airport for hours. As we sat at the gate, I noticed a woman traveling alone with her daughter, who had Down syndrome. The woman looked utterly exhausted, and I went over and introduced myself. She told me that she had the flu, and she looked as if she were at the end of her rope. I knew the feeling— you're so sick that you count the hours until nap time, when you can lie down with the kids. I offered to watch her daughter, whose name was Logan, while she took a walk or went for a cup of coffee, and she appeared so grateful for the break I thought she was going to French-kiss me. Three seconds later, she was sound asleep on a chair.

Logan was very active, and we had to move chairs into a circle to barricade her in. She climbed among our laps, hugging us and kissing us. Jantsen and Crista were laughing hysterically and thought she was the funniest kid they had ever met. Mike and his wife Diane had a daughter, Megan, who had been born with many challenges, physical and mental. She was wonderful, and having her in our lives was a real joy. Though her life was far too short—she died at the age of ten, a year before this trip to Disney World—she blessed my children with the ability to see past the labels others loaded her with—*disabled, different, unlucky*—and they loved her for exactly who she was: a beautiful, bubbly young girl. It did not, therefore, freak them out that Logan was different. She even reminded us of Megan with her blond curly hair and chunky little body. That day at the airport, Jantsen flew paper airplanes that Logan would go and retrieve. It kept her busy for hours. Jantsen and Crista would cheer for her every time, and she responded as if she had performed a miracle. People around us looked at the scene with pity or frustration, and some even moved to another section because we were so loud. But none of us cared, and when our plane was finally called to board, we all felt a little sad to have to say good-bye to Logan.

Of all the experiences on my "perfect" vacation, that scene is what I always remember the best. When the credit card bill came shortly after we returned home, and I saw how much the vacation had cost us, I knew the money had been worth it: We had gotten to spend those few hours with Logan.

A few months after this vacation, Randy and I went to watch a football game at Jantsen's school, as we often did. We'd pack some snacks, put on sweaters, sit in the stands, and cheer for the team. During the first quarter on this particular weekend, I noticed a couple in their mid forties walking up the bleachers. The man was carrying an Asian baby in a carrier strapped to his back. I knew that I wanted to meet this couple, and after they sat down I went over and introduced myself. Their names were Marvin and Carol Harlan, and Kylie, their baby girl, was eight months old. They had recently adopted her from Vietnam.

Now, these people are interesting, I thought.

"That's amazing," I said as Kylie played with my fingers. "How in the world do you even go about doing something like this?"

Carol told me that adopting a child was something they had both always wanted to do, and after having six kids of their own they'd decided it was finally time. She also told me that after visiting a few orphanages in Vietnam, and meeting Kylie, they decided they wanted to do more. The agency they had worked with was difficult, Carol explained, and the process had been so expensive that it kept the option out of reach for many families. After coming home, they began to raise money to build orphanages in Vietnam that would be more about helping orphaned children find loving families, and less about making a profit.

I was intrigued by what they were doing, but the more I thought about them, the more I came to envy them. That's hard to admit now, but it's true. Seeing how meaningful their lives were, and how centered and grounded they seemed, only reminded me of how screwed up and lost I was. How does somebody get to be a woman like Carol? I wondered. How come her weekends were spent fund-raising for orphans while mine were spent in the Spiritual Healing section of the local bookstore and seeking life advice in television commercials? I hated how unfair it seemed that my life would always be defined by laundry and pillows, and hers by things with meaning. Maybe this was God's work. Maybe he chose the people who were meant to have a meaningful life, just as he decided who was intelligent, and I had not been chosen for either of those things.

A few weeks later, Princess Diana died. Seeing as she didn't make a habit out of shopping at the Fayetteville Target, I of course had never actually *met* her, but you would have thought the two of us were best friends given how obsessed I became with her death and, then, the story of her life. As the details unfolded again and again on the nightly news programs, I was offered a glimpse into what it truly meant to live a life of grace. Here was a woman who felt quite broken and abandoned, yet she had found meaning in things outside herself. I watched newsreels of her working in Cambodia with landmine victims, sitting next to legless men whom she wrapped in her arms. Had she made that happen herself, I wondered, or had God chosen her, the way he did Carol? I didn't even know where Cambodia was, or why there were still landmines there.

Mother Teresa dying a few days later didn't help my confusion at all. Nothing reveals how ultimately shallow it is to worry about your hair color better than a reminder of the way this woman lived her life.

After we had been in Arkansas for three years, Randy took a new job that brought us back to Neosho. I was happy to go home. Maybe I'd be happier there. Plus, my kids were thrilled at the idea of being closer to their grandparents and childhood friends. Jantsen couldn't wait to start his sophomore year with his old buddies and be back with Gregan and Darius. Crista could take dance lessons at her old dance studio. Randy's job meant a higher salary, and we bought an even bigger and better house than anything we'd ever owned, on forty acres of land. One evening a few weeks after we were settled back in Neosho, I sat in the backyard with a cup of coffee and just looked at my house. I did love it. When Randy and I were first married, I never imagined we'd have a house like this. At that time, he was making only three hundred dollars a week, and I was pulling in extra spending money by cutting hair. We survived, but I always wanted more. I always wanted *this:* the big, open living room, the huge country kitchen with the brick floor, all the land.

And now that I had it, I still refused to feel content? Sitting there that night, I decided that it was finally time to admit that this was as good as it was ever going to get for me, and simply try to find meaning in the great things I had: my marriage; my family; my two healthy, amazing children. Maybe my life didn't feel like the perfect fit, but maybe that was because this was everything God had intended for me when he created me. And maybe anything less than accepting it was starting to anger him.

Well, for all of the stress this whole thing caused me at the time, I couldn't see then what I believe to be true now: That questioning wasn't angering God. That questioning *was* God.

That voice, that instinct, that constant poking in my heart, telling me I wanted something more, it wasn't me being selfish and ungrateful: It was me finally paying attention. *Okay,* the voice was saying, *it's time for you and me to get real here, and figure out what* really *matters.*

———

Of course, I wouldn't come to understand this until a few months later, when I was forced to stand, broken and annihilated, in the whiteness of a hospital room. It was the day Jantsen died.

GRIEF

Chapter Two

I cannot write about this in the past tense. Doing so might suggest that there's distance between this moment and the day it happened. There is, of course, because it's been nine years, an impossible amount of time, and yet there isn't. A day still doesn't pass that I don't replay it all in my head. Maybe I don't remember the actual details as often—about getting the phone call from my sister Cheryl, or the overly antiseptic smell of the hospital waiting room, or what it felt like when I met Randy's eyes right after the doctor told us Jantsen was dead—but I do think, every day, about how much I love him. And each time I do, I am not here, nine years away. I am right there.

———

I am right here. I whisper it to him.

Pressing my body close to his, I lay my head on his chest, and touch his face, feeling the soft stubble of young hair on his fifteen-year-old cheeks. I will his chest to move, his lungs to fill with air, and sense nothing but the gaping emptiness, my own sudden exhaustion, and a deep, gnawing desire to change what is happening.

What is happening? It's not that I can't remember, I just can't make sense of anything. Time is so confused. Cheryl called me at the hair salon around 1 PM. *Come quick,* she said. *It's Jantsen.*

It's Jantsen.

I am leaving the salon and going next door to Randy's office. We are driving to Cheryl's house, and I'm telling him what she told me on the phone. After football practice, Jantsen and Darius were both meant to mow the lawn. But it was raining. So they went to Cheryl's house to watch a movie. She said that we needed to hurry. She didn't say what was wrong. She didn't say anything else.

Not that he'd had an asthma attack. Or that he'd broken his leg at football. Or that he'd decided to mow anyway and fallen off the lawn mower. She wouldn't have thought to say it was his heart. His heart was perfect.

I don't see him outside when we get there. I knew deep down that I wouldn't, but I had allowed myself that last desperate hope, and the disappointment I feel is crushing. My brother-in-law Mark is telling me that medics have arrived and are inside with him, and as I listen to him talk, the fact of the ambulance in the driveway slowly starts to make sense to me. I immediately start toward the house, but Mark reaches out for my arm, telling me they need their room. I see my father, whose house is right next door to Cheryl's, standing on the lawn. I see Darius and Dallas, Cheryl's oldest son. Everyone looks so scared. Then Jantsen is coming out the door on a stretcher, carried by people I've never seen before. I'm trying to get near him, to see his eyes, but someone is keeping me away again, close to the white picket fence. I am still near enough to see that he is not breathing on his own and I feel myself sinking under the weight of it, knowing this is all terribly wrong. They are loading him into an ambulance, and then they are taking him to the hospital.

Now Cheryl is driving. The ambulance is in front of us, but I don't see it, because I can't bear to look. Cheryl tells me everything again. They had very early football practice. Afterward, they made breakfast and put in a movie. She walked into the room and said something to Jantsen. He didn't answer. He didn't move. She tried to shake him awake, and he didn't move.

Please, God, just let him be alive.

We are in a waiting room, a place that feels cold and foreign. I see that other people are here: my parents, our good friend Warren. I see my three sisters and my brother Ralph. Randy is outside in the hall, pacing the whiteness, back and forth. People I know are coming into the room, and everyone is asking me what's happening. What's happening is that my son is in another room possibly dying, and I can't do anything to help him. There is too much noise and finally I hear myself screaming out loud. *Shut up and start praying.*

The minister from our church appears. He takes my hands, I bow my head, I close my eyes. I am screaming, but it is silent this time. *Please, God, just let him be alive.* Let him be brain-damaged if you need to, but give me back his body and I will be okay. I will take care of him. *Just let him be alive.*

The doctor walks into the room. He says he has bad news. He says something about Jantsen's heart, and then he tells us he is dead.

I look at Randy, standing a few feet away from me across the room, and immediately I know: He is now a different man.

The floor is giving way underneath my feet and a million thoughts are ricocheting inside my head like a parade of bullets. How am I going to possibly survive this? How can I live without my baby boy? I feel a sickness spreading through me like cancer and acid, and I think that I am going to die, right here, in this foreign place.

Then one thought takes hold and I can think clearly again. Jantsen is still very near to me, and he needs me. I ask to see him, and then I am running as quickly as I can down a fluorescent hallway.

I am right here. I am whispering it to him. His body lies on the cold table, and it's far too exposed. How cruel that he had just endured all of those procedures and I was not there to tell him it was okay. I lay my cheek on his skin, trying to cover him, and that is when I know that he is really gone. Another doctor comes in. There are tubes in Jantsen's mouth, and he pulls them out. My son's chest quivers, and a sound escapes his throat. Oh, God, he is alive. All of the sickness that has taken hold is immediately released, and I'm filled with a sense of gratitude I didn't even know possible. What a cruel joke, and what a gift, I think. *He is alive.* I wait for him to take another breath, before I sense the hand on my back and the voice of someone apologizing. He is sorry. Someone else is scolding him about how he should have removed the tubes earlier. He is dead. Again.

My father is standing next to me now, and I notice how bright red his face is, and how swollen his eyes. He kneels down next to me and speaks in a voice so tortured and weak, I barely recognize him.

We did everything we could, Pam. We got to him as quickly as we could, and we tried to save him.

He is begging me to believe him, and I see the panic in his eyes. Of course you did, I say, holding on to him, consumed with fear that this man—the strongest, most stoic, and kindest one I know—might collapse from his sorrow. Of course you did. They all did. He, my sister, my brother-in-law, each of them giving my son CPR, trying to pass on their breath to him. It occurs to me how scary and intense it must have been for everyone there with Jantsen in the moments before the medics arrived. And what a blessing that he was in such a comfortable and familiar place, near people who adored him, who would have given their own lives for him.

Some other person is in the room now, asking us if we want to donate Jantsen's organs. They are sorry, they say, but it needs to be a quick decision. I do not know. I do not really care. Yes, I am saying, take what you need. Randy and this person talk more. This person explains that the only organs that are certainly still useful, especially because we still do not know the exact cause of death . . . *he is dead* . . . are his corneas. Randy tells this person to take Jantsen's corneas.

There are people lined up against the walls. Most of the faces I cannot recognize, but I assume they are all friends and family. I see my mother-in-law and Crista and remember they had planned a special Girls Day together that afternoon. I ask where Jeramiah, my nephew, is. I do not know why I ask for him, I just wonder right then where he is.

Nobody knows what to do next, so Randy starts to speak, assuming the role that will come to define the next few months, if not years, of his life: the leader of this family, its rock. He is talking about how lucky we are to have had Jantsen for these fifteen years. How afraid we had been the day he was born that we were going to lose him too soon. My husband is remembering now how he had begged God not to take his son that day, so we'd have the opportunity to get to know him.

We leave the hospital and despite the fact that it's June, it's very cold. My blood feels like ice. We are taken to someone's car in the parking lot, and I look around for Crista. I need to have my one living child with me right then, and in the car I lay my head on her lap.

Then we are driven home. Although it no longer feels like that.

That night there are people all over the house, their cars filling the driveway and lawn. I stay in my bedroom with the door closed, twisted and clenched on my bed, trying to make sense of everything, telling myself this is probably not even real. If I close my eyes and concentrate, maybe I can make everything the way it was before, the way it's supposed to be. The four of us are sitting down to dinner right now. Crista is showing us that she has written her name on the ice cream in the freezer so that Jantsen doesn't eat it all, and he's making fun of her for it. Randy is grilling steaks in the backyard, tongs in one hand and a newspaper in the other. While we eat, Jantsen tells us about football practice and watching a movie with Darius. He says that afterward, they rode their four-wheelers in the hills behind the house, and then Randy and he talk about going fishing on the weekend. While I do the dishes, Crista and Jantsen get ready to do their homework. We argue, probably, about how much time they have to spend on it.

This reminds me. My last conversation with him was an argument. He had left his baseball glove outside last night and it rained, and his glove had gotten soaked. I had called him at Darius's house earlier that morning, only hours before he died, and told him I thought he had been irresponsible. He was so nonchalant, as he was about most things. What had he said to me?

Don't worry, Mom. I'll find another one.

Another left-handed first-base glove? I asked him, doubting that he would. Had I told him that I loved him before hanging up? I can't believe how much I love him. I can't believe that my son, whom I carried for nine months, gave birth to, the child my body fed for ten months, is gone.

My body feels unfamiliar, like I no longer occupy it but instead float somewhere slightly outside, severed from my senses. People stand around my bedside and my sister Tam is rubbing my feet, although I don't notice this. But I am happy they are here. I want to thank them, but I don't have the language. I try to pull the covers tightly over my head, but my hands feel like they are made of water.

My good friend Traci House, who has been one of my closest friends since high school, has taken charge, standing outside my bedroom door like a gatekeeper, allowing passage inside only to those she knows I want to see. She will stand there, protecting me like that, for several days. I hear people's whispers as they come in and out. Everyone is asking, over and over, what happened, and the details are explained again, like a tragic accident in constant replay.

I can't believe this is happening to us, Randy.

He comes in and lies down next to me. We wrap each other up in our arms, our hearts touching. We try to speak, but we don't know what to say, so we choose words that sound reassuring. But we both know they are only words, and they are not nearly true enough. I still have no sense of time, and eventually my sister Kim suggests we try to get some sleep, offering us a sedative. We do as we are told, because we are clueless as to what else to do, and sleep is as good an option as anything. Later, maybe it's minutes, maybe hours, I fall off the edge and into sleep.

I want to never wake up again, but I do, at 4 AM, lingering in that delicate spot between sleep and consciousness. I have forgotten, momentarily. And then I suddenly notice how sick and tortured I feel and I'm forced to consider why and, of course, I remember. This is exactly how I will wake up for the next several months, having to realize all over again, morning after morning, that Jantsen is gone.

I hear Randy sleeping beside me and I try to quietly lift myself from the bed, as I don't dare wake him. Crista is asleep on an armchair in the corner, her legs propped up on an ottoman. I stand there for a while, watching her sleep. She is so beautiful, this young girl. I have not done enough for her. I have barely spoken to her since the ride home. I want to take her in my arms, and curl and coil around her, but I don't. I won't, in fact, for far too long. Not because I don't want to, but because I am aware in a whole new way of just how much I love her, and how terrifying it would be to lose her, too. It would be enough to kill me, were I not mostly dead already.

I go down the hallway to the living room. The house is strangely quiet. My parents are sleeping upstairs. Warren is on the couch. Randy and Crista are here. Yet it feels completely empty. Warren wakes up when he hears me in the kitchen, standing there, unsure of what to do. He comes to me and takes me in his arms, and then back to the couch, where he covers me with the blanket. He's known us both since Randy was in college, and he loved Jantsen so much. I'm glad that he is here.

"How are you?"

"I'm not sure what happened," I say. I start telling him the details of the day: of getting Cheryl's call, and driving to her house, and going to the hospital, and seeing Jantsen's body. Warren knows this already. He was there for most of it. I slowly talk about Jantsen's heart, trying to form the right words. "Like, did it just stop working?" I ask. Warren doesn't have the answers, of course, nobody does. But if I don't say this out loud to someone, if I don't begin rehearsing this absurd reality that is now mine, how will I ever absorb the fact that it's true? This is actually happening.

The next day, I begin to discover all of the things you have to do in the hours after your fifteen-year-old son dies. Choose a casket. Plan a funeral. Just two days ago, Jantsen was telling us that he had decided what bat he wanted to buy for that season, and Randy and I were discussing if we should get him a pickup truck for his sixteenth birthday. Now we're discussing where to have the service. Where are we going to bury his body? What will his headstone read? What music do we choose?

I try to pull myself together enough to deal with these questions because, well, that is now my job as his mother. But I can't. I can't choose the prayers or think about what he should wear to be buried in. I don't want to tell people what songs might sound nice at his funeral. All I want is for Jantsen to walk through the door and throw his school bag on the floor in the hall. All I want is to feel that dry patch of skin on his cheek, his arms around my waist. I want to hear him say *I love ya, Mom,* in his perfect laid-back way. That, in fact, is all I can imagine ever wanting again.

I later realize that my sisters have stepped in and begun to take care of things. One night I go downstairs and see that the pool table is covered in photos of Jantsen. It's such a strange sight. Why would someone take his photos and lay them around the pool table? Immediately the grief sneaks up on me again and just when I thought I couldn't feel any worse, it flattens me completely. This pool table is where we'd all gather on freezing winter nights, where we'd team up and play long, clumsy games. Why are his photos here? Eventually, I realize that these are the pictures people have chosen to display at his funeral. I realize this, but that doesn't mean it makes sense to me.

The only thing I tell my sisters regarding the funeral is that it needs to be a beautiful tribute to his life, but I don't know how to do that. I do know that I don't want any flowers at the church. Flowers? How can we introduce beauty among the bleeding rawness? I suggest that in lieu of flowers, we ask people to contribute to a memorial fund for him. It's not that I have an idea of how I would use any money we collect, but I know that his memory would be much better served by giving a gift in his name than with hundreds of hollyhocks we'd eventually have to throw away. The idea of people spending money on things that don't last means nothing to me; in fact, it nauseates me.

The service is planned for two days later, which means that when I wake up that morning, I can't just go to the living room and sit on the denim couch for hours, not bothering to even brush my teeth. Instead I have to take a shower, fix my hair. Somehow I do this, somehow I choose something to wear: my black dress, the one I had picked up at TJ Maxx one day thinking it would be the perfect funeral dress when I needed one. I never dreamed it would be for Jantsen's funeral. I find Randy in the kitchen, where he is standing in front of the stove, holding a measuring cup in one hand. He looks at me, and there are enormous tears in his eyes.

"I wanted to make oatmeal," he says, "I know how much to make for Jantsen and me. Four cups of water and two cups of oatmeal. But I do not know how much to make for myself. Do I split it in half? Because he always ate more than I did." His body shudders with his grief. "I don't know how to make oatmeal for one."

I wipe his tears with my hand and press my lips to his, trying to quiet him, to absorb his pain. I would take it all if I could.

"Is he really gone?" he says. "I don't know how to live without him."

Maybe we won't, I think. Maybe we won't survive this.

Our friend Danny, who runs a funeral home, arrives with a car to take us to the church. I do not move, because I don't want to go. But I get up, and I go to the bathroom one last time. In the mirror, I see the face of a woman who looks a hundred years old. I've never seen anyone look this sad, and, for a moment, I almost don't believe it's me. In many ways, it's not. This is a different person: the one who will attend her son's funeral that day. I look at her, and she scares me.

Now we are at the service, and as far as these things go it is beautiful. Nearly a thousand people are here, standing along the walls and crammed into the back. All of Jantsen's friends are here, along with their parents. The boys from his high school baseball team are sitting together, wearing their uniforms, which now have Jantsen's number—16—printed on the sleeve. Jantsen is also wearing his baseball uniform that day. Regan Glenn, his youth minister from Arkansas, helps the crowd laugh with stories about Jantsen and his love for R. D. Mercer, a radio personality known for making absurd prank phone calls to people. Randy's brother Mike talks about how much Jantsen touched his life. I try to listen, afraid to miss the chance to hear people talk so lovingly about my son, but it's difficult. All I see is the polished wooden box holding his body. At some point, Darius and Gregan get up and speak. They say how much they loved Jantsen, and how much they enjoyed being able to grow up with him. Then Jantsen's good friend Brent is up there, getting ready to play something on the drums, as he had been asked to do. The idea, I believe, is something soft and soothing, and so when Brent screeches out a wild, frenzied drum solo, Randy and I look at each other and laugh.

"I'm not sure I've ever heard anything quite like that," I whisper.

"I'm not sure *anyone* has ever heard anything quite like that," he whispers back, taking my hand. Jantsen would have loved it.

The service comes to a close. Randy gets up, and I follow him to the front. Somehow, he is able to speak. Though I am right next to him, I cannot hear what he is saying. The grief in my head is making too much noise, and everything else is just static.

———

Ten days later, Randy went back to work. I, on the other hand, had already decided that I was never going to cut hair again. The idea of having to stand there and pretend like I possibly gave a shit about what the right shade of blond was for someone's skin tone was enough to make me want to shoot myself. I wasn't going back, ever. When I told Tam this, she said she understood. "What are you going to do?" she asked.

"I don't know," I said. "I don't really care."

What I did was sit on my couch, or at the kitchen table, hour after hour, day after day, trying to force down coffee, which tasted terrible. Everything tasted terrible, and I couldn't remember the last time I had eaten. Drinking in the darkness, I vacillated between reading the grief books people had thought to bring me; petting our dog Truman, who barely left my side; and realizing again and again how incredibly stupid and meaningless my life was.

At times, I was with it enough to recognize that I had just spent the last two hours simply sitting there, barely moving. I tried in these moments to open the sliding glass door and walk outside to the pond in my bare feet, or to take Truman down the long country road to the railroad tracks, to prove to myself that I still lived in this world. I tried, but I didn't always succeed.

Randy came home from work the next Friday and reminded me that it was the Fourth of July weekend. He suggested we do something to celebrate. I knew that we should, if only for Crista's sake, but I didn't want to. It was always Jantsen's favorite holiday. He would collect fireworks two weeks before the day and separate them into small piles, carefully deciding the order in which he'd light them. My mom called to invite us over for dinner. I told her we would try to come, but I wasn't sure I wanted to be alive later that afternoon, let alone be eating a hamburger and macaroni salad, trying to speak to someone. But I couldn't say no. Or at least I felt that I couldn't, and so we went. *All I need to do is survive it,* I thought.

At my mom's house, I heard people talking and laughing, but nothing was registering. The only way to avoid a total breakdown was to tune everything out. They were also asking me questions about things that didn't have to do with Jantsen, because (I now realize) they didn't know what else to do. But I didn't want to talk about things that didn't have to do with Jantsen, and I felt the panic rising inside. Two hours in, I simply couldn't take it anymore, and I knew that I needed to be home, where it was safe. I whispered to Randy, "I need to get out of here. Immediately."

On the drive home, he suggested that we stop at the cemetery, and when we pulled the car up the winding, rocky path toward Jantsen's grave, I saw that there were people crowded around it. It was my aunt Joyce and uncle Chester, their two daughters Carrie and Kelly, their husbands Doug and Brian, and all their children: Alex, Mariah, Bryce, and Mackenzie. I was genuinely happy to see them, and I whispered a silent prayer of thanksgiving that they seemed to get it. He may be gone, but this was still his holiday.

Randy and I joined the adults under the dogwood tree that shaded his plot as Crista ran to join the other children. When they were done with the fireworks, a simple and sweet offering to Jantsen, they climbed some of the trees and chased one another around the headstones. It was nice to be reminded that Crista was an eleven-year-old child and not the adult she appeared to have become since Jantsen died, taking care of the things I no longer was able to.

All the flower arrangements that people had placed around his grave after the funeral were gone now, and it was just a simple mound of dirt. Sitting there, I felt peaceful for the first time in weeks. I knew that he could feel me there, and I inched closer to his grave to be closer to his body. I whispered a promise to him that I would finally try to find a proper headstone. I hadn't been able to do that yet—to choose a chunk of marble and inscribe it with his name and the dates of his birth and death. That felt too final.

A few weeks later, I got a call from Randy's brother Mike. Every year at this time, we had all been going on vacation together to Pensacola, Florida, to stay at a condo Randy's parents owned; Mike wanted to know if we were still planning on it for the end of July. This trip had always been the thing I looked forward to most each year. The kids loved it—they'd stay up late playing spoons and get up early to watch *The Price Is Right* before heading down to the beach for the day. We'd grill fresh fish for dinner on the porch, and after the kids were asleep Mike, Diane, Randy, and I would sit on the back deck and share a good bottle of wine we had bought for the occasion.

I didn't know what to do. I couldn't imagine going, but Randy and I decided that the opportunity to escape the blackness that filled the house was too appealing to pass up. As soon as we got there, however, and opened the door to the condo, I began to second-guess our decision. All I noticed was that Jantsen was not with us. How idiotic I had been to think we could leave our heaviness and sadness behind. "Can we do this?" I asked Randy as Crista went to drop her suitcase off in the room she and Jantsen once shared. Can I walk the same beach where he once cast his fishing net for hours, the shoreline where he snorkeled?

"I don't know," Randy said, looking hopelessly at me. "But we at least need to try."

Later that night, trying to act the part of normal, functioning people, we went out to dinner for the first time since he died and were greeted by the hostess, a pretty girl not much older than Jantsen.

"Three?" she asked cheerily, reaching for menus.

"No—" I began, about to say *four*, as I had for the last several years, until I realized that was no longer true.

"Yes," I managed. "Three."

At dinner, I felt like I was eating in a cloud. Everything was strange and foreign, and the only thing I heard was freakish laughter from the people at the table in the corner. What the hell were they laughing so hard about? I pushed the salad around on my plate and tried to eat, all the while envisioning a scene in which I walked over to them and screamed, *How can you be enjoying yourselves when Jantsen is dead?* The anger eventually made room for a far more awkward feeling: total paranoia. I couldn't talk myself out of it, even though I knew it was crazy, but all I could think was that everyone in the place was looking at us funny and talking about us in hushed tones. Did they all know? Did they know we are *that* family, the one that lost a son? As soon as Randy and Crista took the last bite of their food, I signaled for the check, desperate to get out of there.

A few days later, on the morning of July 17, I woke up late and found Randy and Crista in the living room, eating cereal and watching CNN. The broadcaster was saying that last night the plane that John F. Kennedy Jr. was flying, carrying his wife Carolyn Bessette and her sister Lauren, went missing off the coast of Martha's Vineyard. I sank into the couch and couldn't take my eyes off the screen. My mother used to always say that Jantsen looked like a young Kennedy, especially when I dressed him in knee socks and shorts for church. Randy thought it was goofy, but I thought it was adorable.

Why wasn't Jantsen's death mentioned on CNN? I wondered, before the thought passed. They were saying it didn't look hopeful. "We are still searching for more clues as to where the plane might have gone in," a man from the Coast Guard was reporting. "We're going to continue to search for the rest of the day."

Over the next few days, I remained planted in front of the television for hours. When the authorities made the sad decision to give up their search, I pulled myself off the couch and walked down to the beach. High on one of the dunes, I carved out a little spot with my sandal, sat down, and started to bawl. I sobbed harder than I had in days. I had wanted to cry, but the tears wouldn't come. Now they wouldn't stop.

People walked by—a couple with a dog, and then an older man in a red windbreaker. They saw me sitting there alone, grasping my knees and shaking uncontrollably, but I didn't care. I was lost in a thought about something Rose Kennedy said in an interview I had just seen: *My life has been filled with sorrow and joy. I focus on the joy, and that is how I have survived.* Maybe I can do that, I thought, the wind whipping my face and the sand stinging my skin. I can try to focus on the joy. Maybe, in fact, that's the only answer.

I tried to remember the joy: how much Jantsen resembled Randy, and how that had always felt like a special gift bestowed to my husband. How much Jantsen and Crista loved each other. How both he and Darius—his best bud in the whole world—had developed bad stutters when they were first learning to talk, and how the rest of us would cover our ears every time the two of them tried speaking to each other.

But these pained attempts at joy were quickly clobbered powerless by my thoughts of the Bessette family. They lost two daughters that day, and as bad as I felt, I couldn't imagine what they were going through. I wished, impossibly, that there was something I could do for them right then. I started to imagine how we'd all get together. We'd talk about our children, about how they would be defined not by their deaths, but by their lives, and I realized that of everyone in the world, the Bessettes and the Kennedys were the only people I knew of who might be able to understand exactly what I was feeling: how sick I was, and how foreign I felt in my body. As I walked the beach the next few days, I tracked their progress in my mind. It is Day Two, and this is probably what they are experiencing right now. It is Day Four.

Later, Randy came to find me by the pool, where Crista was swimming and I was trying to read one of my grief books. "I just had a thought," he said, handing me a cold Diet Dr Pepper. "I think that JFK Jr. and Jantsen might be together right now. Wouldn't that be wild? Do you think JFK Jr. likes to play pool? Because I bet if he does, then the two of them will become friends and play pool together."

The idea made me laugh, and I agreed. That night in bed, I wrote Jantsen a letter, as I had nearly every night since he died, and suggested they seek each other out.

Most evenings, after the kids had gone to sleep, we sat with Mike and Diane on the porch near the beach, talking about our children. It had been five years since their daughter Megan died, and I could see that the pain they felt was still as pure and raw as it had been that cold November morning when she passed away. I had failed them after Megan's death. I hadn't talked about her enough. I loved that little girl so much, and thought about her all the time, but I had been too afraid to even mention her name, as if doing so would be the one thing to remind them that their daughter was gone. Only now could I understand how ridiculous that was. I thought about the first Christmas without her and how the rest of us had gone back to real life, worrying too much about what to get the kids, and what desserts to make, and making sure the house was perfectly decorated. Mike and Diane had come up from Texas that year to celebrate with us, and when I heard Diane in the basement, sobbing alone, I tried to understand, but I didn't. Not really.

"Listen," Mike said to us one evening as Randy and I stared into the darkness. "You need to know something. You are going to be sadder and your life is going to be harder than you ever thought. But it's going to be richer, too, and much deeper. You will feel things you have never felt before, and have a perspective you would never have otherwise had. It's going to be very bad, but it's also going to be unbelievably great."

I tried to let the words sink in, but I couldn't imagine how they could possibly be true. How could my life ever be richer? I seriously doubted that I'd feel joy again, let alone experience richness. The one thing I knew for sure, sitting there with the sound of the ocean in the background, was that everything that had given my life value and meaning had been taken away. From now on, all I could expect was to be confined in absolute misery, filling the days until I died with ridiculous routines, returning to a life that felt nothing except shallow and meaningless.

We returned home a few days later, and the first thing I saw when we pulled into the driveway was that the tree we had planted in the front yard—Jantsen's tree, which had been a gift from Randy's friend Gene Hall—had been destroyed. The cows that grazed in our pasture had broken the fence and trampled it. Seeing it there, its roots torn out, I was devastated. And enraged. Not only at the cows, but at God. *Is nothing sacred to you?* I thought. *Could you not have at least protected a tree for me? Are you going to take away* everything *that matters?*

The house was so quiet. The people who had been stopping

by those first few weeks to do the dishes and drop off a casserole had gone back to their own lives, and I was happy they were gone. All I wanted was the time and space to be alone with my grief, to be able to give it its rightful and privileged place as the head of this household, without the judging eyes of observers.

Each morning, when I had to watch Randy prepare to travel into the real world in his starched shirt and a diamond-knotted tie, I forced myself to beat away the guilt I was starting to feel. Of course he'd much rather be joining me at the table, flipping through grief books, making pots of coffee we never drank. But he couldn't. He had to go back to work and take care of this family. What was even more upsetting to me was that I was beginning to seriously worry that I was not going to survive this—that vital parts of me were being chipped away and removed—because as hard as I might try, I could not get my brain to function the way it once did. I imagined the day that I was going to wake up and simply not be okay, and either die or be carted away to a padded room. I was trying to do what the grief books suggested: deal with the pain head-on, but I was beginning to wonder if it was worth the price.

On the days that I felt worst, I went downstairs to Jantsen's room and lay down in his bed, in the sheets I still hadn't washed. Sometimes I pulled on one of his dirty T-shirts, whichever one smelled most of his deodorant and scent, and, wrapped in his blankets, I tried to grasp the idea of where, exactly, he was.

Was it heaven?

What was it like when he got there? What was his first conversation with God like? I played different scenarios back and forth in my head.

I wondered if he was hanging out with others his age. I wondered if he still had allergies.

The thoughts felt crazy at times, and other times they comforted me. I listened to tapes of Joyce Meyer and Beth Moore, two theologians I love, and read every Max Lucado book on the shelf, trying to console myself with the idea that my son was safe. But then why did I feel this sad? If heaven was everything I'd read it to be, shouldn't I be celebrating Jantsen's death, and the fact that he had been spared suffering? He was safe now, from all rejection of the world, from heartbreak caused by a girl he loves, or not measuring up to what our world deems smart and valuable. Isn't that what the Scriptures had taught me?

These questions were driving me mad. Meanwhile I was also trying my best to imitate a grown woman—to play the role of a functioning adult who can manage things like shopping and feeding people. This only became harder once the time approached for Crista's school year to begin, and I had to go through the ritual of buying new clothes and different-colored notebooks. I used to love this time of year—my kids actually looked forward to school, and, of course, it meant more free time for me. But as the days grew shorter and the endless back-to-school commercials started airing, I became filled with dread. This was way more than I could handle. I was surprised sometimes when I passed Crista's room and noticed the shiny pink book bag hanging on the door, or the new pair of tennis shoes poking out from under her bed. I guess I was doing it. Somehow, I was doing my job.

I was losing track of time completely. The only way that I noticed that days had turned into nights, creating weeks, and then months, was to notice how others seemed to be moving on. At first they brought Jantsen up less, and then they even seemed to want to hear about him less—not because they didn't miss him, I'm sure, but because they wanted us to stop hurting and maybe if I stopped talking about him, it would mean that I was better.

I tried to be patient when I noticed this, but instead I became preoccupied with reading about how other faiths respond to death. The more I learned, the more screwed up I thought the American Christian traditions were. Here, the attitude seemed to be: *Okay, he's dead and buried, and I've dropped off a tuna casserole, and now it's time for you to rebuild your life and start functioning like a normal person, and we won't talk about your son anymore because that's just too painful.*

I longed for the right to grieve as I needed, for others to allow me to check out of life. After all, if there's anything that gives someone the right to surrender completely to self-pity, it's losing a child. It's everyone's greatest fear, and it happened to me. Therefore, if what I needed was to move into a flophouse on Skid Row and push heroin, didn't everyone else have to simply understand? But people weren't understanding. Instead I found everyone's suggestions that I go back to work, or get out more, or, I don't know, shower every day, maddening. I now understand these gestures were meant to encourage me to fight the impulse to give in entirely to the sadness and hopelessness, but I couldn't see that at the time. All I saw was the way people seemed to be looking at me like I was broken and screwed up and how frustrated they were by my refusal to jump aboard some fast track to healing. It infuriated me. In fact, the anger I felt was starting to consume me, and I spent most of my time fighting the urge to strangle someone.

I was reminded how hard it was to just be myself, and do what I needed to do, every time my mom called to ask me how I was feeling.

Here's what I wanted to say:

How am I feeling? I'm feeling as if my entire body has been turned inside out, and that my organs now exist on the

*outside, torn and swollen. I feel like my heart has shattered
into a million little pieces, which course through my veins,
leaving scratch marks everywhere. The kind that itch.*

But I didn't say that. I knew how much she loved me, and
how it pained her to see how sad I was. So, instead I said,
"I'm good, Mom. Today is a good day. I've done the laundry,
cleaned the house, and now I'm going out for a walk."

Then after I hung up, I would go downstairs to Jantsen's
room, lie down in his bed, and sob until I slept.

I got used to the lying, although I didn't consider it lying as
much as I considered it speaking with footnotes. Sometimes
I would be forced to stop at Jon's Pharmacy or run into the
grocery store and, as is life in small-town Missouri, I'd inevita-
bly see someone I knew. That look would come over their face,
forcing me to brace for what I knew was coming, for having to
make them believe that I was not dead inside.

Oh, hi, Pam, they'd say. *How are you?*

I'm fine, thanks. How are you?[1]

I'm fine. And how's everyone?

They're good, too.[2]

You look good.

Thanks.[3]

Well, I'm running late. It was nice to see you.

Okay. You, too.[4]

Even Crista was getting on my nerves. Sometimes I caught
her laughing with a friend on the phone, and once, after she

[1] I'm miserable. If there were an alternative to toilet paper, I'd never
leave my house.
[2] Well, Crista, my eleven-year-old daughter, is still putting us to bed
each night and making dinner for herself. I doubt she's so excited
about that.
[3] I look like I've been living under the picnic table at the town park
for the last two months.
[4] It wasn't nice for you to see me. Seeing me reminds you of the one
thing you never want to think about: Your child could die.

invited me to watch a movie about a woman dying of cancer, I was crushed. I wanted to scream at her. *I don't think you're showing any grief at all!* I tried to remind myself that she was just eleven years old and that she was dealing not only with the death of her brother, but also, in many ways, with the death of her parents. We were no longer the same people, and I had nothing to give, not even to her. Instead she was the one in charge now, as she had been since the funeral, reminding me that we were out of milk, and making sure the doors were locked each night as we sank into our sleeping-pill-induced sleep. I tried to reach out to her, but I couldn't. Partly because I was still terrified by the thought of losing her, and also because I couldn't stand to see the pleading in her eyes. The look that said, *I'm alive, Mom and Dad. Live for me.*

It was these moments that I tried hardest to be all Rose Kennedy and focus on the joy. And there were many joyous things to focus on. Every time I went to Jantsen's grave site, I saw that the jar we had placed for people to leave notes was spilling over. I took them out and put them in a ziplock bag and sometimes, before I did, I'd read them. There were a bunch from Gregan, whom Jantsen had always considered more a sister than a cousin.

Hey Jantsen. Guess what? I drove for my very first time by myself today and came right over to see you!

Jantsen, I'm stressed and had to come sit with you for a while. I know you understand.

Just came by quick to tell you how much I missed you today.

There was a letter from a girl named Amy Birdsong who, I found out as I read her note, printed on lined paper decorated with red, yellow, and green paw prints, was the first girl Jantsen kissed, when they were in the sixth grade. *Remember when we had the same jeans and would plan to wear them on the same day? That was funny. I really miss you.*

There were a few notes from a boy named Cody Duncan, who played baseball with Jantsen. *Thank you a whole lot for teaching me how to play second base, and telling and showing me how to hit. Remember when I got my very first hit in a game? I owe it all to you. Thank you for everything that you have done for me. I will never forget you and this year I will make it on the Neosho baseball team and I will try out for first base again. If I get it, I will do it as you would, and I won't let you down, Big Guy. Love you.* Later, Cody dropped by again, this time to leave the gold medallion his team had won that year, taking first place in the league championships. A note was printed on a small yellow Post-it, taped to the medallion with thick black tape. *We won. I wanted you to have this.*

As I read through these notes, I realized there was so much about my son that I didn't know, and how quickly he had grown from a baby and a toddler into a young man. I thought about the girlfriends he would never have and the wife and the children we were denied. But I would let those thoughts slip through me as quickly as they could and go home and write my own letter to him inside my journal. One day, I came home to find a letter from the society that had managed the donation of Jantsen's corneas. They were writing to tell me that they had been successfully transplanted. *I am proud of you, honey,* I wrote that night. *I hope they can see everything as beautifully as you did.*

I was most touched the day that Randy came to talk to me, a stack of papers in his hands. "Wait until you get a load of this spreadsheet," he said. "It's amazing." This is not an unusual statement for my exceptionally organized husband. He would probably log and catalog the hairs on my head if I'd let him. But as soon as I saw it, I felt bad about this little joke I made to myself. It was the list of everyone who had donated to the fund we'd established at Jantsen's funeral, and it was seven pages long, in tiny print. I recognized many names, but there were some people I'd never heard of before. I saw that Randy also, impossibly, had been with it enough to note the gifts we had received in the days and weeks after Jantsen died: movies for Crista, Tylenol, detergent, ice, even biscuits for Truman. I didn't remember receiving anything so specific, and I was amazed at how thoughtful these items seemed.

"I got a call earlier from Tina," Randy said, referring to our friend who was managing the donations. "Guess how much money his fund has received?"

"I have no idea," I said. "Two thousand dollars."

"No," Randy replied. "Twenty-five thousand."

I stared back down at the sheets in my hand, then back at my husband. I was in total disbelief. Randy took the list and wrapped my arms around him. "He was very loved," he whispered into my hair. "And we are going to make him proud."

Make him proud.

Over the next few weeks, I became nearly obsessed by the idea of it. Here I was, with one of the most important jobs I'd ever had—spending this money in his name—and I could not think of one thing to do. My first idea was to buy new uniforms for the high school girls' soccer team, on which many of Jantsen's friends played, but when I called the coach to discuss it, he told me they already had money for that. Then I called the Parks Department to talk about building a new playground, but even that didn't seem like a pressing need. And really, were either of these things important enough to reflect everything that Jantsen was?

I knew that I had to pick something that truly mattered to

me, but the more I thought about it, the more I was reminded of how much I struggled with this for years: *Nothing mattered.*

Forced to confront the idea of who I'd been before Jantsen died, I realized that I was beginning to hate that person. Yeah, I had known that I wanted more—that I longed for a greater purpose than wearing the right clothes and driving the right minivan—but I had failed to find it. And in doing so, not only had I failed myself, but, even more disappointingly, I had failed my kids. What had I given Jantsen that was of any real value? He and Crista had the latest clothes and gadgets, they even had their own golf cart to drive around our big lawn, but would Jantsen have wanted to change the world when he grew up? What if all my kids ever wanted was to be like me? What had I ever done that mattered? I never looked outside myself or my family. I sat through the stories on the news about the many tragic things happening around the world, but, honestly, what did any of that have to do with me? It had never even occurred to me that those things fell anywhere near my circle of responsibility. And that had been okay with me. But was it still?

Looking around at the life I had built for myself, and the values I had decided to embrace, all I saw were things that would disappear. I had made my kids do the things I had come to believe were important, even though I hated doing them myself. Many evenings, I'd become frustrated as I helped Jantsen with his homework, trying to make him concentrate on spelling when all he wanted to do was go outside and ride his bike, or watch *Andy Griffith* in the morning before school. Life was simple to him, and we had made it hard. He'd look at us and sigh. "What's the big deal?" he'd say as he reached into the snack cabinet for the tenth time that day. "I wish everyone would chill out."

His nonchalance often infuriated me, because I worried that

I had somehow failed him by not teaching him to value these things I thought mattered. But sitting at my kitchen table, I ached for the chance to return to those days and realize how happy he was just being himself. Why didn't I understand that enough? Why didn't I drill into his head that living for the sake of performance would kill and destroy him? Why didn't I scoop him and Crista up and travel to foreign places, to teach them, and myself, that the world is much bigger than our little Missouri town?

Maybe I hadn't done that for them, but one thing was becoming crystal clear to me now: I needed to begin to do these things for Crista, and for myself. In many ways, my grief was beginning to make me think I had been given a second chance to realize what mattered. And now I couldn't screw it up. I had to find something else now . . . something *more*. It was safe here in my kitchen, in this little grief cocoon I'd built, but what about when it was time for me to return to life? Now that I had been stripped of everything I had once thought defined me, who would I become? Would I go back to shopping with my sisters and become absorbed by things that didn't matter? Would I try to find an easy way out in self-help books and ridiculous decorating schemes? I knew that I didn't want that.

The problem was that I had no idea where to start, and the idea of leaving the familiar life that I had built was daunting. No, maybe my idea of familiar wasn't the best life I could be living, but it was, well . . . familiar. And even bad familiar felt less frightening than the other option: journeying blindly into the unknown.

And more than that, did I even *deserve* anything more?

This was my life now, plagued by doubts, feeling regret, which made it harder yet to return to the real world, but I did try.

I cleaned when it was clear that I needed to, and sometimes, instead of calling Randy and asking him to stop on the way home and pick up a pizza, I went to the grocery store. One day, as I was on my way home from getting Crista at school, I pulled into a Wal-Mart, determined to get the shopping done for the week. But as soon as I got there, the panic welled up inside me and I knew I couldn't do it. Instead, I pulled over in the no-parking lane, grabbed a used envelope and pen out of the glove compartment, and wrote out a list. I turned to Crista. "You have to do this," I said, my tears spilling onto the paper as I realized I really was about to send my eleven-year-old in to do my shopping. "I can't face it today." .

Crista didn't say a word. She didn't say, *Oh, really, Mom? You can't do it, but you expect that I can?* She just took the list, opened the door, and left.

A few minutes later, a policeman walked up to my minivan. By this time, I was sobbing uncontrollably, frightened by the idea that I would never be able to manage something as simple as a trip to Wal-Mart, that my life would never be filled with anything except endless doubt and sorrow. But that didn't seem to concern him. Instead he tapped on my window with his fat, hairy knuckle. "You're going to need to move, ma'am. This is no-parking."

All I could do was stare at him, seeing six of him through the tears swelling my eyes. Are you *kidding me*? I'm sitting here sobbing and the only thing you can think to say to me is that I need to move my car? I thought I was going to roll down the window and beat the living crap out of him. "You big jerk," I heard myself screaming. "My son is dead! Can I not just sit here and wait for my eleven-year-old daughter, who is inside doing this week's shopping? Do you have any idea how hopeless this situation already is, that the last thing I need is to be told that I'm also illegally parked?"

Somehow I managed to move the car and wait, but as soon as we got home I went straight to my bedroom and locked the door. The anger and hopelessness welled inside me, so brawny and muscular it felt like my insides were being beaten to a pulp. WHY DID THIS HAPPEN? WHERE IS JANTSEN? WHY WAS HE TAKEN FROM ME? The emotions were as suffocating as they were the day that he died, and it had been almost four months. *I am not engineered to endure this,* I thought, *and I am never going to feel better.* I felt betrayed and abandoned. I felt exhausted. I felt so *mad.*

I sat down on the gold wingback chair, and it's not that I started talking to God.

No, I started *screaming* at him.

I CANNOT DO THIS ANYMORE. I CANNOT LIVE THIS LIFE. I AM FAILING AS CRISTA'S MOM, AND SHE'S STARTING TO LOOK AT ME LIKE I'M A LUNATIC. I CANNOT FORGE A LIFE OF MEANING FROM THIS SORROW. PLEASE, JUST TAKE ME. OR AT LEAST TELL ME: WHAT DO YOU WANT FROM ME?

And immediately a response came.

What do you want from me?

The voice, which felt like it was emanating not so much from the sky as from my own heart, was generous and clear, and it took me about one millisecond to arrive at the answer:

I want to feel some peace. *Please.*

And just like that, it happened. All the rage and sadness were gone, mid-sob. The feeling was so unequivocal, it was as if I could physically sense the panic exiting my body, atom by miserable atom. I took a breath, a long one, and it felt like the first breath I had ever taken in my life. I felt a thousand pounds lighter. I felt released. I felt . . . *happy.*

And then, for a moment, I felt terrible. How could I be peaceful and happy? Jantsen was gone, I did not have the right to feel anything like this. Wasn't sheer and perfect misery the only thing I had a right to feel, ever again?

But the anger and hopelessness had lost its fight. For several minutes, I sat in my chair, letting the waves of calm sweep through me. I didn't want to question it too much, afraid that the feeling would disappear as easily as it had arrived, and so I stood up, went downstairs, and started to make dinner. Whatever I was doing, it was working, because throughout the day the peace stayed with me. As soon as Randy walked in the door from work, he seemed to sense something was different.

"You feeling okay today?" he asked.

"Yeah, I'm feeling okay today," I said.

Over the next few weeks, I started to play a little game with myself, or with God really. I'd think about having to clean out Jantsen's room, or see a boy his age playing baseball in the park, and I'd feel the terror brewing, and the sickness and the sense that I was losing my mind. When these feelings arose, I simply went back to God, to the one place I knew I could always find him: in the quiet. Sitting on the bench under Jantsen's tree, or on the back porch, or in the gold wingback chair, I let the quiet in. And then:

I want to feel some peace. Please.

And it never failed.

Not knowing what else to do, I decided to talk to God, openly and without fear.

"So what is this all about? Where are you? Are you there, way above the clouds like I always thought you were? Are you hearing me?"

Pam, I am right here. I am sitting next to you on this step. I will not leave your side, not when you feel this bad.

That was it. No grand pronouncements, no magic answers, and, best of all, none of the useless advice everyone else seemed eager to dole out. He never told me that I needed more time, or that I should go out more, or brush my hair, or return to work.

Just: *I will not leave your side, not when you feel this bad. You can do what you need, and I will be right here.* I'm tired today, and I need to sleep. *Then sleep, Pam.* I need to skip dinner at my family's house this Sunday, even though Crista will be disappointed to not see her cousins. *Well, ask someone to take her someplace fun for the afternoon.*

Now, it's not like I'd never talked to God before. Of course I had talked to God, because if there was one word most people would choose to describe me at the time it was *religious.* After Randy and I married, we joined his parents' church. Though I never truly shook the feeling I'd had at sixteen, pretending I belonged there, I did my best to fit in. I never missed a service, which for us meant not only Sunday mornings but Sunday and Wednesday evenings, too. I taught Bible class and bought in to the more conservative rules our church espoused, like attending services in Proper Church Attire, and not drinking alcohol. I even came up with alternative ways of expressing all my favorite cuss words. Well, for the great effort I had put into my religion, I was beginning to realize that up to this point, I hadn't the faintest idea of who God was. I thought about how a friend who was getting a divorce told me that one day she woke up and suddenly realized she'd been sleeping next to a stranger for the last nine years. That's how I was beginning to feel about God. The one I knew was not the type to ever pay me a visit like this, talking to me with such compassion and understanding. He didn't come from my heart, as this voice, or whatever you want to call it, did. No, he was way up there, on a throne somewhere above the clouds. And while I knew he was God, and he loved everyone, I was never wholly convinced all those years that he *liked* me. He was too busy keeping an eye on me, making sure

I didn't disappoint him, always looking for a reason to send me straight to hell someday.

But the more I engaged in these quiet conversations, the more I began to realize that maybe he wasn't the scary, judgmental, punishing force I had thought. Maybe, in fact, what I was coming to find was what I had spent so long searching for: *grace.*

That, or mental illness.

Either way, there was no way I was letting go of it, especially not with what I was facing: winter. It had been creeping up on me like a stalker in a dark parking lot, and that's about as pleased as I felt about it. Not only did I have to deal with Thanksgiving and Christmas, but Jantsen's birthday was approaching, too. Everyone had been looking forward to this year especially, because the Three Musketeers—Jantsen, Darius, and Gregan—were turning sixteen, such a milestone, and this year's celebration was supposed to have been a total blast. I knew I couldn't expect people to give that up, but I also knew I wasn't equipped to handle the celebrating.

All I could hope for was that everyone would try to understand, would leave me alone, and the day would come and go quickly. Maybe I'd bake a cake for the three of us. Maybe afterward I might finally, somehow, find the strength to clean up Jantsen's room, to organize his favorite T-shirts and start on the memory quilt I wanted to make for him.

Maybe.

A few weeks later, I was sitting near Jantsen's grave, thinking about his memorial fund, when I had an idea. I thought about Carol and Marvin Harlan, our friends from Fayetteville. We had stayed in close touch, and I often called them to ask about their work in Vietnam. Carol told me about her frustrations with trying to raise money. She often gave presentations to church groups or volunteer organizations about the need to help the orphans she met find good homes, but although people often seemed moved by the stories, it rarely translated into donations. I knew what that meant for the kids who never got adopted, how they would grow up feeling unloved and abandoned—emotions I could certainly relate to.

In early November, Randy and I drove to Fayetteville to meet the Harlans for lunch at our favorite Mexican restaurant, and to talk about the decision we had made: We wanted to donate Jantsen's money to them for their work in Vietnam. They were touched by the idea, but before they accepted Carol looked at me over her tacos.

"You know," she said, "I'm going to Vietnam over Thanksgiving. Why don't you guys and Crista come along and make sure this is the right place for the money? I don't know if you're up for something like this, but why not?"

Vietnam? I knew nothing about the place, other than old stories about the war. It seemed so far away and foreign. It seemed like the farthest place in the world from Neosho, Missouri, and Thanksgiving dinner and birthday celebrations and family expectations . . .

I accepted immediately.

Chapter Three

November 20, 1999. Dear Jantsen, I went to the cemetery today to tell you good-bye. I was a crazy woman by the time I left. The weeds were overtaking the plots and I was ready to strangle the groundskeeper. I called to complain and was screaming at the secretary, telling her it was unacceptable for a grieving mom to see the grounds around your grave so neglected. She informed me the lawn boy was mentally challenged and had failed to show up for work, and apologized repeatedly. I am a jerk, and out of control with anger. I'm so glad to get out of this country for a while. I miss you so much. Love, Mom

We arrived in Hong Kong around 7 AM three days before Thanksgiving. Thirty hours on four different planes, and there we were, thrown into the chaotic bustle of a crowded airport on the other side of the world. I was exhausted but strangely, I also felt more awake and invigorated than I had in the five months since Jantsen died. We still had a few hours to kill before our final flight to Saigon, and as Carol, Randy, and Crista went for a walk, I stayed with the luggage. The airport felt like the UN. There were flights being called to board to places I had never even heard of, and for the first time in my life I was one of just a few white people around. Since then, I've come to believe that everyone's To Do list for life should include the experience of being in the minority, even if it's for only a few minutes at an airport. It's an experience I've had many times since that day in Hong Kong, and each time seems to change me a little, helping me better understand how absurd it is that we can view our differences as obstacles, rather than as something to embrace and learn from. Anyway, there I was struggling to keep my eyes open, watching people at a nearby store buy bags of crackers and dried squid, when an Asian woman about my age walked over to me and said hello.

"Are you waiting for the flight to Saigon?" she asked in English, with a soft accent I didn't recognize.

"Yes," I said.

"I don't want to bother you, but I'm curious and had to come and ask: Why are you going to Vietnam?"

After I told her, she said that she had been born in Vietnam and was always interested when she saw Americans on her visits back to the country. Her name was Mai Lang. She was short and pretty, with wavy black hair and a delicate smile. "I married an American man and live in Tulsa now," she said.

"You're kidding," I said, making room for her on the floor next to me. "That's only about an hour from where I live in Missouri." For the next hour, Mai and I sat together, sharing M&M's and talking about the best places to visit in Saigon, as well as up north in Phan Rang, where the orphanage Carol worked with was located. When our flight was finally called to board, we hugged each other good-bye.

There's a quote I read once that I've always loved: *A coincidence is a small miracle in which God chooses to remain anonymous.* That's exactly how I think about the moment when I walked down the aisle of that huge Boeing 777 and found that I was assigned to the seat next to Mai. Of course I didn't know it then, but it was a seat assignment that would change my life.

During the three-hour flight, we became two of those people who usually annoy the crap out of me on planes: the complete strangers who end up talking nonstop, sharing the intimate details of their lives as everyone else is trying to quietly read their gossip magazines. I had introduced Mai to Randy and Crista at the airport, and she asked me if Crista was our only child. It was the first time since Jantsen died that I had to confront the question of how many children I had. I told her that I was the mother of two, but my son had recently passed away. As I related the story to her, she rested her hand on my arm.

I was equally moved by her story. She had grown up with nine siblings in Bien Hoa, about twenty miles outside Saigon, and was eleven years old when the first major battle of the Vietnam War broke out in August 1965. Three years later, the fighting hit home for her, literally, during the Tet Offensive, in which the North Vietnamese Army launched a series of surprise military strikes across the nation, including at the Bien Hoa Air Base a few miles from Mai's house. In the months that followed, her family often ran out of food, and they fell asleep to the sound of rockets and mortars directed at the nearby base. After graduating from high school, Mai took a job as a typist for the Vietnamese government, helping to support her family on the meager salary she was paid. In 1974, during a work trip to Da Nang, she stopped for lunch at a hotel restaurant and was surprised when a tall, handsome American man approached her to say hello. He worked for an American company that had been contracted by the Department of Defense. The next time they met each other in the hotel, where he was also staying, he invited her to dinner. For a few months, they corresponded by mail, and eventually her work visits to Da

Nang became more regular. Every time she returned, she and Edward had dinner.

Mai agreed to marry Edward nine months later—but, she admitted to me as our plane soared above the China Sea, it was not because she loved him. "My family was poor and I knew that marrying him was the best opportunity I had to escape the poverty and the war, and help my family." A few weeks after they married, and Mai had settled into Edward's small apartment in Da Nang, Saigon fell to the North Vietnamese, marking an end to the conflict and a victory for the Communist Party. Westerners scrambled to leave the country. Mai and Edward were evacuated in a cargo plane to the Philippines, with the help of Edward's company, and then eventually made their way to Maryland, where they moved in with Edward's mother. "I ended up with a wonderful husband," she said, "but there's nothing I wouldn't have done to escape that war."

Though she eventually became an American citizen, her heart had remained in Vietnam, and she spent a few months each year volunteering with an organization in Saigon that was helping to find shelter for street children: the thousands of kids forced to beg in the streets and sleep in the market or park to survive. They even had a Vietnamese term for these kids, she told me after our plane landed and we exchanged phone numbers: dust of the earth. The description struck a chord in me. I knew precisely how that felt.

———

The exact etymology of the word *Saigon* has long been under debate, but if you ask me it means "City in Which You'll Probably Get Killed by a Motorbike." As soon as we stepped out of the taxi in front of our hotel in the city center, we were immersed in chaos. People on motorbikes were rushing everywhere, even right down the sidewalks. There were few stop signs and fewer traffic lights, and those that did exist were rarely obeyed. Instead, the driving ethos seemed to be, *Okay, you can hear that I'm honking. If I kill you, it's your own fault.* Twice, after we had dropped off our luggage and went out to explore the city—trying to stave off the crushing jet lag and thirteen-hour time difference—I had to pull Crista out of the way of bikes that showed no signs of stopping. One was driven by a man smoking a cigarette; behind him sat a ten-year-old boy and then the man's wife, who was holding a newborn infant in her lap by one arm.

The air felt exhausted by the traffic, and most people wore cloth masks over their mouth and nose to protect themselves from the diesel fumes, which left a bitter taste on my lips. Despite the intense heat, the women wore pants and long-sleeved shirts or jackets, and many had on nylon gloves that stretched up to their shoulders. Others had beach towels wrapped around their faces and heads, secured in the back by a piece of Velcro, and wore big, dark sunglasses. I later learned that women did this to keep the sun from their skin, as dark skin is considered unattractive in Vietnam. Of course, there I was in a tank top and shorts, hoping for a tan.

We pushed our way toward the Ben Thanh Market, a huge bazaar that spanned an entire city block. Even the short walk there was like nothing I'd ever experienced. A group of shirtless men in thin pants and flimsy sandals crouched in a circle on the street corner, eating from steaming bowls of noodles and sipping coconut milk from the shell through a straw. Women fried whole chickens in a pan of oil under a small flame built around rocks on the sidewalk. Everyone seemed so comfortable and at home, as if they were gathered not on a hot sidewalk along a city thoroughfare, but at a comfortable kitchen table about ten blocks long.

Inside the market, which was lined with stalls offering anything you might want to buy and a lot of things you probably wouldn't, the noise of the traffic was replaced by the echo of hundreds of voices: people talking and merchants yelling to us, to bring us into their tiny stalls. Children, some as young as four or five, tugged at my shorts, holding out small packets wrapped in silver foil. "Chewing gum, madam? Buy some chewing gum?"

It felt like a sauna inside, and as soon as we entered, we nearly slipped on the blood spreading on the floor around two women, who squatted on the white tiles skinning snakes. Next to them, young girls in tight jeans sat on plastic crates, holding out five-dollar counterfeit Louis Vuitton and Gucci bags with dull enthusiasm. There were candies, toys, fruits and vegetables I couldn't identify, and seemingly endless rows of spices and dried roots in large plastic bins. The whole place smelled of the earth, and I felt as if we had descended into a deep cavern miles below the soil, an imaginary fairy-tale land. There were smoked pigs' heads, bowls brimming with what had to be fried insects, and dried fish dangling from strings secured to the ceiling. *Oh, look!* I almost expected someone to say. *It's the recipe for the Everlasting Gobstopper.*

Because I no longer had any expectations of anything, I certainly did not expect to find myself immediately enchanted with Vietnam. The energy of Saigon is amazing—the kind that seems capable of identifying the people who might have spent the last five months moping around their kitchen table, grabbing them by the shoulders, and issuing an impossible dare: *Go ahead. Just try feeling depressed and listless while you're here!* To be honest, there had been many times while preparing for our trip that I'd feel a wave of panic: We're going *where*? (This often followed any conversation I had with my family or friends who, when I told them our Thanksgiving plans, looked at me in shock and said, "You're going *where*?") As I packed our bags and told Crista's school we were pulling her out for two weeks, I couldn't help but wonder if the decision had been too impulsive. But then I'd run to the store for something we needed and get home and realize that not only had I managed to get there and back without collapsing, but I was even feeling a strangely unfamiliar emotion under the sadness: *excitement*. I know I should have welcomed it after how hopeless I'd been, but I had grown so accustomed to feeling bad that a moment of excitement made me feel a little guilty, like I was being unfaithful to my grief.

But during those first few afternoons in Vietnam, I decided that maybe it was time to commit to a short affair with happiness and all its trappings: the fresh pineapple juice they served at the rooftop café of the Rex Hotel, a famous hangout for American officers and correspondents during the war; the morning walks through the neon chaos of Backpacker's Alley, filled with Internet cafés and young Australian tourists; and the fact that the one-dollar laundry service at our hotel included returning my underpants *ironed and folded*. It was such a relief to be somewhere this mysterious and colorful and new, where Jantsen's absence didn't seem as obvious. Sometimes I even allowed myself to think that it wasn't that he had died; he just wasn't here. And when we got home, he'd be waiting for us, eager to hear about the trip.

I knew I was only fooling myself, but at least for a while I chose not to care. This was, after all, my fairy-tale land.

You don't have to spend too much time in Vietnam to realize what a paradox it is: a Communist government with a capitalist economy. The government today is a one-party bureaucracy (meaning that leaders don't have to bother with things like elections), and political dissent and demonstrations are avidly frowned upon. But in 1986, the Communist Party implemented a capitalist makeover called *doi moi,* meaning "new changes." It included a move away from a centrally planned economy to one based on free-market principles, opening the door to foreign investment and trade. It now seemed that everyone in Vietnam— including the children—had learned the value of making a buck. On the narrow, leafy streets of Saigon, we could barely walk a foot without a man offering to drive us somewhere on his motorbike or cyclo, a bicycle with a seat over the front wheel. In fact, you have to develop a real knack for ignoring people or you'll find yourself constantly harassed by hawkers: teenage boys with trays of cigarettes and lighters, men balancing cardboard boxes of coconuts and bunches of candy-sweet bananas, and pregnant women weighted down with tall stacks of bootleg videos and xeroxed tourist books. Everything was for sale, it seemed, and given how much tourism has increased over the past decade, American dollars were as widely accepted as dong, the national currency. Once, when I was trying to locate a phone to call my parents and tell them we were still alive, a man pulled out his cell phone and offered it to me. "Four dollars a minute," he said. "Keep it for the day if you like. We can find a good price."

But the flip side of *doi moi* is that, just as in any capitalist economy, there are the upper and middle classes, and then the very poor. Unlike in some American cities, which have done their best to hide their poverty, in Saigon it's impossible to escape. Backpacker's Alley, for example, with its hotels and comfortable cafés catering to tourists, looks as if it could exist in New York. But every time we turned down an alley, I witnessed poverty on a scale I'd never seen before: several generations of families living in crowded one-room apartments; disfigured men sleeping on mats, many with signs noting that they had been injured during the Vietnam War; children with scabies and other skin ailments, begging for money or food.

It was especially hard for me to see the children, and there were so many of them. Kids as young as six or seven, often walking hand in hand, would stop us, holding out a dirty palm to ask for money, their faces contorted into a practiced frown. One evening, as we sat at an outdoor café having dinner, a nine-year-old girl named Huong approached our table, trying to sell us gum. Her teeth were twisted and knotted, and the shirt she wore was at least two sizes too big for her. She didn't go to school, she said, but had learned English from the years she spent working on Backpacker's Alley and talking to tourists. Every afternoon, she came here with her box of gum and candy, and could not go home—a thirty-minute walk, which she did alone—until she had earned ten thousand dong (less than a dollar). That was usually about 2 AM when the tourists at the bars were drunk enough to finally agree to buy two packs of Chiclets. The next day, she woke up, helped her mom with her younger brother and sister, and then headed out again. Randy gave her a dollar for a pack of gum and, after sticking it, all crumpled up, into her shorts pocket, she leaned her head on my shoulder with a dull smile. "Come on, Mommy," she said, "give me some money for a hamburger."

I thought about what Mai had told me about kids like Huong. Many of them, the girls especially, were at great risk of being picked up by traffickers, who would then sell them to a brothel owner in Saigon or, even more commonly, neighboring Cambodia. Because the Vietnamese have lighter skin than Cambodians, they can often fetch a higher price from Westerners whose idea of a vacation is to sleep with a girl. Looking at Huong, who was not much younger than Crista, the idea nauseated me.

———

A few days later, we left Saigon to fly up north to Nha Trang, a breathtakingly beautiful city on the turquoise waters of the

China Sea where many US soldiers went for R&R during the war. As we flew into the small airport, men who had been cutting the grass along the runway with sickles scattered into the surrounding fields, which were dug with ditches once used to accommodate anti-aircraft weapons during the war. We hailed a taxi to take us to our hotel; on the way, we passed groups of workers sweeping garbage into the gutters alongside the road with handheld brooms made of sticks and wire.

When we woke up the next morning, it was Thanksgiving back home. Crista and Carol were still asleep. Randy and I snuck out of the hotel and went for a walk on the beach. Large speakers attached to light poles blared crackly music from a local radio station, a perfect soundtrack for the experience. Even at 5 AM, the beach was filled with people—groups exercising, families gathered on woven mats, eating hard-boiled eggs and bowls of rice. Randy and I sat down on the sand near a man who looked to be about a hundred years old, practicing tai chi. He was silent and focused as he went through the slow, rhythmic motions of this ancient martial art, and it appeared as if he were fighting a phantom ghost in slow motion. As soon as the sun appeared over the horizon, the music stopped and the people gathered their things, heading out toward the town to begin their workday. They were gone so quickly, it was as if they had never even existed.

After breakfast, we all piled into a minivan to begin the two-hour trek to Phan Rang, where the orphanage Carol worked with was located. As we traveled the rough, winding roads of central Vietnam, our driver strictly adhered to the *I Am Honking!* school of Vietnamese driving, jerking aside every few seconds to avoid a child on a bike, or people on their motor scooters, or men crowded atop ox-driven carts. Trying to block out the honking and the chatter, I pressed my head against the window and watched the little villages come and go.

I couldn't believe the living conditions. Every few miles we'd pass a collection of homes: thatched roofs held up with metal poles, bamboo sticks, or bricks, buried in the green pastures of terraced rice fields. Most people in Vietnam practice Buddhism, and the temples were lovely and intricate, with bright, beautiful tiles and slanting roofs. There were orchards of dragon fruit trees, which looked like squat palm trees with a full head of unkempt dreadlocks. Our driver slowed to point out the rubber trees, planted in perfect rows, with slits carved into their trunks, like winding staircases, to allow the rubber to flow down into plastic containers secured at the bottom.

The rice fields were filled with workers, and I noticed how many were women. They stood knee-deep in the swampy, emerald ponds, swinging large, sturdy hoes. Many of them managed this while balancing an infant on their back, secured there by a large piece of fabric. How many of these women had lost a child? I wondered. A lot, probably, as medical care in these rural villages was woefully lacking and Carol explained that families often could not afford even the fifty dollars or so it cost to deliver a baby at a hospital. But here, losing a child didn't mean that a mother could stop working. She couldn't just curl up somewhere, writing in her journal and reading grief books. A day of not working meant a day without eating. What a difference from my experience. I couldn't even handle one day a week at the hair salon.

A few miles outside Phan Rang, we entered a thick jungle that felt ancient and mysterious. As we turned down a dirt road covered by a thick canopy of palm leaves and hanging branches, I rolled down the window to take in the deep rich scent of the earth, and thought about my uncle Phil, who had fought in the Vietnam War. I was eight years old at the time, and captivated by the stories of his "travels," as I thought of them—of how he slept outside with his friends, drank the milk from coconuts they pulled from trees, and was constantly on the lookout for poisonous snakes. When he arrived home, he let me peel through his luggage, and all I could think at the time was how lucky he had been to have had such an adventure. I remember pulling a worn photograph of a young woman out of his wallet. She was the most beautiful woman I'd ever seen: thick black hair, exotic features, and a daring smile. On the back, my uncle Phil had written the name Kim. He saw me looking at the photograph and told me she had been his girl-friend. When I asked him why on earth he hadn't brought her home to America to live with us, he snickered and, speaking to my other uncles in the room, said only, "She's not exactly the type of girl you bring home." I didn't understand what he meant, of course, just as I didn't understand what my uncle Phil had endured, and ultimately survived. Seeing those jungles outside the car window, I couldn't help but imagine the horror of that experience.

We arrived in Phan Rang in time for our Thanksgiving din-ner and chose a restaurant that was small and brightly lit. There was only one menu for the whole place, which we had to wait twenty minutes to see. The tablecloths were orange and pink, covered in stains, and instead of napkins we were given a roll of toilet paper to share. But it was a perfect Thanksgiving feast of noodles, steamed vegetables, and a big plate of spring rolls, and for the first time in years I didn't have to unbutton my jeans when it was time for dessert. Randy suggested that we take turns describing what it was that we were most grate-ful for that day. He began, saying how happy he was that we were all together and experiencing this new culture. Crista said she was grateful she had finally mastered the art of eating with chopsticks without dropping food on her shirt. Carol said she was grateful for us, and our willingness to come and see if this was the best place for Jantsen's money. When it was my turn, I didn't know what to say exactly. Back home, I knew everyone was probably looking forward to the big family dinner. In a few hours, my mom would wake up early to begin preparing the turkeys and cleaning the house. It was such a relief not to be there, and every time I thought about returning home, where the grief waited for us, the panic came again. But to have been given a brief reprieve from it—well, I was more grateful for this than I could possibly explain.

———

As much as I was enjoying the trip and being immersed in the local culture, I couldn't wait to get to the orphanage the next day and meet some of the children who Carol and Marvin had told us so much about. That morning, Carol had scheduled an appointment with government officials with whom she was working on adoptions, and Randy, Crista, and I waited for her outside our hotel, where we watched boys play pool at the bar across the street.

"If Jantsen were here, that's where he would be," Randy said, laughing. I had been thinking the same thing myself, picturing him standing with these boys, acting proper in their blue-and-white school uniforms while shooting pool. Such rebels. When Carol returned, she told us the governmental officials had invited us to have lunch with them, and although she tried to prepare us for it—telling us that to refuse any food or drink was considered rude, and anything short of appearing overwhelmed by their hospitality a real slap in their face—I'm not sure anything could have.

Mr. Chong, who led the meeting, was the director of the humanitarian department in the province. He was tall and creepy, with yellow, crooked teeth in which he kept a burning cigarette tightly clutched. Carol had told us that he called the shots when it came to government matters in this town, and when people didn't do as he wanted, he could make things very difficult. He started the meeting by instructing a young man to bring in a tray of beer, then proceeded to pour each of us a big glass, even Crista. After replacing that with a Coke and sitting down to a table covered in bowls of egg-drop soup, prawn, steak, and grapefruit, the toasts began. Chong got up. He inhaled deeply on his cigarette before saying something loudly in Vietnamese. The interpreter, a small, mousy man, interpreted in the direction of Carol: "I want to drink 100 percent in honor of our good relationship." Mr. Chong linked arms with Carol and downed his beer. He then looked at Randy and me. "I want to drink 50 percent in honor of our good relationship," and then grabbed our arms.

"What happened to the other 50 percent?" Randy whispered as Chong drained another glass. The toasts continued this way for a while, and I did my best to sip as much beer as I could. Nobody but Chong seemed to be enjoying these ceremonies, and Randy, understanding that refusing these toasts would be a sign of disrespect to a man whose help Carol needed for adoptions, pulled it out for the team, matching Chong nearly drink for drink. One for Crista, another for a man whose wife was having surgery. It seemed as if Chong was testing us, and Randy especially.

"You've got to keep up," I whispered as he gazed wearily at a young man pouring him another glass.

"I'm going to end up drunk here," he whispered back.

"I know," I said, "but you're doing it for the kids!"

After the meal, we followed a stumbling Chong back out into the sunlight and heat, and walked to our hotel. I thought he'd leave us in the lobby, but instead he followed us upstairs to Carol's room. There he sat down on the bed and, through his translator, explained that moving forward, he needed to receive fifty dollars for each child adopted through Carol's orphanage.

"In exchange," he said with a smile, "I will personally ensure that things go very smoothly."

———

We finally arrived at the orphanage around 2 PM. It was located at the end of a rocky driveway behind a temple; incense was burning outside. A group of older boys in bare feet stood around a dirt courtyard, passing a deflated soccer ball back and forth. Carol showed us around. There were kids everywhere. Marvin and Carol were doing everything they could to give these children the best life possible, and this orphanage was considered one of the best in Vietnam, but while it was Marvin and Carol's money that funded the place, the government hired and managed the staff and set the rules on how the orphanage would operate. The children here got all the basic necessities—food, clothing, and immunizations—but seeing how many orphans lived here together was heartbreaking. Many of them had been abandoned by parents who couldn't afford to feed them, or by women who had found themselves pregnant and unmarried.

I was most overwhelmed by the newborns, most of whom were sleeping swaddled in blankets on woven mats atop slatted wooden beds or in pink metal cribs corroded with rust. I walked up and down the rows, picking up children and putting them down again. I didn't know any of their names, or how old they were, but I wanted to hold every single one of them. They were so alone. Of course there were staff members around, but it was immediately obvious that none of these children got the love of a mother. After what I had just been through, I couldn't imagine someone making the choice to give up a child. I tried to keep in mind the extreme poverty that likely led parents to have to make this decision, but it wasn't enough to quiet the sense of injustice and sadness I felt.

At the end of one row, I came across a girl who couldn't have been more than two months old. She was wailing. She was tiny, and looked tortured, and I thought my eardrums would burst from the piercing scream she let out. Maybe she was crying because of hunger, but as I picked her up and felt her heaviness, I wondered if perhaps there was something more behind her tears: a sadness for being left here and having to fend for herself and because her future looked bleak and hopeless.

I looked at her, and all I could think was, *Oh my gosh, I know exactly how you feel.* I held her tiny frame before me, and then took her and wrapped her in my arms and held her little body tight to my heart. As I did this, I felt something I had been missing since the morning Jantsen died: compassion.

My sadness and anger over the last five months had me believing that nobody could possibly feel as bad as me. I had the corner on suffering, and for the rest of my life I would walk alone on this earth in a cloud of sadness so thick and dark, the likes of it had never been experienced before. But as I held this young child, I realized how much we had in common and perhaps . . . just perhaps . . . I wasn't the only one suffering in the world. The compassion I felt for her, and for me, was so strong, it warmed my body, and warmed the child in my arms, who was still crying.

Don't worry, I whispered to her. *I'm not going to leave you, not when you feel this bad.*

As I walked around, trying to rock her to sleep, the most wonderful realization struck me: At that moment, I was *exactly* where I belonged. The sense of wholeness and purpose I felt was what I had been searching for all those years. It was what I thought I could find on a Caribbean cruise, and that trip to Disney World, and my countless shopping expeditions. I never would have thought that I'd one day find it here, in a room in Vietnam, in a sweaty T-shirt and no makeup, rocking a crying infant to sleep. I thought about Jantsen's money. It would cost very little to help this child, and his memorial fund—well, it could alter the course of these children's lives, either by helping them find loving homes or by getting them the help they needed here.

As the child in my arms stopped crying and fell asleep, I heard Randy call my name.

"You've got to come here," he said, the strangest look on his face. I laid the baby back on her blankets and followed him to an adjoining room, where a little boy sat alone on a woven mat. Lost in my thoughts, I was envisioning how we could use Jantsen's money to change these children's lives. But as soon as I saw this child, I knew. He was about to change ours.

———

He was born Vinh Thien to a mother who couldn't afford to raise him. She already had three children who were now living with her parents, chicken farmers in Phu Thanh, a rural and impoverished area in central Vietnam. When she discovered she was pregnant with Vinh, this time with her latest boyfriend, her parents refused to take him in, and a few months after Vinh was born—five months before the day I met him—she had dropped him off at this orphanage. She never came back.

"Mom," I heard Crista say beside me, "can you even believe this baby?" He was beautiful—tiny and soft, with huge cheeks and meaty thighs: the only plump kid in a country of tiny people. He was sitting on that mat, in this room by himself, and he was wearing a suit—a blue one, of thick polyester—and white crocheted booties, despite the fact that it had to be over a hundred degrees. Sitting perfectly straight, holding a teacup. It was as if he had just prepared crumpets and a fresh pot of tea, and was now patiently waiting for his guests to arrive. *I'm supposed to meet someone today,* I almost expected him to say to me, *although I don't know who it is.*

I picked him up and, immediately, I was overwhelmed. It was unexplainable. At this point, I had met at least fifty children, if not more. There was something interesting about every single one of them, of course, but Vinh . . . I can't even describe it. There was just something about him. As he settled into me, resting his head on my shoulder, I looked up to see Randy and Crista watching me. I couldn't stop crying, but this time they weren't the tears of misery I had grown used to, they were tears of tremendous hope. I took him and started walking. We went outside, down a cement stairwell and into the courtyard. For the rest of the day, I never put him down.

We could not stay away from him for the remainder of our time there. Randy, Crista, and I were developing bruises on our ribs from how much we'd try to elbow each other out of our way each morning so that we'd be the one to give him his bottle or rock him to sleep. I swear, we were like bratty siblings wrestling over the remote.

"It's my turn," Randy would say as I held him.

"Too bad," I'd say. "I was here first."

Then Crista would appear. "Why do you still get to hold him? I found him!"

There was plenty to do, though, when it wasn't my turn. It was pretty clear that the older kids at the orphanages had likely become accustomed to being passed over for the infants by visitors like us. When I initially tried to engage them, many did their best to appear aloof and disinterested, but it didn't take long to break them down. By the end of the first afternoon, I had teenagers climbing all over me, asking me to take their photograph or take photos of their friends. I went and bought a pair of scissors at a local grocery store; in the evenings, the kids lined up while I cut their hair. Crista was usually sitting on a stool in the corner, surrounded by toddlers, teaching them English words, and learning some in Vietnamese. Carol had brought coloring books and games she had collected from people back home, and the kids loved them. They spread out on the tile floor of the large rooms, among the cots and bunk beds, and colored for hours. I sat down next to a boy who was probably ten years old and asked to see his drawing. It was two adults holding the hand of a child.

———

There is an old Vietnamese proverb: *Hoc an, hoc noi*. It means something along the lines of "people need to learn to eat before they learn to speak." This makes a lot of sense, given how good the food in Vietnam is. In the months after Jantsen died, I had lost at least fifteen pounds (which, by the way, didn't solve all the problems I had once believed losing weight would). Just the day before we'd left for our trip, when we had dinner at my parents' house to say good-bye, I still hadn't been able to eat more than a few bites before feeling full and sick. But in Vietnam, I couldn't wait to eat. Every morning, I'd find a new place to try the pho soup, a spicy chicken broth with flat rice noodles into which I'd squeeze the juice of two whole limes and a thick bunch of mint. In the evenings, I'd start every meal with spring rolls eaten the traditional way: wrapped in a piece of lettuce and pieces of cucumber, and dipped in tangy ginger sauce. Then we'd pile the table with big bowls of steaming vegetables and rice, or a whole fish caught earlier that day.

During the meals, or anytime we were away from the orphanage, all we talked about was Vinh. The second evening after meeting him, Randy was the first to say what all of us were thinking: "That child is ours."

I knew exactly what he meant. This is hard to explain to people who have never adopted, but sometimes, there are these moments when you just, well . . . *know.* "What is it about him exactly?" Randy said to me that night as we sat on the little balcony of our hotel room, watching the city of Phan Rang prepare for sleep.

"I have no idea," I replied. "But he's amazing."

"I know," he said. "I feel blindsided by this sense of knowing right now."

Those first few nights, the conversations never went farther than this, and neither of us ever used the word *adoption.* It seemed evident that this was where we were heading, but it felt bizarre and terrifying. The thought of adopting again had never even occurred to me, and I was pretty sure Randy felt the same. But for Crista, just eleven, it was so simple. Of the three of us, she was most adamant, giving language to what we were feeling. "Why would we not adopt him?" she asked us one morning over breakfast. And then lunch. And then again, at dinner. "He has nobody else in this whole world who truly cares about him. Look at everything we have. Why would you not be the mom and dad to this baby who doesn't have anyone?"

The answer was perhaps apparent the next morning, when I woke up sobbing so hard, I could barely find the strength to lift my head, and felt the familiar, soul-crushing ache in my chest. It was Jantsen's sixteenth birthday. Randy came close to me, our tears wetting the pillows, and we held on to each other. He whispered a few prayers in my ear before we heard Crista stirring in her cot in the corner. She got up and joined us in the bed. My friend Traci had sent a package for Crista to open on this day, and after she unwrapped a beautiful, delicate music box, we held tight to each other, feeling, again, how much we had lost.

Eventually, I pulled myself together—which took every ounce of energy I could muster—and we headed back toward the orphanage. It was our last day here, before we were scheduled to travel north to Hanoi for a few days, and I was filled with dread at the thought of having to get through the day, and, at the end of it, say good-bye to Vinh.

The day before, I had asked someone where I might find a bakery to buy a cake. On the way to the orphanage, we hunted for the address among the barbershops, cafés, and shops selling silks and cell phones, passing monks on bicycles, wrapped in yards of apricot-colored cotton. When I got to where I thought it was supposed to be, I found a mechanic's shop. I was about to turn around and leave when a woman noticed me and waved, telling me to follow her. In the back, past the oily tools and rusting motorbikes, was a bakery.

The woman handed me what looked to be a wedding cake—with big, greasy yellow and red flowers outlining the words HAPPY BIRTHDAY JANTSEN—and told me I owed her seven dollars. I knew that was a ridiculous price for a cake in a town where our hotel room cost fifteen, and that I could have bargained her way down, but I didn't care. I would have paid anything for this simple gesture in memory of my son's birthday.

We carried the cake to the orphanage, and after lunch we celebrated with the kids. As I fed Vinh frosting that tasted like Crisco, I knew that I loved this little boy. It was just as Randy had described it: an unquestionable sense of knowing. I tried to force myself to stay in the wonder of it, but I was so conflicted it felt like my brain and heart had gone to war, and all I could do was take cover and wait to see the casualties. Yes, I loved him, but we were screwed up right now. I, for one, had nowhere near the emotional or mental stability caring for a seven-month-old required. The last time I'd done that I was twenty-six years old, and here I was almost forty. I know plenty of women take on children at that age, but I didn't think that I might be one of them. The woman I saw in the mirror was not a person who could care for a baby. It was just me, the total mess.

By this time, however, Randy had become convinced that we were meant to adopt Vinh. That last evening in Phan Rang, as he held Vinh in his arms, with Crista beside them, I could not take my eyes off the three of them together. Deep down, I knew Randy was right. Vinh was a part of our family now. The feelings I was experiencing about Vinh were more powerful than even my fears. More powerful, in fact, than me. *Of course I can do this,* I thought. *Of course I'll go home, and I'll take care of myself, and I will be able to love and raise this child.* I took Vinh from Randy's arms and whispered a promise to him. "We're going to come back to get you, son."

I just hoped I wasn't lying to him. Or to myself.

Chapter Four

March 2000. Dear Jantsen, I still feel like I am standing on a riverbank and the water is rushing by. The river seems deep and wide. But so be it. Your dad, Crista, and I have decided to take the leap of faith. We're diving in. I love you, Mom

We started the process to adopt Van Alan Cope, the name we had chosen for him during our last days in Hanoi, as soon as we got home. When we told people about our decision, most of them looked at us like we had completely lost our minds. "Everybody says you're not even supposed to make a decision to change your hairstyle when you're in an emotional state," one friend told me. "Certainly you shouldn't be making a decision like this right now." All the grief books agreed. One of them had listed different "levels of grief" you might expect to experience, assigning the appropriate amount of time to be spent at each. It was bizarre, like we had entered this alien universe inhabited solely by grieving people and had to solve clues or take over enough planets before the leader would allow us to graduate to the next level. Randy and I used to joke about it. Once he came home to find me on the kitchen floor, holding Jantsen's photo and sobbing.

"Pam," he had said, taking me in his arms. "This is very Level Two behavior. Our leader will not be pleased." Before I knew it, I was laughing so hard I could barely breathe.

Not surprisingly, that book issued the same warning as most others: No major decisions. While none of them were quite so specific, my guess was that adopting a seven-month-old Vietnamese orphan probably qualified as a major decision.

Randy ignored them completely. "Let them say what they want," he said. "I, for one, am done letting other people think they can dictate how we're supposed to grieve or that they know better than us about what God is telling us to do." The idea that Randy could be happy again was enough to make me do my best to ignore them, too. In fact, I had begun to sense a difference in him since returning home from Vietnam, as if the darkness in his eyes was beginning to fade a little. One day, he came in from mowing the lawn with a peculiar look on his face.

"What's wrong?" I asked as he sat down at the table with a cup of coffee.

"It's weird," he said. "I just caught myself whistling in the garage. I haven't done that since Jantsen died. I guess it's a nice feeling, like maybe I'm feeling hopeful again, but it's also a little sad. Part of me wants to hang on to the misery, you know?"

I did. In some ways, it felt like the misery was the only tangible thing left of Jantsen. Coming home, I noticed how much people had begun to move on, talking even less about him, looking forward to Christmas. I didn't want any part of that. If feeling sad meant feeling closer to Jantsen, then I'd choose to be sad forever. Of course, I didn't have to worry too much about feeling happy, as the joy and peace I'd felt in Vietnam were beginning to elude me completely, clobbered away by a sinking depression—one even more severe, in fact, than what I had felt before we left for the trip. I certainly was not expecting this. We've all heard that time heals all wounds, making it seem like grief is some sort of perfectly linear process. Well, it isn't. The darkness I was beginning to feel six months after Jantsen's death was so deep, I couldn't remember anything so lonely and threatening, not even in the days immediately after he died.

It didn't help that we returned home to a town decorated in reindeers and wreaths—things I thought were placed there simply to remind me of how happy I was supposed to be. They were everywhere I went, often accompanied by one of those Christmas songs that can leave even the happiest person convinced they are not enjoying things *quite* enough. I couldn't believe it was only a year earlier that I was shopping for the kids and eagerly pulling out the stacks of boxes where I stored every Christmas knickknack known to humankind. The idea of doing that now revolted me. Not only because Jantsen wasn't around to enjoy it, but because the whole spirit of the holiday felt manufactured.

I have a friend who likes to warn me after I return from a trip that I'd better not become one of those people who start reminding everyone else that for the cost of that cup of Starbucks, they could feed a village for three years. But part of me did struggle with this after returning home from that first trip to Vietnam. You have to admit, meeting a family of three generations who share a one-room apartment can sort of take the fun out of spending $150 on the perfect loungewear and matching slippers from Victoria's Secret. In fact, I was starting to feel that way about many aspects of my American life. Vietnam was social and alive—the streets and parks crowded in the evening with families eating their meals on blankets, and kids giving each other rides to school on their bikes. Here, everyone on my street pulled their car into the garage each evening, closed their drapes, and probably turned on the television. We had been living in our house for more than a year and still hadn't met the neighbors across the street. I know that most of the people we saw in Vietnam would be considered "poor" compared with us, but when I thought about the way my friends and I lived our lives, theirs seemed so much, well . . . richer.

This only made me feel worse, and the worse I felt, the more I began to doubt our decision to adopt Van. Maybe everyone was right: Maybe it was too soon to make such a momentous decision. With the way I was spiraling downward, I had no idea where I'd eventually land. Had I been crazy to think that I could take care of this child? And even more so, was I simply trying to replace Jantsen? I knew that's not what this was. You cannot replace a child. But others didn't agree. They never told me so outright, but I could see the unspoken sentiments on people's faces when we told them our decision. *Poor Pam. She's just trying to fill a void that she'll never be able to fill.* I'd like to say that after everything I had lost, I no longer cared what people thought, and that I had stopped trying so hard to please people, but it did bother me. Was everyone going to decide that I had lost my mind and abandon me completely? Of course, there I was, just performing for others again.

Although I'd always been honest with Randy about how I was feeling, I didn't want to tell him about my doubts. I knew how much he couldn't wait for the day he could see Van again. When I did mention it, he was understanding but firm.

"Pam," he said, "you have to trust me."

I'd nod and smile and mutter something reassuring, but I wasn't being honest. The only thing I trusted was that I needed to find a way—any way—to stop the searing pain.

This was when I began to daydream about disappearing. The stories of my disappearance were always pretty loose on the details, because it wasn't as if I was actively hoping for death—or planning it—as much as I was allowing myself to entertain the fantasy that I might somehow be liberated from the unbearable sorrow. Sometimes when I was driving, I let the thoughts come: What if I got into an accident? What if someone hit me, traveling too fast down the highway, never leaving me a chance? What if I were suddenly diagnosed with breast cancer—would I seek treatment? No, probably not.

Somehow, I survived Christmas. If I'd had my way, we wouldn't have celebrated the day at all. Randy took charge. He and Crista went out and got a little tree and put it in her room, rather than in the living room where it usually stood this time of year. Mike and Diane came to Missouri for the holiday, and on Christmas morning, we woke up early and sat on the couches and watched the kids open their gifts. Randy's dad handed his mom a small box wrapped in silver paper. Inside was a simple bracelet with two diamonds: one for Megan and one for Jantsen. I felt the tears coming, and I got up and snuck outside to cry. They had lost two grandchildren. What was possibly fair about that? Back inside, as my mother-in-law clasped the bracelet around her wrist, I wondered why we were even going through these motions. What had once been the happiest times in our lives—holidays, vacations, family gatherings—were now the saddest.

After the new year began, my depression began to take a physical toll on me. Where I had once been able to force down food a few times a day, I could no longer manage even that. Even the smell of food made me gag, and days would pass where all I ate was a few pieces of buttered toast.

One night, lying in bed, Randy wrapped his arms around me, and then quickly let go.

"It's hard to hold you," he said. "You're so small and frail, I feel like I could hurt you."

Do it, I thought to myself. *At least I'll feel something.*

It's still difficult to think about the weeks that followed. In February, Randy had to go to Las Vegas for work. It had been eight months since Jantsen died, but I was failing to feel any better. In fact, at this point, I was having trouble even getting Crista ready for school. I'd do it, but it exhausted me so much that as soon as she was out of the house, I'd have to lie down in the dark. As I watched Randy walk out the door for his trip, I felt enormous relief. It was taking too much energy to hide how bad I felt. All I wanted was to be alone.

I don't know how many nights passed that I didn't sleep. Being physically and emotionally exhausted and unable to sleep is an eerie feeling. Not even the sleeping pills helped me. A few days after Randy left, my sister Tam stopped by to see me, as she did most days. She walked into the kitchen and as soon as she saw me, I knew that my cover was about to be blown. There are some things you can't hide from your twin. For most of my life, I had been trying to separate myself from Tam. Though we never looked alike, our mother had dressed us alike when we were young; we shared the same bedroom, the same friends. We didn't really exist as individuals—just "the twins"—until we were about twelve. Then both of us decided it was time for space. But in moments like these, when Tam could take one look at me and know exactly what was going on, I remembered that in many ways we would always share an uncommon bond. "Come on," she said. "Let's go for a walk."

I was still in my robe and felt far too exhausted to change into clothes, let alone walk. "No," I said. "I'm a little tired today."

"Well, I have to run some errands and you're coming with me." She would not take no for an answer, no matter how much I pleaded with her to give me my space. I pulled on a jacket. As

I walked to her car, my whole body hurt. I couldn't focus on anything she was saying; I just lay there with the seat reclined, trying to find peace and the strength I needed to be ready for Crista to come home from school in a few hours.

But Tam didn't take me to run errands. Instead she took me to her house, where she made me lunch and tried to get me to eat. She asked if she should call our mom to come over, or to get Crista at school, but I begged her not to. Although I wanted her there with me, I never would have wanted to worry her with what I knew was happening.

I went into Tam's room and lay down on her bed. I could not move. As I felt the panic growing inside, I knew that today was the day I had been both fearing and longing for. I was either going to end it completely, or get help, but this could not go on.

I probably didn't have the energy to kill myself. So I lay alone in the dark and tried to pray. Even that required too much strength because I was so ticked off at God. *Why are you doing this to me?* I whispered. *On top of everything, you're asking me to adopt a baby? I have just buried a child. Don't you understand? I don't know what to do.*

And there it was again.

I'm not going to leave you, not when you feel this bad.

Then tell me what to do.

Now, it's pretty clear, at least to me, what I meant by that question. What I meant was, Give me the answers to this. Am I supposed to adopt this child, as I feel I am, and Randy is sure of? Am I capable of being his mother? But that was not the answer I got, as the voice inside my heart was obviously far wiser than I. What it said was:

Get up. Go into the kitchen. Tell Tam you need some help.

So I got up, and I went into the kitchen.

"Tam," I said. "I need some help. I think I need to go to a mental hospital or something." I told her to call my mother-in-law, Anne, because she would be able to deal with the situation. When she arrived a few minutes later, I didn't try to hide anything, as I had been doing for so long. I just told her that I could not get control of my mind, and I was probably going crazy, and I was absolutely terrified. I knew I could no longer go on like this.

Anne didn't even flinch. She simply walked to the phone, called Craig Pendergrass, a friend of ours who is a doctor. We were coming to his office, she told him, and we could not wait even one moment in the waiting room. Then we were in her car.

At his office, I could not wait to climb onto the hard examining table. I wanted to curl into a ball and be covered with something and have everything go dark. I was willing to give up. To anything. To death, to drugs, to sleep. I didn't care what they did, I just needed it to end.

Craig forced me to stand up. He took my blood pressure and immediately called the hospital, which was across the street. Then Anne was wheeling me over there in a wheelchair.

At the hospital, I crawled into bed and begged for drugs, knowing that sleep was the only thing that would protect me from myself. A nurse came in and helped me change into a robe. Then she smoothly inserted a needle into my arm. As I watched the IV dripping above my head, the fluid and medicine beginning their short vacation in my veins, I felt my mother-in-law's hand on mine. I tried to thank her but before I could get the words out, I felt my eyes closing, and the room shrinking, giving me what I had been begging for: total and complete blackness.

Later, lost in the haze, I thought I heard Randy's voice.

Randy

It was my voice she heard, and I think it's important that I step in here. That's what I did then, just as Pam would later do for me.

It was terrible getting the phone call that Pam was in the hospital. When my secretary interrupted my meeting to tell me that I needed to call home, I can't even describe what I felt. I was never *really* afraid that Pam would hurt herself, but our world was so different now, and so screwed up, I had no idea what was feasible anymore. Also, after losing Jantsen, I learned that even the most impossible ideas are sometimes possible.

I'm no expert on grief. All I know is what my experience was, and my experience was absolute misery. After Jantsen died, I read the grief books that said that you had to fight denial and work to accept the reality of loss. Well, I think denial is underrated, because, at the time, it was working for me. Every time anyone told me that I was supposed to come to accept that I would never play baseball with Jantsen again, or take him hiking, or cut the grass with him, I refused to believe it. He was *my son*. He looked like me, I knew what he was thinking the moment I saw his face, he had my sense of humor. In fact, he was the only one who got most of my jokes. And he had many qualities that I wanted. He could roll with the punches. I loved that about him, and when I saw how easily he could do that, I'd work to be better at it myself. And now I was being asked to accept that he was gone and "process" losing him? I wouldn't do it, at least not then.

I know that the challenges of staying together are sometimes insurmountable for couples who lose a child, and I can understand why. I certainly allowed myself to entertain the idea of leaving. In many ways, that was the easy route. Of everything Pam was to me, she had mainly become the face of my loss. To even look at her was to be reminded that Jantsen was gone, and of course there were times that I thought the only way for me to continue living was to avoid that reminder by simply walking away from my family.

I got through these times by keeping constantly busy, and I went deep into my work. I also became preoccupied, at least for a while, with trying to understand what, exactly, had killed my son. The doctors who worked on him at the emergency room that day had been able to tell us only that Jantsen had some sort of undetected heart ailment, but I desperately needed more information. I sent his medical file to our friend Leon Blue, who is a cardiologist in Arkansas, and he went out of his way to help me understand the situation better, even consulting four different pathologists. They agreed that Jantsen's heart had an abnormality of the conduction system—which means simply that the part that kept it beating in perfect rhythm was messed up. Though we had no way of knowing this, it was something that he had had since birth. For people with this condition, the first symptom is often sudden death. Leon also explained that based on his research, even if Jantsen had been on a monitor in the cardiac care unit of a hospital at the moment of the actual event, it may still have been impossible to keep him alive.

The information gave me what I wanted: some relief from feeling like I had failed my son. After he died, I was often tortured by the idea that I had not done my job. Wasn't it my job—my most important job—to protect my kids from harm? I couldn't stop questioning what I may have missed that might have saved him. Learning that there was probably nothing we could have done was in some ways a release. The very first thing I did after Leon and I talked was to call Mark and Cheryl, who had worked so hard to save his life that day. I feared they agonized about their own inability to revive him, and it was important to me that they understood this wasn't the case. I am very grateful they were the ones there with him in those moments. If he did feel panic then, I know it was lessened because of the love he saw in their eyes.

As for Van . . . that first moment I saw him was unlike anything that I can explain. I did not go to Vietnam looking to adopt. Like Pam, the thought had never even crossed my mind—until I saw him, and then I could think of nothing else. Before that moment, I had no idea how—or if—we were going to survive the rest of our lives, or how we could possibly start to put together anything that might resemble normalcy. But when Crista called me over and told me I had to see the baby, I knew immediately that he was ours, and that our lives could again have meaning. That moment was definitely one of the greatest of my life—not only because of what I felt for this little boy, but also because of what I saw happen to Pam the minute she looked at Van.

When she first picked him up from that mat, I could not take my eyes off her. Something changed in her, immediately. She cried so hard as she held on to him, and though both of us spent countless days and nights in tears, I knew these tears were different—I can only describe them as tears of deliverance.

Which is why that day, sitting next to my wife in the hospital, beneath my worry and total devotion to her, I was also growing frustrated. I knew she felt the same way about Van. I had known this woman since I was sixteen years old, and there's nothing we have kept from each other. She wasn't doubting her love for him; she was losing faith in herself. It was almost as if she were asking me for permission to give up. I knew that if I gave even an inch—either by joining her in the surrender to grief, or allowing her to think she was right—I would not be loving her at all. The more she gave in, the more firm I needed to be. We had been led to Van and somehow I knew—I *knew*—he was ours. Now we had a choice: walk through this door and find new meaning in our lives, or ignore it and experience tremendous regret. And maybe even our own deaths.

For hours, I stood beside Pam's bed with our good friend Warren. He didn't leave either one of us that night. Together we each held on to one of her hands. "Don't worry," I whispered. "Your boys are here. It's safe."

And then she slowly started to come to.

———

I slowly opened my eyes, and wondered where I was, and then I saw Randy and Warren standing beside me, each holding one of my hands. "It's okay," I thought I heard Randy whisper. "Your boys are here." Knowing I was safe, I closed my eyes again, and slept some more.

When I woke up again, later the next day, Randy was the only one there. As soon as I saw him, and the concern in his eyes, I felt the guilt crushing my chest. I hated having to say the words, but I knew I had to. "I'm sorry, but I can't do it," I managed. "I can't adopt Van. It's too much pressure. Look at me. I can't even take care of myself. Why did I possibly think I could take care of him?"

Randy squeezed my hand, but I could see the disappointment—or was it anger?—in his eyes. I knew he was losing patience with me. "Well," he said, "you can't do it, and I have to do it. I'm not sure where that leaves us."

Craig walked into the room, interrupting the conversation. He told Randy to take a seat, and then started to explain how serious my condition was. He said that he had never seen anyone become as physically depleted from depression as I had been when I arrived at his office three days earlier, and he wanted to get me started immediately on antidepressants. It wasn't as if the idea had never occurred to me—that I needed something more than willpower to feel better—but prior to that moment, lying in that bed, in the ungodly unattractive blue hospital gown, I hadn't wanted to do it. Pills seemed like such a shortcut to recovery—a way to mask the pain and replace it not with joy, but with nothingness. But Craig explained that what I was experiencing was not just self-pity or sadness. Rather, there was a chemical imbalance in my brain that could be controlled by medication. I didn't hesitate even one second before telling him to write me a prescription. My fears and judgments about taking antidepressants seemed ridiculous to me now, lying in a hospital bed. I knew that I had no other choice. None of the things that were supposed to make me happy were ever going to work, even if I had somehow been able to find the energy to do them: exercise, walk in the sun, have sex with my husband, get a new haircut and a bright shade of lipstick. Honestly, I was so tired of feeling bad, I would have tried anything.

All that day, my room was filled with family and friends who came to sit with me or drop off flower arrangements. The gestures were nice, but I felt pathetic. I know how confusing this was for my family—I had been hiding my true grief from them for so long that they were caught totally unaware. Here they'd thought I had gotten much better in the eight months since Jantsen died, and had begun to move away from the grief . . . only to find me tied up in tubes in a hospital, minutes away from possibly giving up completely. When Crista walked into my room with a look of terror in her eyes, I felt horrible. Just twelve years old, and she was having to spend another afternoon in a hospital, wondering if someone else she loved might die. And wondering, still, why she wasn't enough to live for.

I would, of course, have done anything for Crista. Maybe it was my desire to finally make her realize that, or the sleep that I had gotten, or the drugs, but later that afternoon I started to feel better. When I woke up the next day, I wanted to go home.

It may not have seemed like that much to others, but it was something. It was a start.

———

For the next several weeks, Randy was too worried to let me out of his sight for very long. I even had to travel with him on his work trips like a naughty daughter. Or I'd be in the basement folding laundry and he'd casually appear, leaning against the dryer watching me pair up the socks.

"I thought I'd come to say hello," he'd say.

"Really?" I'd reply. "Well thankfully, you're just in time. I was considering trying to drown myself in the gentle cycle."

A few weeks after I came home from the hospital, he asked if I'd go with him to buy a new golf club. On the way to the store, he brought up Van again.

"I'm sorry," I said. "I don't think I can do it."

"Pam," he said, the anger rising in his voice. "You *can* do it. You've got to stop telling yourself you can't. I know this is right for us. Can't you trust me?"

"You I can trust," I said. "It's me I have a problem with. I don't feel like I am strong enough. What if we were to get this baby and I crash like that again?"

"You won't," he said. "You'll see it coming and you'll take better care of yourself. You won't be that low again."

"Are you sure?"

"Yeah, I am," he said. "You have survived this. You survived the day he died, and the day you wanted to die. Your deepest, darkest, most hopeless days are behind you. But if you keep telling yourself that you're weak and broken, then that's who you'll be."

While he went inside to shop, I stayed in the car. I knew that he was pissed, and for the first time in the seventeen years we'd been married, I felt concerned about us. We had never been at such odds about something—and not only something, but *this*. How were we going to get through this one?

A few minutes later, I saw him nearly running out of the store toward the car.

"Okay, listen," he said, opening the passenger door and kneeling on the ground. "I love you very much and I am asking you right here and right now. You have to trust me. You have to trust that this is going to be all right, and that you are okay, and that you are not going to spend the rest of your life feeling this bad. We can do this. You and me and Crista, we can do this. I believe in you."

He took my hands. "But you have to make a decision. Are you going to choose to believe in yourself? That's the question you have to think about."

Over the next few days, I couldn't get Randy's Passenger-Side Grilling, as I had come to think of it, out of my mind. Did choice have anything to do with it? Anybody who has experienced grief, or any type of depression, knows that it's impossible to simply manufacture hope—that's just one of those things that either finds you or doesn't, and it was not finding me. But the more I thought about it, the more I was coming to think that maybe I was waiting for the wrong thing. Maybe instead of trying to muster hope, what I needed to muster was something else entirely: courage.

Not knowing what else to do, I did the only thing I could think of: I went up to my room, locked the door, sat myself back down in the gold wingback chair, and found the silence. On the end table next to me was Van's photograph, and I took it and held it in my hands. I stared at his face. What would his future be like if we didn't adopt him? The best he could hope for was that another family would. But the chances of that happening were minuscule. Saying no to him would likely mean that he'd stay at the orphanage for the rest of his childhood, never getting a good education, never getting enough to eat, and never knowing that somebody loved him completely. Without us, his future was hopeless.

And what would *my* future be like if we didn't adopt him?

I wanted to live a life of meaning, a life of grace, and for many years I had no faith that I would ever find my way. Hadn't I decided, again and again, that I was not like Carol, or Princess Di, or people who did meaningful, interesting things? I remembered those days after Jantsen died, criticizing myself for the choices I had made in my life, for valuing things that were superficial and unimportant. But what was I going to do: spend the rest of my life berating myself for the choices I made, or have the courage to make different ones?

I was still sitting there holding that picture when Randy came upstairs an hour later. He looked at me. Without saying a word I stood up, walked over to him, and put my arms around him. We stayed that way, without speaking, for several minutes.

"Okay," I whispered. "I trust you. And better yet, I am choosing to trust myself." Randy pulled me tighter and when he finally let go, both of our cheeks were wet.

"I just hope that when we get him home I don't collapse again, and end up being taken somewhere to sit and drool in a corner," I added.

"That's not going to happen. And don't worry," he said, kissing my lips. "If it does, I promise to bring Van to visit you as often as I can."

Ten months after our first trip, I was back in Vietnam. This time, to pick up our son.

RESCUE

Chapter Five

August 4, 2000. Dear Jantsen, I have decided I'm no longer going to defend our decision to adopt your baby brother. Your dad and I have spent months getting looks of pity from others who seem to be judging us, who see Van as some sort of "replacement child." I am ready, I want to bring your brother home and be his mom. Love you, Mom

A word of advice? If you ever find yourself wondering if you're equipped to throw yourself back into parenting a baby, try traveling alone on a nineteen-hour flight with a sixteen-month-old. *Who has a parasite.*

By the time we finally got the call that our paperwork had been processed and the adoption was approved by the Vietnamese authorities, I felt much better. Don't get me wrong, I'm not trying to kid myself or pretend that I still didn't experience bad days, because of course I did (and still do). But the decision to say yes to Van, and to myself—and probably the antidepressants—had more of an effect on me than I could have imagined. When Randy, his mother Anne, and I landed in Saigon in August 2000, I was sure not only that I could handle the responsibilities of being Van's mom, but that I desperately wanted to.

When the director of the orphanage handed him over to us on our fifth day there, during a ceremony in a small room decorated with Ho Chi Minh busts and red velvet curtains with bright yellow fringe, Van was dressed in rags—thin jersey shorts with patches sewn on the rear, a tattered shirt, and little plastic gold loafers that barely fit his chubby feet. That first night with him in the hotel was one of the best nights I've ever had. I ran him a bath and removed his clothes. He was perfectly plump, as if he'd been pumped with a tire pump. As he stood before me, I realized that I no longer saw him as the little boy I had met in the orphanage. He was now my son.

When I set him in the bubbles, he had no idea what to do. Unlike my other kids who could spend a whole weekend playing in the bathtub, he just sat there. The only time I had ever seen him bathed was once when a staff member dumped cold water over his head after he had been lathered up; he just stood there taking the punishment. After he was clean, I rubbed lotion over his callused knees, elbows, and feet. I must have used twenty Q-tips on his ears, which were so dirty I swear there was still amniotic fluid in them. Then I clipped his nails and combed his hair and brushed his teeth.

"What are you doing, detailing him?" Randy asked me as I rubbed more lotion into his dry, cracked feet. Van took it all in, barely making a sound.

Crista had packed his suitcase, and I opened it to find that she had organized and labeled her brother's new clothes into outfits. Shorts were pinned to shirts, and socks to hats. I dressed him in a soft one-piece white sleeper (clearly marked in Crista's handwriting as NIGHT #1) and sitting next to Randy on the bed, I fed him a bottle until he slept.

In the end, it took us more than three weeks to get him out

of Vietnam. Compared with some stories I've heard from people who have done international adoptions, we may have gotten
off easy—you never know how long it will take to go through
the red tape. From getting a medical checkup, to a passport to
the interview with the US consulate, you may be stuck there
for more than a month. Ten days into our saga, Randy had to
return home for work, and Van was left with Anne and me. By
this time, we had arrived in Saigon to wait for his passport and
the interview with the US consulate. Every morning, we'd strap
him into a stroller and take him to the zoo, or to see the water
puppets. Anne also had to leave a few days later for a cruise she
had booked, and for the next week I had Van to myself. I loved
every minute. I'd take him downstairs to the beautiful buffet at
the New World Hotel so that I could fill us both up on oatmeal,
the texture of which I've yet to find anywhere else. We'd eat at
a table in front of a huge window that offered a beautiful view
of the park across the street, which was filled with children on
their way to school and teenage couples sitting together under
the large palm trees. We got to know the hotel staff, who let
Van crawl around the empty halls in the afternoons, stepping
over him as they walked between rooms with clean sheets, towels, and buckets of soapy water. Afterward, we'd swim in the
hotel pool and take a nap.

I fell in love with a cozy little restaurant called Sinh Café
on Backpacker's Alley. The ambience was nothing special, but
they had great food and a big open area where Van could run
around, chasing the geckos that scampered back and forth
across the walls. I'd walk him there many mornings, past the
bars that, at 9 AM, were still crowded with young men from
around the world, drinking large bottles of Saigon beer that
cost less than fifty cents. I began to pay attention to how many
teenage Vietnamese girls I saw inside, sitting on stools, their
drunken frames slouched over their drinks; many looked no

older than fifteen. College-aged boys, and sometimes older men, sat next to them, a hand resting possessively on the young girl's thigh.

By the time Van's paperwork was processed and the interview at the consulate complete, I was dying to get him home. Not only because of how badly I knew everyone wanted to meet him, but because with the parasite he had picked up somewhere along the way—not unusual for children raised in Vietnamese orphanages—I was dreading the travel. I knew that it could be easily treated with medication at home, but it was very uncomfortable for him, and a little tricky for me on a trip that was going to take us from Saigon to Hong Kong. And then to Los Angeles. And then to Dallas. And then to Tulsa. With a baby. Who had diarrhea so bad it probably could be considered a lethal weapon.

Things went relatively smoothly until we got to LA. Van barely slept on the nineteen-hour flight, and I spent most of the time walking him up and down the aisles to keep him quiet. Everything I tried to feed him had spilled onto one of us. By the time we landed in California, we could have fed a family with the scraps of food on our clothes, and we were both ready for a shower and some sleep. Of course, we didn't even have time to sit down because we had less than two hours before our connection to Dallas, and had to process the paperwork. This can take a while because this is the point where Van, once he set foot with me on US soil, became an American citizen. As I waited in line at the immigration station, I noticed that he was getting clammy and whiny, a sign that he was about to suffer an attack of intense diarrhea. When we got to the desk, I could smell it. And according to the look on the immigration official's face, so could he. But he was kind enough not to point out that my son had green liquid spilling down his thighs.

After clearing customs and getting our luggage, we had less

than twenty minutes to catch our flight. I was panicked. I hated the idea of missing it and having to spend the night in Los Angeles. So, not even stopping to wash him off, I threw our bags over my shoulder and ran like a madwoman toward security. When I got there, the security guard told me that I had to take Van out of his stroller. I tried to explain that we were extremely late, and he was extremely sick, but she wouldn't budge. With no other choice, I took away his raisins to lift him out of the stroller, which sent him into a fit. He started screaming, and before I could catch him, he threw himself on the ground. *Bottom first.* Runny, green poop flew everywhere—on the floor, on the metal detector, all over him, all over me. The security guard looked at me with a horrified expression that said, *What is that?*

Knowing I didn't have time to clean it up, I did the only thing I could think of: I ran away. With Van over one shoulder, and our luggage over the other, I raced to find a bathroom. I now had fifteen minutes to find our gate, was covered in diarrhea, and had a child who sounded like he was being murdered. On top of that, I was gagging from the stench of his dirty diaper. In the restroom, trying to breathe through my nose, I peeled off his clothes and my T-shirt, scrubbed the poop from his hair and fingernails, threw a fresh shirt on me, and slapped a clean diaper around him.

I could not believe we made it onto the plane. When we boarded, right before they closed the doors, the flight attendant stopped me. "Why is your baby not wearing any clothes?" she rudely inquired.

Ignoring her completely, I found our seats, where I nearly collapsed in tears. Another flight attendant came over, and while I was expecting her to explain that there was a rule prohibiting people covered in baby poo from being able to fly and the authorities were coming to escort us to Child Protective Services, she instead asked if she could do anything to help me. A few minutes later, Van was drinking from a warm bottle and eating a hot plate of rigatoni. Afterward, he lay down on my chest and slept until Texas. I never did get that flight attendant's name, but I swear she saved my life that day.

We arrived in Tulsa at midnight, and Randy and Crista were there waiting for us. Though both of our families had asked to come along to meet our new son, we expected this homecoming would be very emotional, and we didn't want any observers. Also, we knew how much it would mean to Crista to have Van to herself for a few hours. I'd never seen her or Randy so excited. Crista had gotten braces while I was away, and her smile could have lit the airport. Van went to her immediately. She took him away from us and walked around for a while, whispering in his ear.

Randy put his arms around me. "I'm so happy you're home. When I saw how close your connections were, I never thought you'd make it."

I pictured those days and nights after Jantsen died, feeling hopeless; lying in that hospital bed, wishing to die. *I never thought I'd make it either,* I thought.

Van slept in Crista's lap the entire ride home. I know I should have strapped him into the car seat, *but just this once,* I thought. If he were traveling back in Vietnam, he'd be swinging from a woman's lap on the back of a motorbike.

And anyway, watching the way Crista held him tightly against her, I knew he was going to be okay. Maybe we all were.

———

Van brought so much light back into our house, as if the curtains had finally been pushed aside and the black shades lifted. Rocking him to sleep every day for his nap was like a balm on my heart. As he snuggled deep against me, his body melting into mine, I knew that he needed the closeness, and the healing, as much as I did. After we had him home, I even mustered the strength to finally clean out Jantsen's room so Crista could have it, and Van could have hers. That was a very hard day. My mom came over to help me pack Jantsen's things. We sorted out the keepsakes, and I put them in the trunk Randy and I had spent weeks trying to find—the "perfect trunk" in which to store our son's belongings. It was miserable. I remember opening the little nightstand drawer where he kept his most valued possessions, trying to absorb the fact that it had been sixteen months since I'd seen my son. There were golf balls he had retrieved from the golf course pond, baseball cards that were bound with a rubber band, sports medals, a beanie flipper, some coins, and electrical tape because he taped up everything that was in reach. He had needed little to be happy. Oh, and of course there was his paperback Jeff Foxworthy book, which was probably the only book he had ever read all the way through of his own accord.

In addition to taking care of this, and the many other things I had been neglecting, I knew there was something else I needed to do. After our first trip to Vietnam, we had donated ten thousand dollars of Jantsen's money to Carol and Marvin for their adoption work, telling them to use it however they saw fit to help get some of the kids we met into loving homes. We still had about fifteen thousand left. Our initial plan had been to donate all the money to them over time, but when Carol told me they had begun to receive support from some major donors, I started to consider alternatives. The truth is, I hadn't been able to stop thinking about the kids I saw on the streets of Saigon: the teenage girls in those bars on Backpacker's Alley; the boys carrying around shoeshine cases, following Westerners and asking to scrub their loafers; and the little girl Huong who, on our first trip, had asked me for a hamburger. Compared with them, the children I had met in the orphanage seemed almost lucky. I wondered what sort of conditions would make parents send their child to work and live on the streets. Many nights, after putting Van to bed, I'd go down to my little office and try to learn as much as I could about these children.

It is estimated that there are approximately fifty thousand street children in Vietnam—kids younger than sixteen who earn a living on the street. Referred to as *bui doi,* or "dust of the earth," most work in the cities of Saigon, Hanoi, and Da Nang, up north, but come from rural areas where 90 percent of people live in poverty. *Ninety percent?* Though poverty is considered the primary factor pushing kids to the street, others reportedly end up there because they have been abandoned by their parents, are trying to escape domestic abuse, or are handicapped. In Vietnam, as in many Asian countries, being born handicapped can often guarantee a life of begging on the streets.

Ironically, a lot of the poverty in rural areas stems from *doi moi,* or the move toward a free-market economy. While this may have benefited people in cities, along with foreign investors, it has hurt many rural residents. In 1988, the Communist Party ended state subsidies and disbanded the agricultural cooperatives that had provided citizens with health care, education, and a social safety net. The privatization of many services, and the fees now associated with them, keep them out of reach for many rural families in a nation where the average annual income is the equivalent of just $480.

Children working on the street—selling newspapers or postcards, or shining shoes—can earn about twenty thousand dong, or $1.25, a day, a large portion of which they often send home to help support their families. Though all these kids are at risk of getting abused or robbed each night, the most horrifying risk they faced is being trafficked.

I remembered how Mai Lang, the woman I met on the plane to Saigon on our first trip, had told me the same thing. While I understood the general idea, I knew nothing about how bad the situation was until I started researching it. Trafficking was first defined in international law only as recently as the year 2000, through a protocol adopted by the United Nations General Assembly. Known as the Palermo Protocol, it defined human trafficking as the recruiting or harboring of people by means of force or coercion, or paying others for the control of a person, such as their own child. Despite the fact that 117 nations have ratified the Palermo Protocol, and are thus required to enact specific policies making trafficking a serious crime and setting appropriate penalties for those found to engage in it, the problem has not become any less severe. Though there is no exact count of the number of children who have been trafficked, either in Vietnam or worldwide, one report by the UN states that "the numbers are enormous, and the trend is on the rise." In fact, human trafficking has become one of the most lucrative and fastest-growing transnational crimes, generating up to ten billion dollars each year. This is partly due to the fact that as more international resources are committed to combat drug trafficking, the criminal networks once involved in the drug trade have increasingly begun to divert their attention to developing human trafficking networks. As another UN report notes, it has become less expensive and less risky to buy and sell humans, children especially, than it is to traffic drugs or arms.

Children are sold to work in factories or as domestic servants, or to beg on behalf of their sponsor, but trafficked children in Vietnam—girls especially—are most commonly bought to work in the sex trade. It's been estimated that nearly twenty thousand children under eighteen years old have been sold into prostitution, and the number continues to increase. A common tactic used by traffickers is to lure young girls with the promise of a well-paying job in a café or shop, only to then take them to a brothel and sell them to a madame. If the girls refuse to take clients, they are often beaten or locked in a room, and their families threatened.

Sometimes girls are even sold to sex traffickers by their own parents, who need the few hundred dollars a trafficker will pay in order to survive. Afterward, that money is considered the girl's debt; she will be forced to work until the debt is repaid. But between having to pay back the cost of the clothes she's given and her room and board at the brothel, the debt never actually decreases.

Thousands of Vietnamese children are also being trafficked to other countries—Singapore, Thailand, Taiwan, and even the United States—but the most common destination is across the border in Cambodia, which, despite the fact that it ratified the Palermo Protocol, has become renowned as a destination for sex tourists. According to a UNICEF report, nearly 60 percent of the estimated forty-five thousand prostitutes in Phnom Penh, Cambodia's capital city, are Vietnamese. An attractive Vietnamese virgin younger than sixteen will cost a Cambodian brothel owner between $350 and $450; older girls, nonvirgins, or those considered less beautiful, just $150.

In 1998, Vietnam's prime minister enacted new laws to combat child trafficking and child abuse, but according to the information I was finding, members of the military and Communist Party officials are themselves part of the problem. One report I read estimated that up to two-thirds of Vietnamese government officials were known to visit karaoke bars or massage parlors to hire prostitutes, their activities even financed through government agency "slush funds." And prostitution has become so accepted that business deals with foreign investors looking to put some money into the local economy are often closed with an offer of girls.

Reading these facts and figures, I'd think of Huong, and the idea that she could end up at a brothel, being forced to do unspeakable things; or of Van, picturing him walking around Backpacker's Alley, begging American men to let him shine their shoes. These images reminded me of something I had once read in a book called *The Dream Giver* by Bruce Wilkinson, about a boy who had died alone: *It certainly cannot be God's will that any child die alone and abandoned. Surely God placed a particular set of interests and abilities in one person, somewhere in this world, and put that person in a time and place where great things could happen—should have happened—for that boy.*

Those nights, unable to sleep, I could not get that idea out of my mind. I had always believed that the only children I had been assigned to care for were my own. But that idea, and so many others I had about my place in the world, had begun to shift, and I was coming to understand my responsibilities as much larger. I don't know when, exactly, this shift happened—maybe the afternoon in the emergency room with Jantsen, or the night Huong laid her head on my shoulder and asked me for a hamburger, or the moment Van stopped being a Vietnamese orphan and became my son. Or maybe I had known it all along. Maybe, in fact, it was this idea that had been nagging at me those years, stuffed inside pillows and paint cans and self-help books. Maybe *this* is what it had always meant for me to live a life of meaning.

One night, as I clicked off the light beside my bed, thinking again about the children I had met in Vietnam, I realized I no longer had the energy to quiet that voice in my heart. Daunting or not, this was it. It was time to either make the meaning happen or be resigned to a life spent wondering *what if?*

And no, maybe I couldn't do anything to end child trafficking in Asia, but I could do one thing.

The next morning, I picked up the phone and called Mai Lang.

———

Mai's house in Tulsa was large and beautiful and, in keeping with the tradition in Vietnam, didn't have a stitch of furniture beyond a kitchen table downstairs, and a bed upstairs. After driving around for a while with the address she had given me over the phone, I finally spotted the yellow house with white trim and a pretty porch, out in front of which sat a pair of the smallest shoes I'd ever seen. This had to be it.

Mai had prepared homemade pho soup for us. As we ate, she told me how happy she was that I had called, and that she had thought about me often since we met on the plane to Saigon. I brought her pictures of Jantsen, Crista, and Van, and she showed me photos of her son Kelly and daughter Karen, two of the most beautiful children I'd ever seen, who were grown now. We talked more about our lives, and she told me how difficult it had been for her when she first moved to the United States with Edward. Shortly after they got settled in Edward's mother's house in Maryland, Mai found out she was pregnant. A few months later, Edward received a job offer to work in Taif, Saudi Arabia. Mai couldn't go with him because her visa was still being processed, so—two months after he left—she had their first child alone. When her son was almost three months old, the two of them finally moved to Saudi Arabia. There Karen was born three years later. Then, in 1984, they moved back to the United States again, settling, this time, in Tulsa.

It was hard for her—a Vietnamese woman married to an American man. In the beginning, when they lived in Vietnam, she said that people often labeled her a prostitute, thinking she was one of the many women who had sold themselves to foreign soldiers to help support their family during the war. After they escaped to the United States, Mai had no way to contact her family and friends, and it was nearly three years before she got word that they had survived. It was a lonely time for her, and even after she became an American citizen, she never felt truly accepted in her new country.

"I've never been pretty or popular, and I've grown used to feeling like an outcast," she said, sitting next to me on the mauve carpeting, holding the scrapbook filled with photos of her family. "When I was a child, I was poor and people would ridicule me. Then I came to the US, where people saw me only as an immigrant. I've never felt good enough."

This was partly what led her to feel such a connection to the street kids and prostitutes in Vietnam, with whom she worked when she went back to Saigon a few times each year. She told me about some of the children she had gotten to know. K'Sally, who was sixteen and from the Ma Tribe, lived with her mother, who tried to make a living selling lottery tickets and doing odd jobs after her husband up and left. Twice, while K'Sally was home alone as her mother worked, she was raped by a neighbor. After the second time, he threw her into a dry well and covered it, hoping to bury her alive. She was eventually rescued by neighbors who heard her screams. La Thi Ngoc, who was five years old, was a dwarf. Raised by a single mother who did odd jobs, she was guaranteed a life of begging. When twelve-year-old Kiet The's father became paralyzed in an accident, the mother abandoned the family, and now he and his siblings worked the streets of Saigon selling cigarettes and lighters.

A few weeks later, Randy and I invited Mai and Edward to dinner at our house. Over hamburgers and salad on our back porch and three weeks before Mai was scheduled to return to Vietnam for another three-month stretch, we told them about Jantsen's memorial fund, and the decision we had made. We wanted to use the remainder of his money to help kids like

K'Sally and La Thi Ngoc. We couldn't do it without Mai's help, and we asked her how she thought we might spend the money.

"Get the children who are on the street off the street, and keep others from ending up there," she said without hesitation. "They are there, mostly, because they are not going to school, and also because many have no other place to go. If I could do anything, I'd enroll them in school, get them educated, and let them know they have a safe place to live for as long as they need it."

"Well, if you're willing to help us, I think that's what we should do," I said.

Mai was speechless for a few moments, and then we all came to a decision. We would focus on prevention, doing what we could to keep at least some kids from having to work on the streets. When she got to Saigon, she would rent an apartment big enough for fifteen children, hire a houseparent, and enroll the kids in school. "Are you sure you'll be able to do that?" I asked her.

"There are so many kids in need of help," she says. "I'm sure I can do it."

When I asked her the cost of this, it was my turn to be speechless. Twenty-five hundred dollars for one year. This included food, shelter, tuition, clothing, and medical needs for fifteen children, and a salary for the houseparent. I couldn't believe it, silently going down the long list of frivolous things I'd spent at least that much money on. At that amount, I began to imagine everything we could do with fifteen thousand dollars, and I felt like writing her a check that moment for the remaining money. But since neither Mai nor I had any idea what we were doing, I knew it was best to start with fifteen kids, make sure we didn't do any major harm, and move forward from there. Also, Randy and I were both sure of one thing: The kids that were helped through Jantsen's money were not going to be looked after only until they were a certain age, or done with school, but for as long as they needed it, even if that was for the rest of their lives.

I was on pins and needles for the next few weeks, waiting for news from Mai. Finally, one evening during her third week in Vietnam, not long after I finally managed to get Van to sleep, the phone rang. I knew it had to be her. There was singing in the background when I answered, and I thought for sure I was hearing her wrong. "We did it!" she said. "We found an apartment, got the kids, and now they're here at their home!" They were the ones singing. Mai had identified the children with the help of a woman named Sister Minh. She and her husband Thao had been doing street outreach in Saigon, often bringing homeless and vulnerable children to live with them and their three sons in the one-room apartment where they lived. Some had been trafficked, others orphaned. The ones who did have families were being cared for by single parents, many of whom had drug, alcohol, or mental health issues, and all of whom were very poor. In every instance, after Mai explained that she wanted to take their child to live with Sister Minh—who had happily agreed, with her husband, to be the houseparent—and enroll them in school, the parent gratefully accepted. Though some of the children were initially hesitant to go with Mai, once they walked into their new home, where new mattresses waited for them on the floor and a huge dinner simmered in the kitchen, their fear subsided. When Mai explained that none of them would have to work on the streets again, or beg for food or money, a huge celebration erupted. Within a few days, the fifteen children had become part of a new family, and Sister Minh was always there to dole out as much love as they needed. And the best part, Mai told me, was that the following morning, they'd all be starting their first day at school.

It was exciting to hear Mai's stories about the children, but over the next few days, underneath my excitement, I was beginning to grow worried and more than a little intimidated. Now that this was real, I didn't know what to do. It had been only an *idea* and, let's face it, one that I never trusted I could make happen. If I had, perhaps I would have better thought through the fact that Jantsen's money wasn't going to last forever. With what was left in his fund, we could only guarantee support for those fifteen children for five years, and that wasn't going to work. So now what?

So now I do whatever I need to, I thought. Randy and I decided that we would start contributing a portion of his salary to Jantsen's fund, and if and when we ran out of money, we'd figure it out. But the thought kept occurring to me that I wanted to do a little more. The more I read about the extent of the problem in Vietnam, and the great risks many of these children faced, the more I wanted to tell people what I was learning. Sometimes at church, guest speakers would come to discuss larger issues outside our community, or missionaries would speak about the problems in the countries where they worked. Maybe I could do something like that, too, I thought. And maybe if I could, if people heard the stories about kids like K'Sally and La Thi Ngoc who were now living with Sister Minh—if people could understand the fate that Van may have escaped—maybe they'd want to pitch in and help. The only problem with this idea was that I absolutely hated it. I had never spoken before a crowd of people in my life, and even imagining it was enough to make me nearly collapse with stage fright.

Which is why I should never have mentioned the idea to my friend Penny.

Penny is far more like my sister than she is a friend. We'd

met in cosmetology school eighteen years earlier, when we'd sometimes carpool to class. But we didn't truly become friends until after Jantsen died. One day, a few months afterward, she arrived at my doorstep with a small gift for me, a little prayer book inscribed with Jantsen's name. We hadn't spoken in years, and the gesture was so kind. I called her a few weeks later, and since then she's been one of my closest friends. She is the warmest, funniest, most gracious woman I know. And at times—like when it comes to talking me into things I know I should do but don't *want* to—a real pain in the ass.

After I mentioned my idea of trying to talk to people about our work in Vietnam, Penny assumed the role of my uninvited publicist, and because it's hard to say no to her, the invitations to speak started to roll in. The first one was before a lunch meeting for a group of women who did volunteer work. Randy agreed to stay home with Van, and I put on my best dress and picked up Penny. The whole way there I was so nervous, I had to fight the urge to turn the car around and go home. We had put together a slide show with photos of K'Sally, La Thi Ngoc, and the other kids. This was before the PowerPoint era, and I had borrowed an old, creaky slide projector from someone. At the meeting, Penny sat in back and tried to manage the slides. Every time she pressed the button, the machine made a huge clunking noise, like someone opening fire, and everyone in the room would jump out of their seats. This is Hong, she was homeless for many years after being raped by a sixty-year-old. *Clunk-clunk-clunk-clunk-clunk.* This is Le Nguyen Vuong, his father beat him for many years until he escaped to the street. Without our support, who knows what could happen to him. *Clunk-clunk-clunk-clunk-clunk.*

When I finished, I was surprised to find that the whole room was in tears, which made Penny laugh with delight. "This is great!" she whispered to me as I joined her in the back. "There's not a dry eye here. They're going to empty their wallets." And she was right. At the end of the meeting, the chairwoman passed around a basket and asked everyone to be as generous as they could. Penny and I grabbed each other's hands. Our first donations! We watched the women pour checks and cash into the basket. When it got back to the organizer, she looked very pleased. "This money is going to go a long way toward funding the upcoming Christmas home tour," she said. "Thank you ladies for being so generous. And thank you, Penny and Pam, for such an enlightening talk." I saw Penny's face drop. The money was not for us. Not knowing what else to do, we smiled and started to pack up our things. On the way out, a woman stopped me.

"Pam," she said. "I have a question for you."

"Of course," I said, getting ready to tell her I'd take either a check or cash, and anything at all would be helpful.

"I heard that you were once a very good decorator," she said, handing me her business card. "I'm looking to redo my kitchen and was wondering if you could help. I'd be willing to pay."

Our next several speaking engagements weren't much different. We'd go to lunch meetings for different volunteer groups and *clunk-clunk* our way through the stories, but we'd still leave empty-handed. The best talk I ever gave was before a group of professional men. By this time, I had worked out most of the kinks in our presentation and was able to hide my jitters better; I was very pleased at the end of it. The organization's president stood up and gave me a lovely and heartfelt thank-you. He then turned to the group. "Okay, we need to get down to business," he said. "We're here to talk about the bathrooms at Big Spring Park. They're disgusting, and people are starting to complain. How are we going to raise the money to fix this problem?"

The *bathrooms*? In the car on the way home, Penny could not stop laughing. "You're joking me. Half those men could have bought all of Vietnam, and we didn't get a dime!" she said, wiping the tears from her eyes. "The bathrooms!"

After a while, I didn't know if I could do one more talk. It felt as if I was nothing more than a lunchtime distraction, a way to fill an hour of time. Was I just naive to think that people were going to care about orphans halfway around the world? All I seemed to be good at was making people squirm, check their cell phones as I talked, go for a bathroom break. I knew the information I was sharing was uncomfortable and depressing, of course, but that was *my whole point*.

The churches I tried next were hardly any better. Any donations we got were usually things people simply no longer wanted—old shoes and winter coats (not so necessary in Vietnam). I cannot tell you how many times we got a call to come pick up a donation and found a garbage bag full of used McDonald's Happy Meal toys. People seemed willing to give away the things they no longer wanted, but is giving away something you no longer want truly *giving*?

Trying another strategy, I picked up the phone and started to call some of the more prominent businesspeople Randy and I knew to ask if I could come in for an appointment. While many were generous with the time they gave to me, I could not get to them to understand why a child halfway around the world was possibly their problem. Instead, I started hearing the same question, again and again: *Why Vietnam? Why not Neosho, or Newton County, or somewhere in America? We certainly have our fair share of problems here, Pam.* It's not that I didn't expect this question, or understand why people felt drawn to ask it; it just didn't make sense to me anymore. *Because,* that's why. Because a child is a child regardless of where they live, and only by the grace of God did we end up living in a country with a welfare system and soup kitchens. Because the minute I set foot in that first orphanage, a nagging started that hasn't stopped yet. Because this is what I feel I have been called to do. Every time Mai called to ask if we could find a way to help a few more kids in need, which she did quite frequently, what was I supposed to say? *Yes. As long as they are American.*

I gave up trying to explain this to people. Instead, I tried to remember that these children felt distant, and their stories were more than a little hard to hear. In fact, I was getting the same looks I'd once gotten when I wanted to talk to people about Jantsen after he died. It was too painful to think about, and much easier to try to get away from me as quickly as possible and return to the things we've found to distract ourselves with: park bathrooms, and dinners, and bigger houses and cars. It was easier to buy in to the idea that this is simply how the world worked: We are American and privileged, and these kids are third-world and poor. It's not my problem. *Well, it's become my problem,* I thought as I shook another hand and thanked someone for their time. *And you can say no to me, but that doesn't mean I'm going to stop.*

That's not to say I wasn't getting extremely frustrated, and that part of me didn't want to stop. Many nights, I'd come home, join Randy on the back porch, and show him what I had raised. "Am I wasting my time?" I'd ask him. "Maybe I should just give this up."

"No," Randy said. "Remember, there's a benefit in just telling the stories. It can't become about the money. Keep it about the kids, and everything will follow."

And it seemed that every time I felt discouraged something would happen to encourage me. Once, I got a call from a teacher at the local elementary school. Her students had raised $150, most of it in rolls of pennies and crumpled dollar bills, and they wanted to donate it to my work in Vietnam. Another time, a friend came by with beautiful bags of toys and school supplies for each of the kids, tied up in colorful string, and a big check.

I tried to remember these tremendously thoughtful gestures a few months later while Penny and I were driving home from another talk with an envelope containing ten dollars and a garbage bag full of broken toys and used shoes. Exhausted by my frustration, I clenched the steering wheel so hard my knuckles turned white, and a passing headlight caught the diamond on my wedding ring. I just looked at it. I have always *loved* my wedding ring. Seventeen years earlier, when Randy proposed to me, he handed me the exact ring I had always wanted: a solitary diamond in a marquis cut. It was beautiful, and the only time I ever took it off was to have it cleaned by my friend Stephen, who is a jeweler. Every time I did, he'd comment on its perfect cut and clarity.

But looking at that ring that night, I felt something different: I felt like a total hypocrite. Here I was, annoyed at everyone else for their unwillingness to sacrifice, judging them for the decisions they made, but what about my decisions? What was *I* sacrificing? Yes, maybe I had changed my way of thinking, but had I done anything to change my way of living? Was I any different from the woman I'd been before Jantsen died? Maybe it was time that *I* gave up something that I valued.

The next day, I went to Stephen's jewelry shop, and I never saw that diamond again. I don't think I got more than fifteen hundred dollars for it, but that was more money than I had raised to date, and it felt like a lot. Plus, it was almost one year of support for those fifteen kids. When I later asked Randy if he had minded that I sold the diamond, he laughed. "I can't think of a better expression of our love," he said.

Looking back now, I know that my decision to give up that ring was the moment that things really started to happen, because it was at that point that I began to take my work—and myself—seriously. I deposited the money in the account with the remainder of Jantsen's fund, and that night Randy and I decided that we'd give a name to the work we were doing: Touch A Life. And it couldn't have come at a better time, because the next day, I got a call from Mai.

"Okay," she said. "I think we know what we're doing. The shelter is operating great, the kids are happy, everyone is doing well at school. We did it, Pam."

"That's great," I said, allowing the relief to wash over me.

"So what should we do now?" Mai asked.

I looked down at the simple gold band I now wore on my finger. "Easy," I said. "Let's go get fifteen more."

Chapter Six

Christmas, 2000. Dear Jantsen, I sometimes think I will stop breathing when I see Crista and Van together laughing. Your dad and I are surprised every time Van does something that reminds us so much of you. Your similar characteristics are a sign that he truly is our special gift. He would love you so much. Merry Christmas sweetheart. Love, Mom

In February 2001, Penny called and asked if she and her husband could come over for dinner. They absolutely adored Van, and as they explained to us that night, they had decided that they also wanted to adopt. They already had two biological sons. "I just know we have a lot more love to give," Penny said. "When I think about adopting a child who has nobody, the question isn't why would we do it. It's more like, why *wouldn't* we?"

Before bringing Van home, I often wondered how people would react, expecting that we'd have to become accustomed to funny looks now that we were the pale white family with the Asian baby. But I couldn't have been more off the mark. A few months after Van came home, the local paper did a story on us, and before long I was inundated with calls from people wanting to know how we had done it.

At the time, Carol and Marvin were beginning to explore Cambodia as a place for adoptions, and when Carol heard that Penny was considering adopting, she asked if she'd be interested in being a pioneer family for the new program. Penny was thrilled by the idea. Within two weeks, she was sent a photo of MaiLia, who was less than one year old.

MaiLia's Cambodian name was Rom Doul, but after she was found in a box that had been placed on the grounds of a hospital in Kampong Spoe when she was only a few days old, she became known as Rath, the Cambodian word for "unwanted child." The idea that a mother could abandon a newborn like that may seem heartless, but the reality is that for people who live in extreme poverty, it's often a courageous act of love—a parent's hope that the child will be found and brought to a better life. Before long, a woman walking through the hospital grounds spotted the box and took MaiLia home. She cared for her for several days, but—unable to afford to raise her forever—she brought the baby to the village chief to ask for guidance. He decided MaiLia would be taken to the orphanage where Carol had recently started working.

Penny fell in love with her the moment she saw her photo. We spent many hours going through the paperwork together. Less than three months later, she got the call that the adoption was approved; she could travel to Phnom Penh to pick up her daughter. Penny was a mess of excitement and nerves, and called me one night with an idea. "I've never done anything like this," she said. "And I think you have to come along. You'll help out with the adoption stuff and with MaiLia, and we'll have a blast."

I was dying to go to Cambodia. Knowing how many Vietnamese girls were trafficked there to work in the growing sex trade, I was curious to see the situation for myself. For a few days, I wavered back and forth between my strong desire for another adventure and my fear of leaving Van for the first time and looking like a horrible, neglectful mother. But hadn't I decided long ago that being a good mom meant showing my children that the world was bigger than our family? I kept asking myself: What would ultimately be more valuable to Van—having me there for another two weeks, doing the things Randy and Crista—now sixteen years old—would be happy to do, or someday being able to show him my photos of Cambodia and tell him about everything I learned there? And yes, I was a new mom again, but that didn't mean I should stop trying to find balance in my own life. The thing I kept coming back to the most was the idea that my mother never would have even considered taking a trip like this when my siblings and I were young. That's not what mothers *did,* after all. Well, the truth is, I would have loved it if my mother had done something like this. A few weeks later, I was back on a plane to Asia.

Despite the fact that Cambodia and Vietnam border each other, they're quite different countries. As soon as we landed in Phnom Penh and went outside to hail a taxi, I felt there was something about the city—something indefinable—that was chaotic and lawless. Driving toward the city center, past the large, ornate building housing the Ministry of National Defense, we passed pickup trucks crowded with men hanging from the back, their faces and heads wrapped with kromas, the traditional red and white checkered Cambodian cloths that once symbolized membership in the Khmer Rouge. Only their eyes could be seen. It wouldn't have surprised me to find that the men had machine guns tucked between their knees.

Though the country is now at peace, Cambodia has been thoroughly shaped by war, violence, and, especially during the last thirty years, genocide. In 1975, two weeks after the fall of Saigon and the end of the Vietnam War, the Khmer Rouge assumed power under the despotic leadership of Saloth Sar, a fifty-year-old radical Marxist better known as Pol Pot. His ascension to power marked an end to a brutal civil war that had wreaked havoc on the nation for five years, but the worst was yet to come. Harboring an idea of an agrarian utopia, Pol Pot embarked on one of the most brutal restructurings ever attempted of any society. Proclaiming the year 1975 as "Year Zero," he set out to erase the nation's history and create a peasant society by cleansing the nation of all intellectuals and foreign influences. During the four years he held power, the cities were emptied, and every Cambodian was made to march to the country and work in agricultural communes or forced labor camps. Money, private property, and religion were abolished. Flights in and out of the country were mostly halted.

Pol Pot decided that only two million of the seven million people living in Cambodia were needed to fulfill his vision, and the others—anyone thought to be loyal to the old regime, old and infirm people, and all educated citizens (who were commonly identified by the fact that they wore glasses or knew a foreign language)—were simply to be killed. The world watched these horrific events unfold, but for the most part remained silent, allowing Pol Pot to oversee the genocide of as many as 1.7 million people. As he bluntly stated to the citizens of Cambodia over the government-controlled airwaves, "To keep you is no benefit, to destroy you is no loss."

In 1975, Pol Pot transformed what was once a secondary school into an internment camp called Tuol Sleng. Here up to seventeen thousand people were imprisoned and interrogated. It's a museum now; the quiet rooms that had once been holding cells display photographs and relics of the horror. I spent a few hours here, walking slowly among the portraits of prisoners, taken upon their arrival at Tuol Sleng: All bear a number scribbled on a board tied around their neck, and a look of terror in their eyes. Many of the women held children in their laps. After being photographed, the prisoners were forced to strip, their possessions were taken, and then they were led to a cell not much larger than a coffin, or to one of the large holding rooms, where they were shackled to the floor.

They could not speak to one another, spent most of their time unclothed, and were hosed down every few days. They were rarely fed, and sometimes forced to ingest feces and urine. On display were many of the tools used during interrogations to try to coerce the prisoners to confess whatever supposed crime had brought them there. They were electrocuted, seared with hot poles, cut with knives, and beaten with sticks. Their heads were held under water, their fingernails pulled out.

Most prisoners died within a few months of their internment, from either the disease that was rampant inside the prison, starvation, or the beatings they were forced to endure. In 1979, the Khmer Rouge began operating Choeung Ek, one of the largest killing fields, about nine miles outside Phnom Penh, which I also visited. Here, in what was once an orchard tucked among the vast rice fields and coconut trees, thousands of people were exterminated. Babies were ripped from their mothers' arms, their heads beaten against a tree until they died. Adults were tortured and killed, their bodies buried in mass graves among hundreds of others. Today the skulls of more than five thousand of the estimated seventeen thousand killed here are on display in a glass monument. Human bones, teeth, and clothing can still be seen buried in the dirt among the mass graves and trees.

Before leaving Choeung Ek, I flipped through a book that had been placed on a simple wooden table, where visitors were invited to leave comments. Tourists from around the world expressed their sorrow and outrage for what the citizens of

Cambodia had to endure here. *Let us never forget this horrible atrocity so that it cannot be repeated,* one person wrote.

One afternoon, I hired a driver to take me to a neighborhood called Svay Pak. Here, about fifteen minutes from the city center, on a dusty road lined with smoky open-air cafés and dingy beer bars, groups of young girls sat together on folding chairs in front of rusty, crumbling shacks. They painted one another's fingernails, played card games by candlelight, and stared blankly toward the street. This was the city's main red-light district, and many of the girls sitting here were prostitutes, a majority of them Vietnamese. I rolled down my window, breathing in the sticky, diesel-soaked air, and watched a man—white and in his sixties—as he got off a motorbike taxi in front of one shack. He was approached by a boy who looked no older than twelve. "Yum yum or boom boom?" the boy asked. I knew what that meant. *Yum yum* implied oral sex, which could be had for a few dollars; *boom boom* was intercourse.

Though most of the girls I saw looked to be between sixteen and twenty, I knew that inside, much younger girls—children—waited. It's estimated that one-third of the prostitutes in Cambodia are children. A man looking to have sex with a six-year-old, a twelve-year-old, simply had to do what this man did: hail a taxi for the fee of one dollar and be delivered here. Inside these shacks, in dimly lit rooms, he could summon girls as young as five to line up and lift their skirts and tops for inspection. He could take the one he chose to a room in the back, not much larger than a coffin and with nothing but a slatted, wooden bed. He could spend an hour with her, or longer, if he was willing to pay. He could do anything he pleased.

But first, of course, the money would be exchanged. Thirty dollars for a teenager; more for a child whose chances of having AIDS were lower. For a virgin, he could pay three hundred.

These activities were hardly confined to the Svay Pak dis-

trict. In the evenings, Penny and I ate dinner at one of the outdoor cafés near our hotel along the Mekong River. At most of
the tables around us, single men sat alone, sipping iced tea or
Angkor beer. Groups of girls walked by, heavily made up and
wearing tight jeans and low-cut tops that sparkled in the street
lights. One evening, I watched as the men scoured the groups
of girls, keeping a close eye on them until they spotted the one
they wanted. One man—an older, overweight Westerner in cut-
off jean shorts and a tourist T-shirt from Thailand—called to a
young girl with big brown eyes and red barrettes in her hair. As
he led her to his table, the confidence and bravado she displayed
while among the other girls disappeared. She became shy and
distant, and kept stealing furtive glances back at her friends.
He raised his arm to order her a drink, and a dull smile crossed
her lips, but it wasn't genuine enough to mask the terror in her
eyes. Eyes not unlike those of the prisoners in the photographs
we had seen in Tuol Sleng.

As the waitress set a beer down in front of her, the man
leaned down and kissed the young girl's neck.

To keep you is no benefit, to destroy you is no loss.

Around us, the other diners paid little attention to this scene,
playing out right before us at table after table, at every café on
this street. On the corner, I watched young girls in short skirts
spilling out of a van and onto the sidewalk under the neon
lights of a karaoke bar, inside which they'd take their place on
bar stools and wait for a man to buy them a drink, and then a
taxi back to his hotel. Next door to us, a sign offered five-dollar
massages, and college-aged American and Australian boys with
pimples and flip-flops peered through the windows, elbowing
each other when they saw something inside they liked.

I thought about Svay Pak. The rooms inside those shacks,
behind where the girls sat staring vacantly toward the street,
were not so unlike the cells where the Tuol Sleng prisoners had

been held. The same size, the same dirty floor, the same horrid secrets. As the Europeans at the table next to us laughed and ordered another round of drinks, and an American couple flipped quietly through a tour book, I wondered what it would take to get people to care more about this. In thirty years, would one of those brothels have become a museum: the rooms where girls took clients kept intact, photos of the girl with the brown eyes and red barrettes fastened to the walls, a guest book for people to express their disgust and dismay that people from around the world had known this was happening, and had done nothing to stop it?

———

Over the next few days, while Penny was busy applying for MaiLia's passport and organizing her medical exam, I wandered through the streets of Phnom Penh. I took a tuk tuk out to the Central Market and walked through the throngs of people shopping for vegetables, and tourists buying Birkenstocks that sold for eight dollars. Children roamed the market holding out their hands, asking for money. Women carrying infants lurked close by, pushing their children toward any Westerner, always perceived as a possible gold mine.

Sometimes, Penny and I would take MaiLia with us on walks along the water, down to where the Mekong River met the Tonlé Sap. We strolled through the Royal Palace and the Silver Pagoda, the official temple of the king of Cambodia. Outside the palace, families gathered in the evenings over ostrich eggs and prawn soup, sold from vendors on the corners. MaiLia, who has very dark skin for a Cambodian, would sit quietly in the stroller or a pack strapped to Penny's back. Everywhere, people gave us looks. Sometimes, women would even stop and poke MaiLia harshly on her arms or face. "Cambodian!" they'd say, ridiculing her for her dark skin.

One day, Penny came back from an interview at the US consulate and told me she had sat in the waiting room with an American man who was also adopting a Cambodian girl. As they waited, he told her about a Canadian woman named Marie Ens, who he had met during his visit. Marie's husband, Norman, died from a heart attack in 1991, and nine years later, at the age of sixty, Marie moved to Phnom Penh, where she and Norman had lived for many years after they were first married, raising their children and doing missionary work. She was now living alone in a tiny apartment in the city and volunteering her time at AIDS hospitals.

"This woman sounds cool," Penny said to me. "Let's invite her over and learn more about her."

We called Marie, and the next night she came to our hotel room. As we got MaiLia ready for bed, Marie sat in the living room of our hotel suite and we laughed and hung out like we had known each other for years. The idea that she lived here alone, in this foreign country, fascinated me. "After Norman died, I knew that this is where I wanted to be. But when I told my children that I was moving to Cambodia by myself, they all said I was crazy," she told us. "I guess everyone thought that because I was sixty and alone, I needed to stay home and do nothing. For a while, I bought in to what they were saying. Then one day, I was out shopping for Christmas gifts and this song starts to play over the store stereo. It was Billy Joel's 'My Life' and I know this is funny, but the words made me stop in my tracks. A few days later, I bought my ticket, and I've been here ever since."

The next day, Penny, MaiLia, and I hopped a tuk tuk and drove out to the AIDS hospital where Marie volunteered. It was one of the few places where people in the region who suffered from AIDS could go. As we walked through large rooms crowded with cots, I saw that not one of them was empty.

Marie knew every patient. Every few feet, she stopped before someone else—so thin and frail—and would hold their hand and introduce us. Seeing MaiLia, just eleven months old, many of the patients smiled and reached out to touch her little feet. "Lucky baby, going to America," they'd say.

We spent several days at the hospital. People here needed very little: a mosquito net, soy milk, fresh fruit, and a loaf of bread could change their lives, yet they were always in short supply. We met many children who spent their days next to the bed of a dying parent as their other parent worked at the market or begged on the streets. In the mornings, we'd stop at a store and spend twenty dollars on several bags of bread to take to the hospital. When we handed a loaf to the children, their whole faces smiled, as if this were the best gift they could even imagine receiving.

On our final night in Cambodia, Penny and I took Marie to dinner at a café near our hotel. It was here she told us that while she loved her work at this hospital, she had much bigger plans. The hospital was necessary but in reality, it was nothing more than a place for people with AIDS to come and die. For years, she had been dreaming about opening a center somewhere outside the city where people with AIDS could live comfortably in cottages with their families while getting treatment. If a parent did die from the disease, the children could still live there for the rest of their lives. She had found the land to purchase and had drawn up the plans for the first sixteen families, but was still fifteen thousand dollars short of being able to move forward. "This is what I want to do because I see how many children end up on the streets of Phnom Penh whose parents die from AIDS, and it's heartbreaking what can happen to them."

Just then, at one of the tables near us, a Cambodian girl who couldn't have been older than fifteen, approached a table where a man had been dining alone. He stood up and embraced her before she sat down at his table.

"That's exactly what I mean," Marie said, a look of disgust clouding her face. "So many girls like her feel as if they have no other choice than to work in the sex industry, which is supported by men like him, who come here to do unspeakable things. To him, it means almost nothing to shell out three hundred dollars to sleep with a virgin. To her, that's three times what her family earns a year. These girls are not only being exploited, they're being brutalized."

———

Back home, Penny and I could not stop talking about Marie. As Van and MaiLia ran around the grass and played with each other's toys, we'd sit on lawn chairs sipping Diet Dr Peppers and talk about how much we wanted to do something to help her get the center built.

"She's so close to making this happen," Penny said to me. "How can we find a way to scrape together that last fifteen thousand?" That night, I pored over the Touch A Life account. Mai had called a few times to tell me about a child she'd met who was a great student but couldn't afford college, or another who was struggling to feed her family, and we'd been sending extra money in bits and pieces to help out. There was $11,500 remaining—just $3,500 short.

I knew that the only way I could operate Touch A Life without completely losing my mind with worry was to ensure that we always had a cushion. The stakes were too high to risk running out of money. Not paying the bills for those thirty kids in Vietnam meant they'd end up back on the street. But every time I looked at the balance, I couldn't help but think it was ridiculous to keep this money when it could get Marie so close to what she needed to build the center. A few nights later, Randy and I discussed it. We'd give what remained in the Touch A Life account to Marie and somehow find the funds to support our work in Vietnam, even if we had to use more of our own money. Making that decision, however, meant we had to start making some real changes in our life, and we decided that from that point forward, we would adhere to an all-cash budget. Up until then, I had used my credit card for almost every purchase: to buy clothes for me or the kids, dinners out, movies, gas, school supplies. We did this mostly to build up mileage for another trip we knew we wanted to take to Vietnam, and we did pay off the bill at the end of each month. But the problem was that I never knew exactly how much I was spending. Anytime I bought something, I'd simply pull out the Visa, sign my name, and never think about it. It was all so, well . . . thoughtless. When I did look at the credit card bill, I'd see the balance and think, *What in the world did I spend all that money on?* Eighty dollars at Target, another thirty at the bookstore . . .

By this time, Randy was making a comfortable salary, but rather than figure out what we could afford, we thought about how much we felt comfortable spending. We looked at what the average American family spent and decided that at the beginning of each month, I'd go to the bank and draw out a set amount of cash. That was what I could use for everything we needed. When the cash was gone, it was gone until the first of the month. In short, no more credit cards for me.

It was definitely an adjustment in the beginning because our new budget was significantly less than what I had been spending each month. But I also knew that it was the only way that I would be putting my money where my mouth was by living at a different standard. And even if we never got one more donation to Touch A Life, we were still going to support those kids. We had made that commitment, and doing so, we had to take full responsibility.

I'm not saying we lived on ramen noodles and water. We still went out to eat and to see a movie sometimes. My kids still wore clothes and shoes. What changed most was our idea of what was essential to us and what was not. I, like many of us, had bought in to the idea that more is better. But after trying to live more simply, I've come to believe that's not the case. More is *tiring*. Everything you acquire is one more thing to take care of. This decision was one of the most liberating I've ever made. There is so much freedom that comes from living within your means. Every time I had to pay for something, I had to count out the bills and watch my wallet get thinner, rather than just scribbling my name on a credit card slip. It felt very deliberate.

In the end, we scraped together a loan for the remaining thirty-five hundred dollars. When we called Marie to tell her, there was silence on the other end of the phone for several minutes. Finally, through her tears, Marie spoke. "I can't tell you what this will mean to these families," she said.

Of course, our decision to commit to an all-cash budget was hardly the most important one Randy and I made at the time. A few months after Van came home to us, we knew that we wanted another child—not only because of all the fun we were having with him, but also because we had much more love to give, and we wanted Van to have a sibling his age to grow up with. At the time, Carol and Marvin were thinking of adopting a young girl named Huong from the same orphanage where Van had lived. When Carol showed me Huong's photograph, I thought she was the sweetest, most beautiful girl I'd ever seen. She was two years old and her mother, whose name was Lan, had gotten pregnant by a boyfriend, bringing great shame to her family. They kicked her out of the house, and Lan's brother often beat her, punching her over and over again in the stomach, hoping to cause her to miscarry. She didn't, but Huong was born almost two months prematurely, and now that she was two, she was beginning to show signs of cerebral palsy, walking with a severe limp and experiencing muscle weakness in her upper body. Carol and Marvin ultimately decided that taking on a child with medical needs was too much of a hardship when they already had seven children at home. When Carol called to tell me this, I could not stop thinking about Huong and looking at the recent photograph Carol had sent to me. Huong was standing on the balcony staring out into the courtyard of the orphanage. She looked frightened and alone, as if she were just waiting for her family to come and claim her.

One day, Randy came into the kitchen where I was sitting, staring at her picture. "What are you waiting for?" he said. "Let's go get that little girl."

In October 2001, we welcomed the newest member of our family: Tatum Diane Cope.

———

Before we left for Vietnam to get Tatum, I spent a lot of time worrying that I'd be too worn out and weary to raise two toddlers. As soon as we had her home, however, those thoughts disappeared—but only because I no longer had time to think about anything so complex. Instead, most of my time was spent playing games, cleaning up spills, and helping Van adjust to this stranger in a bow.

To say he was a little hesitant of her at first is kind of like saying that Tiger Woods is slightly athletic. He had grown accustomed to being absolutely doted on by Randy, Crista, and me. Who was this little girl with whom he had to share his toys and, more importantly, our attention? I wondered if he'd ever stop resenting her, but everything seemed to change the day he realized that Tatum had a few disabilities. A couple of times a week, she'd lie on a blanket in our living room and we'd do a series of exercises her therapist had showed me, designed to build up the muscles in her left side. Van would sit and watch us. One day he asked me why we did this.

"She just needs a little extra help with things," I told him. Later that day, instead of ignoring her the way he typically did, I noticed him following her out to the backyard. A few minutes later, he was nudging her up the slide, hoisting her up on the swing.

Tatum, meanwhile, pushed him academically. From the moment I took her out of that orphanage, I knew that she was an eager learner. She was fluent in Vietnamese, and I worried that it would be difficult to teach her English—but by the time we got on the plane to come home, she was explaining to the flight attendants and fellow passengers, in English, how excited she was to go meet her brother, sister, and father. She did, however, struggle a little with the accent, especially when it came to pronouncing our state. When people asked her where they lived, she'd look at them and say, "My family lives in Misery."

Before long, Van and Tatum were such an important and natural part of our family that I almost couldn't remember a time that they weren't lying on the couch watching cartoons, their legs intertwined, or begging Crista to take them to McDonald's. And they love each other's company. Once, after a particularly scary dream about a shark, Tatum asked Van if he wanted to sleep with her. They haven't slept alone since. Every night, knowing her brother's need to save face and not look like he needs the protection of a *girl*, Tatum finds him and says the same thing, "Hey Van, you wanna sleep with me tonight?"

"Oh, okay," he says with a shrug. "I suppose I could do that."

Watching the two of them together, I just know that they were meant to be part of our family.

Chapter Seven

March 2003. Dear Jantsen, I don't know if I will ever throw away your prescription bottle of Allegra I keep in the bathroom drawer. It is the one thing I need to see every day: a reminder of your allergies, and the fact you once walked on this earth. It's been four years: Time has slipped away so quickly. Van and Tatum are healing us all. I miss you so much. Love, Mom

When Jantsen and Crista were young, I never would have imagined that I could handle working forty hours a week while raising them. After Van and Tatum were home, however, it didn't even occur to me to stop my work with Touch A Life. In fact, though filled with challenges, the work ultimately proved to be much easier than I could have ever imagined, probably because I enjoyed it so much. All those years wasted because I didn't think I could do something like this, or was unsure of where to start, or had somehow convinced myself that only people with a master's degree in some obscure field could make a difference. All of those *if onlys* . . . when all I needed was the courage to try.

Slowly, I began to have more luck with fund-raising—often

receiving the most generous donations from people I least expected, like single moms, a neighbor I knew did not have much extra cash, even complete strangers. It was extremely encouraging, not only because it made me feel confident that I was doing a good job, but because I wanted to continue to expand our work. At the time, however, that was on hold. Mai and I had decided to wait one year before renting a larger apartment and bringing home more kids, wanting first to make sure we could continue to manage the thirty we had, and give them everything they needed. Plus, we were running into some problems. A few months after we established the first shelter, the police had shown up. They had gotten word that Sister Minh had taken in children and enrolled them in school. Convinced this was only possible through funding from outside sources, like foreigners, they demanded a share. After Sister Minh explained that they did not have extra cash, and that granting their bribe would mean the children would not be able to continue school, the police left. A few days later they came back, this time with more officers. They separated Sister Minh and her husband, and kept the children at bay in the sleeping area, attempting to find one of them in a lie. Sister Minh knew that if they gave in, the threats would only continue, and the police would come back again to demand another payment, and likely a larger one. A few nights later, Sister Minh and her husband packed up the children and their belongings, and moved to another house. It didn't take long before the police found them again. In the first six months the shelter operated, the children were forced to move four times.

Being chased around Saigon by the Communist government probably would have caused me to panic, but Mai, who was in Saigon at this time, reacted with her typical aplomb, refusing to be intimidated. This was just one of a million times that I felt grateful for having met her that day, a total stranger in the plane seat next to mine. She was perfect for this job. She refused to take any money for herself as a salary, and always paid her own way to Vietnam, which she visited at least four months each year. She even covered all her expenses once she got there, using the money Edward earned and, after he retired, his pension. She could also stretch a dollar farther than anyone I had ever met. In fact, her attitude toward frugality sometimes bordered on the obsessive. During one of our many phone calls, I asked her if the children needed anything. "Do they have enough food, clothes for school?"

"They're fine," Mai said. "Nobody is hungry and every child has one school uniform, and they're very good about washing them out every night."

"Only one?" I asked. "How much are uniforms?"

"About two dollars."

"Mai!" I said. "Will you stop being such a cheapskate and buy them another set?"

I was also learning a lot about myself, and what it takes to run a program like Touch A Life. In some ways, it became the college education I'd never had: learning to balance the books, make presentations, and write a short newsletter that I'd e-mail out to my family and friends. While I learned a lot from the small successes along the way, I learned far more from all the mistakes I made. My first lesson: Beware of preachers in Haiti who can't explain what they did with two thousand dollars.

In spring 2003 my friend Cary Kelso and I accompanied Carol to Haiti, where she was going to check out a few orphanages as possible places to coordinate adoptions. Haiti is a very interesting place to travel, especially for women. When we landed in Port-au-Prince, we were "welcomed" by men in camouflage and carrying machine guns. The director of one of the orphanages Carol worked with met us at the airport, and as soon as we got into the van he grew very stern, warning us to never go out by ourselves after dark. Get what we needed done before sunset, he told us, and after that stay in our hotel room with the door locked. He was so serious, I half expected him to reach under the seat and hand us each a semi-automatic. You know, *just in case.*

Our hotel was like a prison: There were gates around it, topped with barbed wire and shards of glass from broken bottles. Most houses were enclosed behind locked gates. The country itself felt very dry and depressing. Unlike the rousing energy of Vietnam and Cambodia, everything—and everyone— seemed to be half asleep.

When we weren't out visiting orphanages, we tried to stay put in our hotel as we had been instructed, but that felt so, well, boring. We wanted to be safe but we also wanted to experience more of the culture. One morning, Cary, Carol, and I decided to take a taxi to the market and back, which taught me another lesson: Negotiate the price *before* you get into the cab. When the driver stopped in front of our hotel, which wasn't more than ten minutes from the market, he told us that we owed him three hundred dollars. That was almost what we had paid in airfare! We tried to argue with him, but he kept yelling at us in Creole. Finally, with the help of a clerk at the hotel, we got the price down to fifty, which was still a ridiculous amount.

One evening, we were invited to dinner by a man named Etienne, whom Carol knew through a church she worked with in Port-au-Prince. He was tall and lean, and in his forties; he volunteered as a preacher at a local church. He told us how much he'd always wanted to build an orphanage through which he'd try to place kids in good homes, and how he would take very little money for himself. His goal was to recruit families who wanted to adopt but couldn't afford the typically hefty costs of international adoptions.

As soon as he said this, I knew that I wanted to help him.

I was constantly getting calls from people who told me how much they wanted to adopt a child and were wondering how we had done it. After I explained the process, the same question always came: And how much did it cost?

In total, it cost us about twenty thousand dollars each to adopt Van and Tatum, including the costs of the paperwork, adoption fees, and travel to get them. We eventually got a tax credit of about ten thousand, spread out over three years, but we did have to find that amount of cash up front. When I told people this, I could immediately detect the change in their voice. "Oh," they'd say. "That's too much money for us."

I always hated that. Here were families who desperately wanted to adopt; who were willing to take and love a child who had nobody else and who would never know what it meant to be part of a family. But they couldn't do it simply because they didn't have enough *money*?

Maybe this was the answer. Haiti was an easy flight from the United States, much cheaper than travel to Vietnam and Cambodia, and there was a great need to place children into good homes. So many of the orphans we met were not getting the attention they needed, and the orphanages we visited had become a breeding ground for scabies and other health issues. Etienne seemed like the perfect connection: my Haitian Mai. But helping him build an orphanage would be a huge under-taking, and after I got home, Randy suggested that rather than jumping in immediately, we should first test our relationship with him by setting up a food pantry. Ideas like this did not even occur to me at the time. It was more like, *You mean, I'm not supposed to just wire the balance of our bank account to a guy in Haiti I met once?* When I called to discuss the food pan-try idea with Etienne, he was very interested, and said that for five hundred dollars each month he could feed many families in the community and help get them on their feet. We agreed to support him for four months, and the next day I wired him two thousand from the Touch A Life account.

A month later, he called me. "I need more money," he said.

"What for?" I asked.

"I used it all."

"On what?" I asked, surprised.

"On feeding people," he breezily replied. "As we discussed."

"Etienne," I said, "that was for four months."

He explained that it was difficult to stay within a budget when there were so many people to feed. I understood and tried to sympathize with what it was like for him, living there and seeing a need and knowing he could meet it with the money he had. Randy decided to run down to Haiti for a few days to check out the situation. We felt strongly that we wanted to work there and did not want to make any hasty decisions to terminate the work. Randy spent five days visiting orphanages and hanging out with Etienne. Our final conclusion was that as much as we may have liked Etienne as a person, we did not know if we could partner with him. It was a very difficult decision for me, but at the same time I knew that there was a lesson in this. I had to trust my instincts, which were telling me not to move forward.

Here's the third lesson: Never travel with more than two people. In the fall of 2003, after so many people I knew told me that they would love to go to Vietnam and Cambodia to see the work we were doing and meet the children whose photos were plastered around my house, I decided to organize a group trip. After all, the more people who saw the issues firsthand, the greater the chance they'd want to do something to help. Penny agreed to come along, and worked with me to organize the trip. While our kids were at school, we spent our afternoons researching hotels, renting vans, hiring drivers, and planning visits to shelters, orphanages, and AIDS hospitals. Finally, a few weeks before Thanksgiving, I boarded a plane with *eleven* others and headed out for ten days in Asia.

Two days in, I thought I was going to blow my brains out. Prior to this, I had come to believe that I'd made a lot of progress in my struggle to stop being such a people pleaser. Boy was I wrong. Rather than doing what I needed to do for Touch A Life while I was there, I became obsessed with making sure everyone was having a good time: that the hotel was okay, and they liked the restaurants, and did they mind the fact that there were lizards in their room? I know that part of this was how much I wanted everyone to fall in love with the country and the culture as much as I had, but part of it was simply because I didn't want to disappoint anybody.

On one of our first days in Cambodia, I rented a bus to visit Marie's shelter. On the way, it suddenly became very warm inside. Someone was yelling and pointing at the clouds of smoke seeping from the floor. We started to throw our bags out the window when the smoke turned to flames. We couldn't exit through the front door because of the fire and instinctively, we all ran toward Taylor, the eight-year-old who had come with us, trying to shove her out a side window. Once she was safe outside, we started to crawl out ourselves. As I watched my friends squeezing through the small windows, their arms and legs getting banged and bruised, all I could think was, *Welcome to Cambodia, everyone!*

A few days later, we rented another bus to take us across the border to Vietnam. It was the rainy season and the road was flooded in many places, causing the bus to constantly fishtail. At one point, in a very rural area surrounded by rice fields, the bus slid off the road and into a swampy ditch. Mai, who was traveling with us, instructed everyone to get out one-dollar bills and hold them out the window. We did as we were told. Before long, men and boys came running from the rice fields toward the bus. They took the money and then used all of their might to push the bus forward. "Okay," I said to Penny after the bus was finally freed from the ditch. "Perhaps my calling in life does not include tour guide."

Things got continually more frustrating, and I survived only due to the fact that I could look forward to the time when everyone went to their rooms to sleep and I could sneak out and meet Penny for a Tiger beer.

———

But that's not to say that this trip was a waste of time. In fact, it was a very important trip, because it was when I met Peter Stone. Should you ever find yourself worrying that maybe you've taken things in your life for granted, spend a minute with Peter. He was born in 1966 during the Vietnam War and contracted polio as an infant. His disability may have been the reason his parents chose to abandon him on the streets of Saigon, as good as dead. He was eventually discovered and taken to the Sancta Maria orphanage outside the city. When it was established in 1964, there were only a handful of kids. By the time Peter arrived three years later, there were nearly eight hundred, many of them orphaned because of the war. There was never enough to eat, the conditions were abominable, and many of the children there died of sickness. Sometimes money was in such short supply, the director of the orphanage sold his own possessions to buy food for the kids.

Peter tried to make the best of his days at the orphanage, and with his ability to walk on his hands for long periods of time—which he had learned to do because the lower half of his body was paralyzed from the polio—he was well liked by the other children and the staff. He and the other handicapped children formed a family for themselves, spending their afternoons hunting geckos with rubber bands and inventing games to play with rubbish and stones. But of course, life was hard. Peter watched many of his friends die, either from sickness or malnutrition. Many mornings, he and the other kids would watch a staff member take away the covered body of another child. "Every time that happened," Peter told me, "we'd wonder who was next."

In 1975, two years after the US military pulled out of Vietnam, President Gerald Ford announced a US-funded evacuation effort called Operation Babylift. With two million dollars from a special foreign aid children's fund, the goal was to evacuate some of the estimated seventy thousand orphans to the United States, Canada, Europe, and Australia. In April of that year, private and military transport planes began to prepare for Operation Babylift, and the director of the orphanage where Peter lived was told to gather two hundred children immediately who would be among the first sent to the United States. It was decided that the handicapped kids would go first, as their chances of ever being placed into a home in Vietnam were slim. Peter, who was eight at the time, was among those chosen. However, when the bus arrived to take the children to the waiting plane, Peter was in the medical clinic being treated. He missed the bus. When staff members at the orphanage realized what had happened, they rushed Peter to the airport. As they pulled up, they watched the plane, which carried more than three hundred children and accompanying adults, beginning its takeoff. They were too late.

That may have been the luckiest day of Peter's life. About forty miles outside of Saigon and twenty-three thousand feet in the air, an explosion blew off the airplane's rear doors. Somehow the US Air Force pilots commanding the plane were able to turn it back toward Saigon and crash-land in rice paddies about two miles from the airport. The plane skidded and bounced before hitting a dike and shredding into several pieces. More than half of the children aboard died; many who survived were tragically injured.

Peter did eventually make it on to another cargo plane, this one headed for Australia, where he was eventually adopted by Brian and Kathleen Stone, who had three children. Peter found a loving home in the Stone family, but he never fully trusted that he'd amount to anything special. After the Stone's youngest son Phillip died unexpectedly from an acute asthma attack, Peter spiraled into a deep depression. In high school, he ran away from home and became involved in dealing drugs, and then developed an addiction himself. He lived this way until he was twenty-one, until the day that he decided that his future was up to him: He was either going to work to make something of his life, or kill himself. He gave up drugs, moved home, went to college, and turned himself around. A few years later, Peter returned to Vietnam. What was going to be a short visit turned into something else: He remained in his homeland and dedicated himself to helping the children he met who lived in extreme poverty.

It had been his dream to open a shelter for children, and after meeting him I decided that Touch A Life would help him achieve this dream. We helped fund his first shelter, which he called House of Grace. The operation would start small and focus solely on handicapped children. That was dear to my heart because of my niece Megan, who had been born with many disabilities; I thought we could do this work in honor of her life. Peter started gathering children for the shelter and bringing them one at a time to House of Grace.

About seven months after I returned home from the trip, I received an e-mail from Peter. He was writing to tell me that he had read a story in the local newspaper about a young Vietnamese girl named Phoo Twee Do. Her parents, who were both married to other people, had fallen in love, and before long,

Phoo's mother discovered she was pregnant. Knowing their families would never approve of their relationship, the young couple made a decision after their daughter was born: They'd rather die together than live apart. One day, holding tight to Phoo, who was fifteen months old at the time, they strapped themselves with homemade bombs and lit a match. They both died instantly. Phoo somehow survived, although both of her legs were blown off just below the knee. This had happened a few weeks before the article was written, and Phoo was now staying at a clinic in Da Nang.

Peter is the type of guy who, when he reads a story like this, has a hard time closing the newspaper and going out for a sandwich. He decided that he had to meet this little girl. He, perhaps better than anyone, understood how bleak her future was as a handicapped child in Vietnam. A few days later, he was on a bus, traveling the eight hours to the Da Nang hospital where Phoo was battling serious infections and awaiting treatment on her legs. He hung around for a few days, playing games with her and keeping company with her grandmother, who now had custody of the young girl. In the photos he sent me, the old woman looked like a bag of bones, and she told Peter that she couldn't possibly afford to care for the young girl. From the look of it, the old woman already carried the weight of the world on her shoulders.

I spent a long time gazing at her photos. Bandaged and thin, she looked miserable there in the clinic. Peter was afraid she wasn't going to get the medical attention she required, and the chances that she could die from her infection were frighteningly high. Even if she survived, the best she could hope for was a life of begging. Though Peter originally thought he'd bring her to live at the House of Grace, he knew he didn't have the resources to help her.

Now, I can't *really* explain what happens to me in these

moments. The best I can say is that the inner voice that I was growing better able to hear, or at least more willing to acknowledge, started speaking, and it would not shut up. *You need to help this girl.* I admit, I did try at first to stuff a pillow in it, so to speak. All the self-doubt that was still hanging around in my mind was fighting for its life here, and it was ready for battle. What could I possibly do to help this child on the other side of the world whom I'd never even met?

It was Carol's idea that I look into bringing Phoo to the United States on a medical visa. These were special visas that allowed foreigners entry into the US for medical procedures they could not get in their home country. I had no idea what the process was to apply for one, and so I called the US consulate to find out. After several attempts, I finally spoke to a woman named Amy, who helpfully explained the steps that had to be taken before Phoo would even be considered for a medical visa. I needed support from doctors, who would agree to cover the costs of any medical procedures. And a hospital that would allow the doctor to take on a case like hers. And a family to host her while she was here, at their own expense, and a way to get her a passport, and pay for her transportation to the United States.

It was so daunting, I almost regretted making the call. Part of me expected that the only thing I had to do was write a letter or fill out a bunch of papers or pay for a plane ticket. Those things I could have handled. But this?

I was floored by the response I got. Crista, who was turning seventeen, had recently begun to date Zach Austin. He lived in Neosho and attended a different high school; whatever free minutes the two had, I'd find them studying together at the kitchen table or taking Van and Tatum out for ice cream on a Friday night. Zach's mother Kim was a nurse at the local Freeman Hospital. After Crista told Zach about Phoo, he went home and told his mom. Kim called me right away with the phone number for Dr. Melvin Karges, a rehabilitation specialist she knew, and suggested I speak to him.

It took Dr. Karges about two milliseconds after hearing Phoo's story to agree to be her sponsoring physician. He also put me in touch with his friend Frank Ikerd, a prosthetist, who offered to fit Phoo with prosthetics after her surgery. Dr. Ganesh Gupta, a surgeon and pediatric orthopedic doctor in Kansas City whom I had been taking Tatum to see for help with her cerebral palsy, also signed on to help. So did my friend Stephanie Stewart, a nurse practitioner; and Dr. Benjamin Rosenberg, a dentist in town, who agreed to fix Phoo's teeth, which had been splintered to nubs through the explosion. In fact, there was not one person who heard Phoo's story that did not offer to assist her in whatever way they could. We even received a check for five thousand dollars—our biggest contribution to date—from our neighbors Kim and Carol Mailes, to assist us with Phoo.

When I called Peter a few weeks later to tell him the good news, he was stunned. But, he explained, the real challenges still lay ahead. Phoo didn't even have residency papers, which was going to make it extremely difficult for her to get a passport to travel to the United States if her visa was approved by the consulate. He'd also have to get permission from her grandmother to turn over custody to Randy and me.

A few days later, Carol and Marvin suggested I call Mr. Lei, a man they worked with to help facilitate adoptions in Vietnam. He was in his twenties, lived in Phan Rang, and was a master schmoozer. "Tell him it's an impossible task," Carol said, "and I bet you he'll rise to the occasion. He's the fixer."

I liked Mr. Lei the first time I spoke with him. "Hello Miss Pam!" he yelled into the phone. "I do a good job. I do A-okay, A-okay! I figure everything out and get you everything and you come to Vietnam and we give you baby Phoo!"

"Okay," I said, "I hope you're telling me the truth because I'm planning on coming to Vietnam to get baby Phoo."

"Yes, yes, yes." He giggled. "You have any problems, you just call Mr. Lei."

"How are you getting this done?" I asked him.

He giggled again. "Do not worry, Mrs. Cope. You do not worry. It take a little money in people's hands, but we get it done."

And that was the day I set up another column in our financial records for Touch A Life: THE FIXER FUND.

Mr. Lei was true to his word, doing everything he could to get Phoo's paperwork in order and being constantly available to me. Many nights I stayed up late to call Amy at the US consulate—trying to reach her first thing in the morning her time—and she was amazing, walking me through each step along the way. Without either of them, there's no way that I could have succeeded, but a few weeks after I'd first talked to Mr. Lei, everything was in order: A couple we knew from church had agreed to host Phoo while she got her treatment, all the doctors were prepared to take her whenever we were ready, and Phoo's grandmother had signed custody of her over to me.

The trip to meet Phoo and take her for the interview at the US consulate in Saigon and, hopefully, back home with us afterward was set for the end of October 2004. I really do have the coolest set of female friends. When my good friend Shelly Shepherd heard that I was going to go to Vietnam again, this time to go get Phoo, the legless baby, she said she was coming with me. Even though she had six children at home, she had always been so interested to hear my stories about my trips, and she wanted an adventure of her own. I was thrilled to have her come along.

The plan, according to Mr. Lei, was that Shelly and I would find our way to Da Nang, in central Vietnam, where we'd be met by a driver. He would then take us to the very remote jungle village where Phoo was living with her grandparents. It was not going to be easy traveling, Mr. Lei had warned us, and much of it would have to be done on a motorbike, as the roads where we were going were not passable by car. A week before the trip, Randy came to find me in the bedroom, where I was standing in front of my dresser trying to figure out what one wears on a motorbike in the jungle.

"Do you think this whole thing is a little bizarre?" he asked.

"What do you mean?"

"Well, you and Shelly are going to this remote mountainous region of Vietnam to get a legless baby, escorted by a twenty-year-old guy you've never met, and who you have no idea if you can trust."

"That's not true," I said. "Mr. Lei is A-okay. He's A-okay. Also, he's at least twenty-two."

"Well, if you're sure," he said.

Now, before I explain how brilliant the idea I had at this moment was, I have to first explain "The Troubles." This is the name I've given for this time in my marriage, which I now think of as a sort of brutal but short-lived war. It had been five years since Jantsen died, and I was dealing a lot better with my grief. That's not to say I wasn't still grieving, and, in fact, there were many times when, just as I finished congratulating myself for how well I was doing, I'd wake up the next day feeling as sad and desperate as ever. But in general, I had arrived at a much more stable place. I missed him desperately but had found a new life for myself in mothering Van and Tatum, and in the children I was trying to help; and in these efforts, I had discovered a renewed sense of hope and energy. But something else had changed, too: One day I turned around to find that Randy was no longer beside me. Where we once shared our feelings openly and provided a constant source of comfort, he had grown distant and quiet. When he wasn't at work, he was in the garage, or on an all-day bike ride, or mowing the lawn that didn't need mowing.

I didn't realize soon enough that he was finally mourning our son. Since the moment five years earlier when the doctor told us that Jantsen had died, Randy had been on overdrive, methodically going through the motions so that our family didn't sink too deep. Without him, I don't know how we would have survived.

And it's probably because I had begun to feel better that he pulled away and sought refuge in himself. He no longer needed to take care of me the way he had those first few years, and when that responsibility ended, he was able to recognize how completely out of gas he was. It was his turn to check out.

I know that I should have been understanding, but I wasn't, at least not initially. Now that we had two toddlers at home, I needed his help, and I was frustrated by how emotionally absent he felt. It's not that I questioned his love for our new family. He spent a lot of time with the kids—taking Van to baseball games, accompanying Tatum on long walks through the park. But he was a lot less present to me, and my first response was anger. As I gave Van and Tatum their bath each night, or got them ready for school in the morning, I'd shoot him a frustrated look. "Don't forget," I'd remind him. "Adopting again was your idea, too." A few weeks earlier, I had even threatened to leave him—to take the kids to his parents' condo in Florida and stay there until he pulled himself together. The only thing that stopped me from doing it was the fact that the condo was being used by others.

Looking back now, I'm not surprised that this moment in our marriage arrived. If anything surprises me, it's that it didn't occur earlier. Losing a child creates such a gaping hole in a marriage that it sometimes feels impossible to fill. And even when the hole did seem as if it were being closed, it was difficult to trust it to stay that way. Instead, it was being constantly pried open by sadness and hopelessness and that nagging desire to make things different than what they were.

But that day, as I stood there packing my bags to head out on my latest adventure while he stayed home and *took care of everything,* I realized what a jerk I was being. Instead of resenting him for what he felt he needed to do, it was time to do for him what he had done for me. All those days I could barely get out of bed, those nights in the hospital, I'm sure the thought occurred to him that maybe it would be a hell of a lot easier on a farm in Idaho with three dogs and satellite television. But he didn't do that. He gave me the push I needed when I needed it, and maybe it was my time to push him to the one place I think people experiencing grief should go: outside themselves.

I also knew that convincing him to come to Vietnam with me to get Phoo would take a little finesse, as there were a million excuses to keep him home. When I first brought up the idea that day, he uttered every one of them: missing work, Van and Tatum, dealing with the two weeks it took to recover from the jet lag when he got home. Over the next few days, I tried to persuade him with well-honed arguments. *It will be good for you to get away from work and take a break. We'll get more respect at the consulate interview if there are two of us. It'll be hard to find the village where she lives, and you're really good with directions.*

But for every reason I gave him why he should come, he gave me six why he couldn't. I knew I had to draw on every bit of wisdom to deal with this man. And then finally, it dawned on me. I had already been given the wisdom. No, not "the voice." The comedian Jeff Foxworthy! Jantsen had loved him, and as I sat on the floor with Tatum a few days later, helping her with her physical therapy, I remembered one thing I had heard him say: Men are not that hard to figure out. If you want them to do something, just offer them a cold beer and the chance to see a naked woman.

That evening, after Van and Tatum were asleep, I put on the one nightgown I had that could be considered even remotely sexy, pulled out a six-pack of Sierra Nevada, and went to find Randy.

The next morning, he seemed surprisingly more open to talking it out. I made us some eggs, poured him coffee, and explained how much it would mean to me if he accompanied me to Vietnam, how much I wanted us to go on this adventure together, as a couple.

"I've missed you," I said to him, and as I reached across the table to take his hand, I remembered the words from the Passenger-Side Grilling he once uttered to me in a shopping mall parking lot. I began: "I love you very much and I am asking you right here and right now. You have to trust me. You have to trust that this is going to be all right, and that you are okay, and that you are not going to spend the rest of your life feeling this bad. We can do this. You and me, we can go to a mountainous region of Vietnam and rescue a little girl who needs our help. I believe in you."

"I know what you're doing here, Pam," he said.

"Shut up, I'm not finished," I said. "But you have to make a decision. Are you going to choose to believe in yourself? That's the question you have to think about."

A few hours later, he was packing his bags for Vietnam.

———

Later that week, we dropped Van and Tatum off at my parents' house and the four of us—Shelly's husband, Rob, had decided to come, too—headed off to find Phoo. We flew first to Singapore, where we had a thirteen-hour layover, then on to Saigon. The next day, exhausted but excited, we left our little budget hotel at 5 AM to catch a flight to Da Nang. When we landed, the two men Peter had arranged to escort us—Mr. Twee and Mr. Twa—were there waiting. With them was a young woman who they introduced as our translator.

"Hello," I said to her, extending my hand. "I'm very glad you're going to be helping us because, unfortunately, I know maybe three Vietnamese words." She looked at me confused, as if she didn't understand. "I can't speak Vietnamese," I said again, loudly and slowly. She looked at Mr. Twee for help, and then at Mr. Twa, but they both shook their heads. With a shrug, she turned to walk toward the van.

Mr. Twee, Mr. Twa, the translator who apparently couldn't speak English, and the four of us drove for about four hours in total honking chaos. The driver sped along, weaving past motor-bikes and people on bicycles. Children ran along the side of the road on their way home from school, and as our van sped by them, coming within inches of their swinging arms, Shelly let out a little shriek.

"I can't even watch," she said, sinking her forehead into Rob's shoulder.

The paved road eventually ended, giving way first to a gravel street and then to a narrow bumpy dirt path cut through thick brush. Knowing how important it was that someone could help translate when we got to Phoo's village, I kept talking to the translator, seeing if I could pry the English from her memory.

"So, do you have children?" I asked her.

"Yes," she said.

"How many?"

"No," she answered.

A few minutes later, I tapped her shoulder again.

"No, I mean how many children do you have?"

"Yes," she said, and turned to look out the window.

Randy couldn't stop laughing. "Keep at it, Pam," he said. "Really, ask her favorite color. Find out if she has allergies."

As we drove, it became clear how carefully this mission had been planned. We kept stopping in small villages where a man would jump in the van and hand us a folder of paperwork, or another would be waiting with Phoo's residency papers on a street corner. Eventually, the driver stopped the van alongside the road, near a group of men sitting on idling motorbikes. We each hopped on the back of one and began the slow, treacherous trek up the steep mountain. The beauty was incredible, and the air was moist with the smell of the jungle. The road began to level off as we neared the top of the mountain, offering us the most spectacular view of central Vietnam, and acres and acres of beautiful rice fields. The rocky road turned into a narrow grass path, and the motorbikes sputtered under our weight and over the sticks and rocks in our way. I kept stealing glances back at Randy, hoping he wasn't wondering what exactly I had gotten him into, but every time I looked, he was hysterically laughing.

About thirty minutes later, we arrived in Phoo's village, which was nothing more than a collection of a dozen homes: thatched roofs held up by large sticks and branches. The men stopped the motorbikes in front of one of the tinier houses. Phoo's grandfather was in front waiting for us. He wore no shirt, and his body was thin and frail. His wife was on the porch. When she saw us, she ran into the house and came out a few minutes later wearing a clean, colorful dress. She grabbed a handful of grain from a large canvas bag and threw it force-fully onto the concrete porch. She then took a hand broom made of sticks tied together at the end, and started sweeping the grain onto the grass. I wondered if this was some sort of local custom and looked at Randy, sure he was wondering the same himself.

"You should ask the translator to explain what's happening," he said with a smirk.

As we walked up to the house, people from the village started to gather around us. They walked out from the jungle behind the houses, men and women of all ages, and many children. I saw a young girl who looked to be about seven years old walking toward us, holding a little girl with no legs. Phoo. She was tiny and beautiful and she carried a toy horse made of woven reeds. Shelly and I walked over to the little girl, and Shelly reached out and grabbed her. Phoo didn't make a sound. She settled into Shelly's arms, and reached up and started to play with her blond hair.

Some of the villagers brought a table and plastic chairs, setting them up on the dirt in front of their house. The grandfather motioned for us to take a seat. A man approached and explained (in English, thankfully) that he was a government official and asked to see our passports. He pulled out papers that we had to sign, as did the grandparents, turning over custody of the child to us. Phoo's grandmother kept hugging each of us again and again, thanking us for getting Phoo the help she needed. She then took my arm and led me into her house. There, in the simple front room, which had a spotless, white-tiled floor and a thatched roof above, was a little shrine to her daughter, Phoo's mother. Her photo hung on the wall; on the floor underneath, many candles were lit, next to a plate of cookies and a jar of cigarettes.

Back outside, the scene had become downright chaotic. At least two dozen people were gathered now, and so many were talking to the government official that it was impossible to tell what was happening, or who was in charge. Finally, after the papers were signed, and passports checked, it seemed that we were free to go. This became more evident when Mr. Twee came over, stomped a foot, chopped the air with his arms, and said, simply, "Finished."

I looked at Randy and mouthed to him, "Let's get this baby and get out of here quick."

We had brought along a baby pack to carry Phoo on the motorcycle back down to where the van waited. Randy got it and held it up to his chest. He tried to strap it around one way, and then another way, but neither way was right. I tried to help him. Maybe it was upside down? Shelly came over and turned it over, then flipped it back, but she couldn't get it right, either. We thought the baby was meant to be carried on his chest, but maybe it went on his back? "Rob," Shelly yelled, "do you have any idea how this thing works?"

As this was happening, we failed to notice that the crowd of people who'd gathered around the table now stood silently watching us. We looked up at the same time, and nobody said a word. But the look on many faces was clear: These people can't strap on a leather and plastic thing, how are they going to fix this girl's legs? Clearly, they are all idiots. We tried to offer reassuring smiles and finally, we figured it out. Phoo was tucked snugly against Randy, and we all hopped back on the motorbikes and began the long trek down the mountain. Reaching an overgrown area of the path, my driver slowed, and Randy's bike pulled next to mine. When I looked at him, it felt like time stopped. The jungle air, the bumpy road, the baby on his chest: It was one of those rare moments when you have the privilege of thinking, *I was meant for this moment.* I could tell by the look on Randy's face he was feeling the same thing. We reached out our arms, but our bikes were too far apart, and our hands couldn't quite touch. "We did it, Pam!" he said through the wind. "I can't believe we did it!"

I wasn't sure which part of the story he was referring to

exactly—that Phoo was now ours to help or that we had done it together—but it didn't matter.

"I knew we would," I said.

———

For the first two days with us, Phoo appeared to waver between sadness and fear, but on the third day, I swear she woke up and decided that she was going to make this work. *These people—the two chicks in particular—are at my beck and call,* she seemed to say. She loved Shelly and came to absolutely adore Rob, reaching for him in the mornings and falling asleep on him at night. She'd crawl around the floor on her arms and knees and everywhere we went, people would look at our group and *tsk,* shaking their heads in a manner that asked: *Why would those two white couples possibly want to hang around with that handicapped child?* But Phoo didn't seem to mind. She'd sit in her stroller giggling, holding her sippy cup and waving her stumps.

Randy, however, was a whole different story. He wasn't even allowed to look at her. Every time he did, she let out a terrified wail. Finally, he realized that she liked Band-Aids, so one day he went for a walk and came back with a bagful of them. Later, I found them sitting together on the hotel bed, both giggling, their cheeks, arms, and legs covered in colorful bandages.

The day of the interview at the US consulate, Randy and I went in with Phoo while Rob and Shelly stayed outside, praying she'd be approved. I went to the bulletproof window and asked to see Amy, and I was as happy to meet her as she was to finally meet the little girl she'd been hearing so much about. "Good luck," Amy said, "I can't help you from here. It's up to the interviewing officer now."

I was a nervous wreck. I've clearly never been much of a Plan B type of thinker, and I hadn't let myself even consider what I'd do if Phoo was denied. We took a seat in the waiting room. Phoo crawled around on the floor and pulled off my sandals. She then strapped them to her stumps and tried to walk, laughing the whole time. It was more than an hour before our names were finally called. The interviewing officer read her file and asked us questions. My voice cracked as I answered; I was glad to have Randy there, always my rock. "Okay," the officer finally said. "The whole office has heard about this girl, and everyone here wants to make sure she gets the best treatment possible. I'm approving her. Come back next week to get her passport, and then go fix this child's legs."

———

Randy and Rob left for home the next day, leaving Shelly and me to have Phoo to ourselves while we waited for her passport to be processed. The three of us had a blast. Shelly's daughter was getting married in a few months, and we spent our afternoons at the Ben Thanh Market searching for fabric for the bridesmaids' dresses and finding outfits for the flower girls, which cost just seven dollars. Even after everything she'd been through, Phoo was such an easy, happy baby, and seemed wise beyond her years. She never complained, and ate everything we fed her, using her chopsticks like a toothbrush.

One morning, Shelly and I decided to go to church, and there we met an American woman named Yvonne. She told us that she volunteered at an orphanage for handicapped children. When we explained that we were stuck in Vietnam for a few more days, looking for meaningful ways to spend our time, she invited us to come with her the next day.

The orphanage was funded by the French government and run by a woman named Irene. Though it was considered one of the best facilities in the country, it was still far below the standards of how children should be raised. The kids, who suffered from many different kinds of handicaps, were everywhere, some of them in wheelchairs, others so sick they were strapped to their beds. I'm sure Irene and the others were doing the best they could to take good care of the kids, but they obviously didn't have the resources they needed, and it was mind boggling how sad a place it was. The children seemed absolutely starved for attention, reaching out to grab us whenever we came near.

As we went around saying hello to the kids, a young boy on crutches ran over and greeted us in English. "This is Tuan," Yvonne said, scooping him up. Then, whispering to us: "He's my favorite." I could see why. His eyes were the brightest little things, and he was happy and energetic: a spot of light amid the misery. I couldn't imagine why he was here.

As he and Phoo played together in the dusty courtyard, Yvonne explained that about a year earlier, when Tuan was four, he had fallen and broken his leg. Something as simple as mending a broken leg was a major and expensive medical procedure here in Vietnam. His mother could not afford to have it treated, or to raise a special-needs child, and she turned custody of him over to her sister. But she didn't have the means to keep him, either, and so she took him to this orphanage. Neither of them had ever come back to visit him.

He eventually got the surgery he needed, but the doctors had butchered it, leaving him with a horrible infection in his hip bone that spread throughout his legs. He could only walk with the help of crutches and Yvonne said that despite his sunny demeanor, he was often in excruciating pain. She called Tuan over and unwrapped one of the bandages on his legs to reveal a wound that was raw and swollen, oozing white pus.

I looked at Yvonne, and understood better why she had been eager to bring us here to the orphanage. "Do you think you can help me get him out of here, and to the US?" she asked hopefully. "If you can do one medical visa for Phoo, can't you do another one for Tuan?" I told her I would try, and explained that she'd have to start the process here in Vietnam. Like Phoo, Tuan didn't even have residency papers.

I stayed with Yvonne at the orphanage while Shelly took Phoo back to the hotel for her nap. I was happy to give the two of them some time alone, as I had noticed the bond that had developed between them. Phoo loved Shelly and each night, they fell asleep wrapped around each other. When I got back to the hotel, Shelly and I took Phoo to a nearby café for dinner. Over our meal, Shelly was quiet, and when we finished she turned serious. "Is this crazy?" she asked me. "But I honestly feel like Phoo is my child. I am so in love with her, and never imagined I could feel *this way* about a child I hadn't given birth to."

I was pretty sure I knew what Shelly was experiencing. It's almost impossible, I think, for any mother to meet a child in need and not become immediately convinced she's meant to adopt. I've done it a million times myself, believing that every second child I met at the orphanages I visited was *mine*. And then I'd get home and remember that it was hard enough to raise two six-year-olds, and while I may have felt a deep sense of caring, even love, for many of the children I met—it didn't mean I was supposed to take them all home.

"I understand what you're feeling," I said to Shelly. "But you're just caught up in the emotion of everything right now."

"I don't think so," she said, looking at Phoo. "I believe she's supposed to be my daughter. And that she already kind of is."

A few days later, it was time to pick up Phoo's passport and visa, and get the required vaccinations. The woman at the consulate gave us the address of the medical clinic where these were administered, and Shelly and I were horrified when we walked into what was basically a thatched shed with syringes lying on a table. It was dirty inside, and I prayed that those needles were clean as a nurse stuck Phoo over and over with several different shots.

On the morning we were scheduled to fly home, I hailed a cab to go back once more to see Yvonne. I brought with me a list of everything she'd need to do to help us get Tuan a medical visa. I'd work on it from my end, but I told her it was vital that she find Tuan's mother and get together the paperwork that would give us permission to bring him over. "It won't be easy," I told her after hugging Tuan good-bye, "but keep at it. Don't give up, and eventually it will happen. I truly believe that."

The trip home with Phoo was equal parts fun and annoying. We had to show her papers at least a dozen times, and it was a hassle trying to carry her and our luggage and explain yet again why we were bringing this child to the United States. But we quickly figured out that as soon as anyone met Phoo, they couldn't say no to her. Balancing on the counter, waving her stumps, she'd giggle at the person who would giggle back, and then wave us on. In fact, we started to get some special treatment. One airline employee gave us free passes to the VIP lounge; another pulled us to the front of the line at security. And who were we to turn that down? On the last leg of our trip, we had a long layover and booked a room in a hotel at the airport. That night, I woke up to the sound of crying and found Shelly in the bathroom, her eyes swollen.

"I don't know if I'm going to be able to say good-bye to her," she said. The couple who had agreed to sponsor Phoo and give her a home while she underwent her surgeries were going to be at the airport in Tulsa to meet us.

"I know," I said, putting my arms around her. "But you'll get to see her. You can go visit her whenever you want."

"It's not enough," Shelly said, pulling away for more tissues.

I didn't know what to say. "Caring for her would be hard work," I tried. "You know how much your back hurts now after just two weeks of carrying that stroller up and down stairs. It's not going to be easy for the family who takes her on."

"Yeah, but with my six kids at home, they could help. And I know they would love her as much as I do."

We barely slept at all that night, and we arrived at the terminal early the next morning, trying to steel ourselves for what was going to be an eighteen-hour flight and then having to say good-bye to Phoo. Over coffee, Shelly and I hatched our plan. Propping Phoo up on the counter as we checked into our coach seats, Shelly began telling the man behind the desk about Phoo: about the explosion and our trip up the mountain and how exhausted we were, and how *nice* it would be to get bumped to first class. Well, it didn't work. Apparently pointing out that the infant with whom you are traveling doesn't have legs is not a very convincing argument as to why you need the extra legroom.

I was worn out when we landed in Tulsa, and felt physically sick about the idea of having to watch Shelly hug Phoo good-bye. But we got through it, and afterward, I walked with Shelly to the parking lot, where she had left her car. She opened her door but couldn't speak. We hugged each other tightly for several minutes. As she pulled away, she was sobbing.

The experience had utterly exhausted me. All I wanted was to get home and spend the next few weeks hanging out with Randy and the kids, and staying in my robe. I knew Van and Tatum were counting down the days until I returned, and not only because they missed me. They both loved to hear the stories about the children we worked with in Vietnam, and I knew they'd want to see every photograph I had taken of Phoo and the trip. When I finally pushed through the front door, Tatum ran to meet me. She had just returned from school and was wearing what I have come to identify as a *Randy Is in Charge* outfit: two clashing shades of pink, tennis shoes dug from the pile of clothes I had set aside to donate, and a lumpy ponytail.

Crista came and hugged me, and noticed the look on my face. "Don't look at me," she said. "I tried to get her to change, but you know how much she loves her father."

The next day, I called Shelly as soon as I woke up. "How are you?"

"Great," she said, lying completely. She told me she had gotten lost on the way home from the airport—a drive she had probably made at least six thousand times—and the typically one-hour drive had taken her almost four. "I know it's wrong that Phoo is not here with me," she said. "I couldn't even concentrate enough to find my way home. Call me crazy, but I love that child, and she'll always be a part of this family."

Chapter Eight

September 2005. Dear Jantsen, I have paid a high price to be living the life I am experiencing now. I see things so clearly now and love you even more for leading me to my purpose. This may not be the life I'd have chosen, but it is the one I now choose to embrace. Love, Mom

The way I look at the whole experience with Phoo now is that she was the one who opened up opportunities for so many other children. When we got her home, Rob, Shelly, and I took Phoo to her first appointment with Dr. Karges. In the waiting room, I started to tell them about an e-mail I had recently received from a missionary working in Cambodia. She had met a baby girl named Claira who had been born with a hole in her heart. I pulled out Claira's photograph, which the woman had sent. She was tiny and frail with arms and legs like twigs, and it was clear she would die if she did not get surgery to fix her heart soon. I wanted to help Claira, but I didn't think I could find a doctor or a family to sponsor her in time. As I was explaining this to Rob and Shelly, Dr. Karges called us into his office. After examining

Phoo, he mentioned that he and his wife had long been considering adopting a child. They had three teenage daughters and one son. I told Dr. Karges about Claira, and that she was suffering from a heart condition. He was quiet for a few moments, then told us that three of his children had been born with heart problems; all were very healthy now. Rob, Shelly, and I looked at one another, our eyes nearly bulging out of our heads. Without hesitating even a moment, Dr. Karges told us that if there was any way he could help Claira, he would do it. A few months later, Claira was in the United States. I was able to line up a wonderful team of doctors to help her—Dr. Shari Smith and Dr. Elizabeth Frazier—who both moved mountains to get Claira into a Little Rock hospital for open-heart surgery. The Karges family gave her a home.

Now, if only Tuan's story were as sunny.

In the months after I returned home, I spent so much time on the phone with Yvonne in Vietnam that I was sure the phone company was going to invite me to serve on their board. Yvonne was working to locate Tuan's mother for permission to bring him to the United States for help and, meanwhile, I was able, with Dr. Karges's help, to secure the medical sponsorships I needed. The Karges family also agreed to give Tuan a home. They had fallen in love with Claira, who had been living with them for a few months after her first heart surgery, and they were happy to help.

It was several weeks before Yvonne, with the help of another fixer named Mr. Tweet, found Tuan's mother. She said she would help to get his residency papers, but because she had signed custody of him over to her sister, there was little more she could do. It was up to her sister now, but the two of them had lost touch, and she had no idea where she lived. And so we were at it again—trying to locate a woman with no known address in a disorganized city. Even Mr. Tweet couldn't find her.

As the months passed with no good news, people appeared to be giving up hope. The longer Tuan was denied medical care, the greater the chances he'd never recover from the infection. But I couldn't give up. Tuan was a Touch A Life child now, and that meant I was going to fight for him the way a mother fights for her own child—the same as I would for Crista, Van, or Tatum. The way I would have liked to have fought for Jantsen the day he died. Finally, I decided that I needed to go to Vietnam myself—my seventh trip there in six years and just twelve months after my last trip—to see if I might have better luck.

Cary Kelso and my friend Cindy Daugherty, who is a nurse, agreed to travel with me. If we did get custody of Tuan, which I believed we would, I needed someone to help me care for his infected leg. We arrived in Saigon on an October afternoon in 2005 and, exhausted from the travel, went right out to try to find Tuan's aunt. Mai, who was in Vietnam at the time, had tracked down a potential address. Long after the sun had set, we were still walking around the back alleys of the city. It wasn't as if the houses here had addresses nailed to the front. Along the way, Mai stopped every person we passed to ask if they knew of this place. Finally, we found a woman who nodded and pointed down a tiny alley. We stepped over the debris and through the puddles of still water, and inside a tiny one-room house, Tuan's aunt was making rice on a small stove on the floor.

After Mai explained the situation, and the help we wanted to give Tuan, she agreed to sign him out of the orphanage the next day so we could take him to a hospital for a complete checkup, then bring him to stay with us at Yvonne's while we tried to get his papers in order. That was wishful thinking—in the end, it took us ten days to get Tuan out of the orphanage. But when he did finally walk out of there, stumbling along on his crutches, I don't think I'd ever seen a kid so happy. Every day we spent with him, he had always asked the same thing: *Are you going to get me out of this orphanage? Can someone really fix my leg?* That night at Yvonne's house, I swear Tuan thought he'd died and gone to heaven. We filled up the bathtub with hot water and Matchbox cars and afterward, Mai prepared a big dinner of rice and vegetables. Cindy had to leave the next day, so she showed Cary and me the right way to keep his leg sterile. It was like showing two monkeys how to change a tire: Every time we tried, the bandages ended up wrinkled and twisted. We couldn't even get the tape to stick. Cary and I had been sharing Yvonne's big bed, and that night Tuan, wearing his new pajamas and smelling like a million bucks, crawled in between us, grabbed a pillow to prop up his sore leg, and fell soundly asleep.

The next day, Mr. Tweet called. We had asked him to try to expedite the process to get Tuan's passport. With the severity of his infection, we were racing against the clock.

"I'm sorry, but I can't get him the passport any quicker," he said. "It's going to take at least a few months."

"You're kidding me," I said, willing myself to not use the curse words filling my mouth like marbles.

"I'm sorry but I'm not."

"Well, we don't have a few months," I blurted out. "Surely there's someone we can bribe."

He was quiet.

"How much do you need?" I asked.

"I think eight hundred dollars would do it."

That's a boatload of money in a country where the annual income is less than five hundred, but it was our only option. I went to the bank, drew eight hundred off my credit card, and delivered it to Mr. Tweet. Just once, I thought, it would be nice to stay somewhere within my budget on these trips. A few days later, he told me that the previous problems had been resolved, and the passport was being processed.

Six days later, we decided that Yvonne would take over from here. Cary and I had been away more than two weeks, and we needed to go home. Besides, all that was left after getting Tuan's passport was to go to the interview with the US consulate, which, after everything we'd been through, would be the easiest step. Or so I hoped. Before we left, I carefully labeled the paperwork and walked Yvonne through everything she had to do.

"Just give them this folder," I said, "and don't say too much."

Back home, I woke up the morning of the interview feeling nervous and excited. When Yvonne finally called, she was so hysterical, she could barely speak.

"They denied him!" she said.

I tried to stay composed. "Tell me what happened."

"They said they didn't think his condition was life threatening enough."

I thought I was going to punch a hole through my kitchen wall. How *absurd*. This six-year-old kid had been living in excruciating pain for two years and could die from his infection. In fact, Yvonne had recently called to tell me that Tuan had to have emergency surgery because his infection had gotten worse. That sounded pretty "life threatening" to me. I called Dr. Karges, who called the orthopedic surgeon, who wrote a letter explaining that if Tuan's infection got into his bloodstream, a real possibility, he could go septic and die. I faxed that to Yvonne immediately.

She called me again two days later. And once again, she was hysterical.

"They are still denying him!" she said through her tears.

Apparently the woman who led the interview this time claimed that we were trying to circumvent the adoption system. Because Tuan didn't have anyone to return to in Vietnam—essentially, nobody there would say they wanted him afterward—they could not let him go.

Not knowing what else to do, I called my US senators, Kit Bond and Roy Blunt. Someone from each of their offices agreed to write a letter in support of Tuan's application, but I knew that wouldn't be enough of the push we needed. That night, unable to sleep, I crawled out of bed, went down to my little office, and got on the Internet. I was researching other possibilities when I came across information on something called humanitarian parole. Considered the last chance route for people seeking to come to the United States for "urgent humanitarian reasons," it could be used in cases of medical emergency, and was granted on a case-by-case basis. It was administered through the Department of Homeland Security, which had been put in charge of immigration issues after the attacks of September 11.

For the first time in weeks, I felt hopeful. Tuan met every single criterion for humanitarian parole, and I knew that this was exactly what I had been searching for. The next morning, as soon as Van and Tatum left for school with Randy, I picked up the phone and called DHS in Washington. As I waited on hold for what was beginning to feel like forever, I thought about where I had been five years earlier. It was Christmastime again, and that first holiday without Jantsen was among my worst, most desperate times. I thought about those nights I had spent questioning if I would go back to who I had been—decorating my house and filling my life with superficial things and mindless routines. That day, waiting for someone to answer the phone, I laughed out loud. I guess I got my answer to that. This year, instead of decorating my house, or buying the gifts I was supposed to, here I was, researching the heck out of something called humanitarian parole.

A woman finally answered. When I finished telling her Tuan's story, and why I was calling, I thought I heard her snicker. She then proceeded to tell me that "she did not have time to hear my sad sob story about a little boy in Vietnam dying." Because he had twice been denied a medical visa, she said, there was nothing she could do. And then she hung up.

I put the phone down and I seriously thought I was going to throw up. At that moment, right then, I knew that Tuan was going to die. He would not survive this latest rejection. It made absolutely no sense to me. I thought of all the people who had gotten Tuan this far, stretching back to Crista's boyfriend Zach, whose mother led me to Dr. Karges; Amy at the US consulate, who was willing to patiently teach me the steps I needed to take; Dr. Tupper, who agreed to do the surgery; and on and on. And then we could be this easily stopped in our tracks by one person?

Well, screw that.

I went right back to the Internet and found that the director of the Humanitarian Office at DHS was a man named Kenneth Leutbecker. I couldn't find a phone number for him, but I did come across the number of a man with the same last name who lived in the Washington, DC, area. I picked up the phone and dialed. When a man answered, I asked to speak to Kenneth.

"You have the wrong number, but Kenneth is my brother," he said.

"Oh," I said, surprised. "Of course. I'm desperately trying to get in touch with your brother. Do you have his home number?" And, well, yes he did!

That evening, Kenneth Leutbecker answered on the first ring, and he was very nice. When I explained why I was calling (so sorry to bother you at home, of course!), he told me that he was just walking out the door for Christmas vacation.

"I'll just tell you quickly then," I said, launching into the details of Tuan's story. "But according to my research, he's a perfect candidate for a humanitarian parole visa. He fits every single criterion."

When he told me to e-mail the paperwork to his office so he

could personally look into it after the holidays, I thought I was going to jump on a plane and take him to dinner. Well . . . what a tease. A few days after Christmas, I called his office. A few days later, when I hadn't heard back from him, I did it again. Finally, I dug his home phone number out from under the papers on my desk. This time, however, my call was not answered. Nor were any of the other calls I placed to his home or office the next few weeks. I suspected I was probably being deliberately ignored, and I imagined that his staff was fed up with me and saying to one another: The Crazy Lady from Missouri called again today. There was definitely a time where I would have been intimidated by the idea that educated, accomplished people in an office in Washington, DC, thought I was some sort of uneducated buffoon. But I didn't have time to let my pride get in the way, and if making a fool out of myself might help Tuan, what did I care?

In fact, I sort of took a liking to my new *Crazy Lady from Missouri* routine: Wake up, get Van and Tatum ready for school, make my coffee, call Kenneth Leutbecker at home, call Kenneth Leutbecker at work. Every time I told the receptionist my name, click. Right to voice mail. If I did get humans on the phone, they all asked the same thing: What do you want us to do? It wasn't brain surgery. I wanted them to do their jobs!

Finally, after several weeks of this, someone at the Department of Homeland Security called Cheryl Karges. They told her that as Tuan's sponsoring family, she and Melvin could present his case, but they wouldn't work with Crazy Lady anymore. It was great news! I helped them with the paperwork, and a few weeks later, as I was pulling out of the McDonald's drive-through handing Van his double cheeseburger and Tatum her garden salad (yes, I do have a seven-year-old who orders a salad at McDonald's), Cheryl called my cell phone. Her voice was quivering.

"They denied him, Pam."

I didn't even wait to hear the rest of it. I hung up and called Randy. He had a friend at the Associated Press. "Okay," I told Randy. "It's time to bring in the big guns."

A few days later, the AP sent reporter Marcus Kabel to Neosho. Over coffee at our kitchen table with the Kargeses, we explained the whole drama, telling him that the only reason cited by DHS for denying Tuan was that the application "appears designed to circumvent or shortcut normal immigrant visa processing requirements." Marcus's story was picked up by newspapers across the country, and that Friday I got a call from a producer at the *Today* show in New York City. She explained that she had read Marcus's article, and the show was interested in doing a segment on Tuan. They wanted to fly Dr. Karges and me to New York for an interview that would air live that coming Monday.

Well, that sounded *great*. And to help them out, I gave the producer Kenneth Leutbecker's home phone number. Unfortunately, she called back later to say that Mr. Leutbecker told his side of the story, and they were no longer interested. That weekend, I felt devastated, ready to give up. *Forget this,* I thought. *We got that kid's hopes up and now he's screwed.* I was done. No more new projects, no more fund-raising. And, to be honest, I was almost done with God. I mean, who does that? Lead me, and more importantly Tuan, so close only to then abandon him as quickly? I was outraged. I marched myself back up to the gold wingback chair, and he and I had a very serious talk. It was something along the lines of Who do you think you are? And why are you messing with me like this? Didn't I do everything I thought I was being told to do?

"Forget it," I finally said out loud. "I'm going back to being a mom and taking care of the things in this house. The rest of you are on your own."

I woke up early on Monday, feeling awful. As I was making the coffee, the phone rang. It was Cheryl Karges.

"We got it, Pam!" she yelled into the phone. "DHS just called. They granted him the humanitarian parole and are faxing the paperwork over right now."

When I hung up the phone, I went back upstairs, back to my chair. "Uhhh, sorry?" It was all I could manage.

In the end, I never did learn why Kenneth Leutbecker changed his mind. Maybe it was the potential of bad press, or his desire to get me out of his hair, but I choose to believe he realized how many people here cared about that little boy.

Cindy agreed to return to Vietnam to escort Tuan home, and a few weeks later Randy and I went to the airport with the Karges family. Well, not only them, but half the residents of southwest Missouri, every balloon that existed in Newton County, and, of course, Claira, who would soon be his new sister. When Cindy and Tuan came marching toward us, the entire terminal erupted into cheers and hugs. People could not wait to meet this little boy; it felt like a reception for a king. Tuan fell easily into people's huge embraces, a huge smile plastered to his face.

It had taken one and a half years from the moment I met Tuan to this moment right here. So many times, I had come *this close* to giving up completely because it was too hard and too frustrating and too annoying. As I watched Cheryl and Melvin Karges gently approach Tuan before wrapping him up in their arms, I knew, of course, that it had been worth it.

He was here. Finally. He was home.

———

Three years have passed since then. Claira has successfully undergone major open-heart surgery and is doing extremely well. She and her brother Tuan live on a huge, beautiful farm in the

Our wedding day,
May 1982

Randy, Jantsen,
and me, after nine
days in the ICU

Jantsen and his new
sister Crista,
her first week home

Jantsen and me, 1990

High school
football,
Fayetteville, 1997

Gregan,
Darius, and
Jantsen with
their new
braces

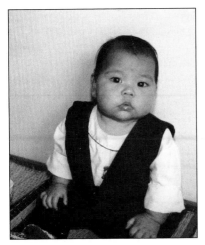

Thanksgiving Day, 1999,
when we met Van at the
orphanage in Vietnam

Tatum, two years old,
with her caretaker at the
orphanage, 2000

The whole family, 2008:
Zach and Crista Austin, Van, me, Randy, and Tatum

Touch A Life kids in Vietnam, 2007

A new bike for a Touch A Life child in Vietnam, donated through our first bike drive

Tuan, the day he was released from the orphanage, on his way to the US for medical treatment

Randy with Phoo, later named Haven, leaving the mountain village near Da Nang

Haven Shepard, 2008

The Magnificent Seven at the Village of Hope, 2007: Richard, Sarah, Kofi, Kojo, Mark, John Arthur, and Hagar

Crista and me during our first trip to Ghana, with Prince and Mark, January 2007

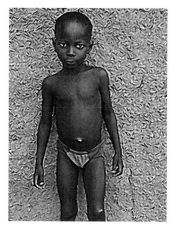

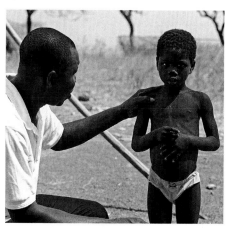

Mark in Sofoline, the
village where he worked,
on the day of his rescue,
December 18, 2006

George Achibra and Kobi,
rescue day

Mark and Kobi at
the Village of Hope,
August 2008

Walking the
children to the
Krachi Queen
on rescue day,
March 2007

Teteh, the day we met him on
Lake Volta, March 2007

One of the many trafficked
boys we met on Lake Volta
who still haunts our memories

John Arthur, me, and Ezekiel, August 2008

Ebenezer, Teteh, Aimee Molloy, Kobi, Israel, and Regina, on the children's first night at George's house

The first building of the Village of Life, completed September 2008

The twenty-one Touch A Life children in Ghana, all freed from slavery on Lake Volta, at the Village of Hope, August 2008

country with their four siblings. Tuan endured many painful surgeries, and spent months in a body cast. But not only does he walk without crutches now, he also rides a bike, plays soccer, and runs circles around the other nine-year-old boys.

Phoo, whose American name is Haven, is now five years old, and on her third pair of prosthetic legs, with many more to come. She is a runner, a cheerleader—and the best part? Shelly and Rob did end up adopting her. She's now the youngest of seven children in her family.

On a recent afternoon, Shelly brought Haven to our house to play with Van and Tatum, as she often does. Penny stopped by with MaiLia and her two sons and she, Shelly, and I took the kids to the backyard. It was such a riot. Tatum, Haven, and MaiLia were in one corner of the yard with their purses and makeup. Van and Penny's sons were in another, dressed as superheroes and jumping off the porch. In the middle of the lawn were Haven's prosthetic legs, which she had taken off because she often prefers to crawl around on her hands and knees. It probably would have been a funny scene to walk into: six kids from different corners of the world, playing in our little yard in Missouri, a pair of artificial legs in the middle.

But you know what? Despite everyone's differences, we didn't even notice. Those sorts of details had long escaped us all.

Chapter Nine

October 2006. Dear Jantsen, You have taught me how to love differently. Losing you has helped me find the depth of compassion I need for these children. Thank you for helping me see beyond myself. Love, Mom

There have been many times, like after I returned home from that nearly three-week trip to help Tuan, that some of my friends or members of my family have looked at me with what I'm quite sure is a hint of judgment, and asked how I can leave my family for so long, especially with two young children at home. I'm not saying that it's easy for me to leave them, or that I don't miss them while I'm away, because I flat-out like my children. It's just that I know that what I'm doing is best for them in many ways.

The concept of a bad day for my kids is when the cable goes out, or there's not enough milk for their Lucky Charms. I want my kids to know a different life than that; to have a different understanding of what constitutes hardship. The best way for me to do this is to do what I regretted not having done for Jantsen: teach them, through the way I live my life, that the world is not as big as we think and it's my responsibility—and will someday be theirs—to take care of people who need our help, even if those people look nothing like us, or live someplace that seems far away and foreign. I see many of my friends trying to shield their kids from pain and disappointment the way that I did when Jantsen and Crista were young, but I can't continue to do that. I don't want them to be crippled by fear. I want them to take chances and live adventurous lives. I want them to live their dreams, and the best way I can teach them to do that is to let them watch me live mine. And yes, maybe that means I haven't been there every night to tuck them into bed and I may have missed a Halloween or two, but they've survived. In fact, every year Tatum tells me the one thing she wants for her birthday is an updated passport so she can go and meet the children she considers her brothers and sisters.

It wasn't, however, always that easy for Crista. She was a teenager during the years that I began to travel a lot. And as any parent can attest, raising a teenager has its more, shall we say, trying moments. She'd sometimes make a joke that the only children I cared about were orphans overseas. This would have bothered me more if I didn't know that underneath her practiced annoyance, she truly supported me. Before every trip, she'd come home from the dollar store with bags of treats to leave with the children I was going to meet. She'd make popcorn, gather Van and Tatum on the living room floor, and show them how to tie the candy and gifts in beautiful paper and bright bows. Such gestures of support meant the world to me, and I tried to keep them in mind every time I felt the distance between us, and the guilt rising for not being there when she may have needed me. Only once did I truly question if my work with Touch A Life was coming at too great a cost to Crista. It was the time she decided to locate her birth mother. Not only did she do it without talking to me about it first, she did it while I was in Vietnam, trying to help Tuan.

I had called Randy one evening from an Internet café, on a lousy connection, and I could tell from the tone of his voice that something was wrong. He explained that Crista, on what I can understand only as a teenage whim, had called the adoption agency in St. Louis to ask for information. We'd had no contact with her birth mother since we'd adopted Crista seventeen years earlier, and the agency was prohibited from sharing information without the written consent of both the birth and adoptive parents. The woman who answered the phone, apparently having no idea about that rule, or how resourceful my daughter could be, told Crista her birth mother's name, and that she lived in Connecticut. Within a few minutes on the Internet, Crista had found a phone number. So what did she do? She picked up the phone and called.

Her birth mother was thrilled that Crista had found her. We didn't know this, but she had been sending letters to the adoption agency over the years, asking for information on what had happened to her daughter. She and Crista talked for a while, and decided that they would eventually plan to meet.

"Don't be mad," Randy said to me that day. He assured me that he had also talked to Crista's birth mother, and the situation was under control. He also made Crista promise to not contact her anymore until I got home.

I wasn't mad, I just felt caught off guard, and completely unprepared to deal with another person claiming to be my daughter's mother. I also felt guilty. If there was one moment I should have been there beside Crista, this was it. I knew that she had long been curious about who her birth mother was. We had never hid from her the fact that she was adopted; in fact, every year we celebrated the anniversary of the day we brought her home from the adoption agency, which we all called Gotcha

Day. I'd cook her favorite meal—poppy seed chicken—or let her pick a restaurant, and Randy would come home from work with flowers or a gift. She would sometimes ask me: What do you think my birth mother looks like? Where do you think she lives? I was curious about those things myself, and had planned that we would both try to find her together one day. It just wasn't *that* day when I was standing alone in a noisy Internet café in Saigon, halfway around the world. When I later asked Crista why she had chosen to contact the agency and call her birth mother right then, she offered a typical teenage response: *I'm not sure. I guess my curiosity just finally got the best of me.* Okay, then.

As soon as I returned home from Vietnam, I called her birth mother, who was now married with two children. We tried to figure out a time that she could come to Missouri to meet our family, but Crista was preparing to start college in Texas the next year, and we couldn't find a convenient time.

I carried the guilt I felt for not being there for her that day with me for a while, and I tried to make it up to her. But we struggled, and the distance between us deepened—until the day, not too long afterward, everything came to a head. It was the afternoon that she and I have come to refer to as our Jerry Springer moment.

At the time, Crista was spoiled. Perhaps I should find a less obnoxious way to describe that, because it makes all of us look bad, but it's true. She had everything she wanted: a silver VW Bug and her own bedroom downstairs with a separate TV area and a comfortable couch. In exchange, I expected her to help out with Van and Tatum (which she happily did because if there was one thing she truly loved in this world, it was those two children) and help out around the house (which she refused to do). One afternoon, I had plans to follow Randy to the mechanic shop where he was dropping off his car for a tune-up. I had given her a list of chores. When I saw Randy pull into the driveway, I grabbed my keys and purse and went to check on her. While I expected to find her pushing a vacuum, I instead found her sitting at the computer, writing instant messages to her friends while talking on her cell phone.

"What are you doing?" I asked her.

"What does it look like?"

"You haven't done one thing on your list."

"So?" she replied.

"Crista," I said. "Hang up right now and while we're at it, give me the cell phone."

"No."

No?

"Give me the cell phone."

"No."

"Crista Marie Cope," I said, pulling out the ubiquitous three-name warning that I believe has probably signaled the beginning of most major world wars, "give me the cell phone."

"I don't have to."

Now, while parenting books may advise against doing what I did next, before I knew it, I was running at her, trying to grab the phone out of her hand. She jerked her hand away, and my nails accidentally caught her wrist, leaving a pretty deep scratch. You would have thought that I had just pulled out every hair in her head (which I sort of attempted to do about five minutes later) the way she screamed in agony. But it didn't mean she was going to give up the phone. Instead she curled up in the office chair, protecting that phone the way a lion would shield her cub from a predator.

"You have the crossed the line," I yelled. "Give. Me. The. Phone."

She stood up and tried to push past me out of the office. I grabbed her waist with one hand, her hair with the other, trying to get to the phone from behind her. It was this moment I noticed Van and Tatum standing in the doorway watching us. For a moment, I considered just letting Crista go, if only to save my two six-year-olds thousands of dollars in therapy bills years later as they attempted to process this moment. But when Crista tried to run toward freedom, I was knocked to my knees and dragged along behind her. So instead of letting go, I heard myself screaming, "Sister, you are GOING DOWN!"

It went on like this for several minutes, and through many rooms of the house. The more she dragged me around, and the more I felt the rug burns on my knees, the more irate I became. And the more she sounded like I was pulling out her heart with my bare hands. "You're hurting me," she yelled. But I didn't care. I was going to get that cell phone even if I had to spend the next several years in prison.

And then the moment came. Probably exhausted from dragging me from the office to the living room to the kitchen, or her attempts to pull out my hair, her grip on the phone weakened, and I reached in and got it. I stood up, my hair a mess, my makeup smeared, my knees bloodied, and I held the phone in the air. I looked like Rocky after he won his first big fight, holding the phone above my head, relishing the moment of victory. Crista started crying, and Van and Tatum just stood there in silence, their eyes nearly bugging out of their little heads.

"What's going on?" Van whispered.

"I don't know," Tatum responded. "But I think Mom's being naughty."

I knew I had to get out of there, find some room to breathe. I was heading to the car when I heard Crista behind me, running toward the car door. Inside, I was fumbling for the locks and panicking at the idea of her getting in, as if she were some sort of carjacker. She squeezed in through the passenger door and started yelling at me to return her phone. It was ugly and intense and beneath my anger, I felt numb. She clearly had little respect for my authority and was pushing far past acceptable boundaries. In that moment, all I could think was that maybe we were so dysfunctional, she and I would never have a healthy relationship. I told her to get out of the car, but she was demanding the phone back like a junkie needing her fix.

I was in the middle of screeching out a long, incoherent list of all the things she'd never be allowed to do again—which basically included everything short of brushing her teeth—when Randy walked up to the car.

"Is there a problem, ladies?" he stammered.

Crista and I both started yelling out our side of the story, like two teenage rivals who had been caught by the principal.

"Crista, get out of the car this minute," he said. And of course, as she usually did, she obeyed him without a word.

"Do you think that means she can't drive us to school anymore?" I heard Tatum say.

I didn't stick around to answer her. I started the car, pulled out of the driveway, and went for a very long drive. Later when I came back, I hid the phone in Randy's tools in the garage and went straight to bed.

The next day, I woke up feeling furious, sore, crazy, and more than a little guilty. Crista and I had planned to spend the day together at the mall, and even though I was still very angry at her, and she downright hated me, we went anyway. A few hours later, we still hadn't said a word to each other. But then, standing before a rack of sale items, I looked over and saw the scratches on her arms and legs. She looked back at me, at the hard-core *I don't like you right now* look on my face, at the rug burns on my elbows and knees.

"You look like you were in a bar fight," she said. Before I knew it, I was picturing the way she had dragged me around the house and I was laughing so hard I thought I was going to wet my pants. And so was she. I went over to her and hugged her.

"I'm sorry," I said through my laughter.

"Me, too, Mom," she said. "I wish we had taped that, though. Think of the daytime talk shows we could have appeared on."

As ugly as this moment was for us, it was as bad as it ever got and, in some ways, it helped Crista and me begin to heal. Maybe the Jerry Springer moment really was just about a cell phone, but probably not. Part of me thinks it was also her way of expressing the pent-up anger she felt toward me for failing to mother her the way she needed, not only because of the trips I took, but in all the months and years after Jantsen died. I definitely understand that. I thought about how many nights I had watched her sleep on the chair and ottoman in our room seven years earlier; how much I had wanted then to wrap my arms around her and make her feel my love for her. I wasn't able to do it then, and our relationship had suffered a lot in the ensuing years. The barriers I had put up to protect myself included more than a few against her. I wondered if she trusted that I would ever heal, or be a good mom again. But that afternoon, as I fought her for the cell phone, I think that in a slightly twisted way she saw me as a parent fighting for her, telling her that I loved her enough to stand up to her and be the disciplinarian we both knew she still needed, despite her unwavering sense of independence. She had stepped over the boundary, and it had scared her. And there was no way that I wasn't going to stay there and show her that as mad as it might make her, I was going to protect her. From harm, when needed, and also from herself.

Of course I would do that, because I am so in love with Crista it's impossible to describe. She is an amazing daughter, and a wonderful young woman. To this day, every time I see how she is with Van and Tatum and how much she loves those kids, I am awed by her, and I often regret that I didn't—because I couldn't—do more for her when her brother died. I love how she has worked hard to make Tatum into a little carbon copy of herself—a strong, independent girl who is not afraid to speak her mind or compete with the boys. I know it's mostly because of Crista that Tatum doesn't feel weakened by her physical disabilities, and why it's easy for her to tell the other kids who ask why she limps, "Oh, God made my leg special. I just walk a little different than you, but it's no big deal." Then she'll apply the lip gloss Crista got for her at Bath & Body Works and go back to her Junie B. Jones book. I love how she has decided that she, too, is one day going to travel the world, and meet the children we've worked with, and do what she can to change their lives.

Thinking about this as I held on to Crista in that store that day, I was finally able to say what I knew I needed to.

"I'm sorry if I hurt you," I whispered to her. And of course I just didn't mean for the scratches and marks I had left on her skin.

———

In addition to beating up my oldest daughter and taking care not to traumatize the younger ones during this time, I was also trying to manage at least forty hours a week with Touch A Life—fund-raising, managing the medical visas, helping families who wanted to adopt assemble their dossiers, which I had begun to do more and more. In fact, in the seven years that have passed since Van and Tatum came home, our little town of Neosho and the surrounding communities have become home to more than thirty adopted children from all over the world. There are Nian Wheeler and Nathan Jackson from China; Cobi Marble and Kai Kelso from Vietnam; Madison and Carson McCary and Davy, Davin, Seth, and Chantal Benz from

Cambodia; Gabe Bradshaw from Guatemala; Max and Marcus Duncan, Evanson St. Clair, and Caben White from Haiti; Gracie and Caleb White from Taiwan; Katya Roelfsema from Kazakhstan; Barrett Freed and Mateo Kaempfe from Nicaragua; and Sammy Cook from Ghana. Penny also adopted again: another daughter, KeSey, from Cambodia. Our families often get together for pool parties or to go to the park, and it's not unusual that we get odd stares from people. It often takes me a second to remember, *Ohhhhhh, right, these children don't look like us!* I have a friend who has six kids, two of them adopted from Africa. He says, "I have six children and two of them are adopted, but I don't remember which." I love that.

In January 2005, I decided I was ready to take the next step. Up to this point, we had raised nearly fifty thousand dollars for Touch A Life, but had been operating under Carol and Marvin's not-for-profit organization, Ventures for Children, so that these donations could be tax-deductible. It was helpful, but it meant that Touch A Life always felt a little distant to me, and that month I began applying for our own not-for-profit status. After starting the process, I learned that one of the first requirements was to create a board of directors. It felt so official! Someone recommended that I consider inviting some of the business owners in town, or try to get experts from one of the local colleges involved. While that sounded like it would be helpful, it didn't sound like much fun. For years, our friends Bud Reed and Cary Kelso had been coming over each month to help Randy and me brainstorm ideas. Bud, who is seventy but acts thirty, had been a big supporter of our work since the beginning; Cary was a close friend who had accompanied me on trips to Vietnam and Haiti, and adopted her son Kai from the same orphanage where Van and Tatum had lived. Before long, our friend Warren also joined us. While I know Warren had long been interested in our work, he also has a very good business sense, and my guess is that Randy invited him in order to have backup every time he needed to convince Cary, Bud, and me that we shouldn't give away every penny to whatever problem we heard of next. One morning, over Bud's famous sausage-and-egg Buddritos, I looked around the room at my friends poring over financial records and talking about what to do next, and realized I already had my board of directors. When I told them the exciting news that day, they all happily agreed. (Well, Bud happily agreed on the condition that he wouldn't be expected to wear a suit anytime soon.)

For several weeks, we talked about where we wanted Touch A Life to be heading, and again and again we kept coming back to the idea that all we really wanted was to remain open to identifying the children we knew were Touch A Life kids. There was no formula for it, which made some of the paperwork I had to fill out in the process to become an independent organization a little difficult.

Describe the population you intend to work with.
Children
How will people in your target population be identified?
Well, you see, it's hard to explain. Do you ever just
get this feeling . . .

In the end, I guess I finessed it enough because we did get not-for-profit status, which also meant that I could start applying for grants (a certain type of hell I wouldn't wish on anyone). But even that was good for me, because it forced me to begin to think a little bigger about things. One thing that was becoming clear to me was that the more I traveled, the more I knew that I wanted to go to Africa. It had always felt to me like the biggest adventure—a more interesting, more life-changing place to travel than the moon. And of course, the need is so great. I was spending a lot of time reading about the scale of the poverty there, and the number of children who are orphaned, desperate for help.

The more I read, the more I wanted to understand. We had been introduced to a couple from Liberia, Korma and Cecilia, who were studying for their master's degrees at a local university. One night, Randy and I invited them over for dinner to learn more about the situation in their country. They are a lovely couple in their early forties, and as we grilled steaks and sat near the pool, and their two sons played tag with Van and Tatum, they told us about the atrocities they had witnessed in Liberia: the public rapes, the mass killings, the tribal wars. Cecilia had been publicly raped herself and was severely beaten by members of an opposing tribe. She escaped to a refugee camp, where she met Korma. After finishing their studies in the United States, they planned to return to Liberia and build an orphanage to help the children who had been orphaned by the conflict.

Over dessert, I explained to them that I had become very interested in Africa, and had been thinking about fund-raising in order to expand our work there. When I finished speaking, I saw a peculiar look cross Korma's face. He was quiet for a moment, then set down his fork and leaned toward me in his chair.

"Pam, I have to ask you this," he said. "Why do you talk about needing to raise money?" He waved his hand across the pool, the sprawling lawn, and pointed up toward our house. "You have been blessed with so much. And it looks to me like everything you need is already right here."

I will never forget that moment. At first, I was extremely uncomfortable, and a little angry. *Hey, wait a minute here, buddy,* I thought. *Don't judge me, I am saving a lot of orphans!* But later that evening, as I put away the dishes and wrapped up the leftovers, I couldn't get what Korma said out of my mind. I tried to see myself the way that he and Cecilia had to see me: living a privileged life in a fifty-five-hundred-square-foot house, far more room than we needed, and still talking about hitting up everyone we knew to help.

I took a glass of wine out back and sat down by the pool, dipping my toes in the warm water. As I did this, I was reminded of the time I had done the exact same thing seven years earlier, right after we moved back to Neosho from Arkansas. I remembered how that night, from a similar spot in a different, less glamorous house, I thought about how much I wanted to make decisions in my life that would feel deliberate and meaningful.

That seemed like a lifetime ago. I had become a different person, one much closer, I think, to the woman God had in mind. But something about Korma's words had shaken me, making me admit to myself that even though Randy and I had embarked on this new journey, we were still trying to drag along so much *stuff*. All this time, I had tricked myself into believing that I was proud of my house. After all, why wouldn't I be? It was big and pretty and everyone was always commenting on how nice it was. But the truth was, I didn't feel proud of it at all. All I felt was how much of a burden it was. It required so much effort to live here. All those rooms meant someone had to clean them, and pick up toys from them. And the mortgage we paid. Was it worth it? Of all the things we wanted to spend money on, was this house worth the debt, and all the other things we were giving up? I was surprised that night to be looking at it like this for the first time; it had never occurred to me to ask myself if this house was essential to us. Yes, we needed to have a house, but did we need *this* house?

No, we didn't. It was as simple as that. When Randy and I talked about it, he agreed right away, and once the thought occurred to us that we should consider downsizing our home, it felt like a no-brainer. Randy, especially, was tied down by the mortgage, because it was his salary that had to pay for it.

In the end, we found the perfect house. Our friends Chris and Lisa Parks had always loved ours as much as we did, and had recently put their own home on the market. It was about half the size of ours, and all that we needed. A few months later, they bought our house and we bought theirs, and it felt right. Of course, I was second-guessing the whole thing a few weeks later, as Crista and I spent countless hours unpacking boxes and stripping wallpaper in our new home, our arms covered in burns from the steamer we'd rented. The more we stripped that wallpaper, the more I became convinced that this is what hell had to be like. People would get there and be told that for the next one thousand years they would be stripping wallpaper fifteen years old. When they were done, they'd be brought to another room (like, say, my new bedroom) and have to strip wallpaper that was twenty years old, and had been painted over. It was endless. I was stripping wallpaper in my sleep. The day of the move was hardly any better. I certainly do not recommend trading houses with someone in this way. We'd be moving our furniture into the living room as Chris and Lisa were trying to move theirs out, or pulling our moving van into their driveway as they were backing theirs out.

But that first night in our new house, as I sat alone in the kitchen, I knew that despite the moving challenges, I loved that we made this decision. Randy had recently read a quote to me by the author and poet John Ruskin: *Every increased possession loads us with a new weariness.* I hadn't thought about it like that before, but that night, I became aware of how true it was. In the weeks before the move, I had gotten rid of so much stuff—most of it things I had never even needed. For the first time in years, I felt physically and emotionally skinny.

Looking back now, I know that this decision set so many wonderful things in motion. It was just a few weeks after we sold our house that Randy and I went to New York City with Warren and his wife, Shelly, to see *Mamma Mia!*, where I came across the article in *The New York Times* about Mark Kwadwo, the boy who had been sold into slavery in Ghana. And I know . . . I *know* . . . that it is only because I had unburdened myself—financially, emotionally, spiritually—that everything that happened with Mark was able to, well, happen.

————

As soon as I saw Mark's photo in the *Times* that morning, and read about what he was made to endure as a child slave, I knew that he was a Touch A Life kid. I didn't know how, or if, I could help him, but I knew that if there was any way to get him off Lake Volta, where he fished fourteen hours a day, I was going to give it my very best shot. I also knew that Mark was hardly the only suffering child in Ghana. From what I read, thousands of others were in similar situations—having been sold by their parents to fishermen to work on the lake, deprived of a family's love and an education. They were taken so young and kept so long that in some cases, they no longer remembered their last name or the town where they had been born. And even though the Ghanaian government had enacted a law against these activities, and anyone found to be buying or trafficking children could face five years in prison, the law was not being enforced. For all these children knew, they had been abandoned and forgotten.

The first thing I did was e-mail *The New York Times* at the address I found on its Web site. I got a quick, automated response, explaining that the article had elicited enormous response from readers. It suggested that people interested in helping should contact the International Organization of Migration (IOM), which was headquartered in Switzerland and had, in the previous two years, organized the rescue of nearly six hundred children.

I e-mailed IOM and, a few days later, received a response from a coordinator. He explained that his organization was hoping to raise at least a hundred thousand dollars to fund a coordinated rescue of twenty-five children soon after the new year, and he included an address where I might send a check.

The new year? That was a whole two months away, and a hundred thousand dollars seemed like an impossible amount of money—I'd be carting around that slide projector until I was about two hundred years old before I came close to raising half that amount. I wrote him back that day, asking if there wasn't something I could do more immediately to help Mark Kwadwo. I knew how I probably appeared to him: a well-intentioned but clueless American whose efforts wouldn't do anything to solve *The Problem*. But I didn't have time to worry about that.

The IOM coordinator wrote me again, and while he thanked me for my concern for Mark, he explained that it was far more "cost-effective" to rescue several children at once, rather than one at a time. *Cost-effective?* Weren't we talking about the life of a child? After going back and forth about this a few times, I decided that the *Crazy Lady from Missouri* routine wasn't going to work; it was time to give up on this route. It wasn't that I didn't think that what IOM was doing was necessary and important, I just knew it wasn't the right course of action for me. I had also e-mailed the reporter who had written the *Times* story, Sharon LaFraniere, and kept hoping that would be the connection I needed. After not hearing back from her, I kept at it, sending another e-mail every few days. Just when I was about to give up hope that she'd respond, I woke up to a new message from her in my inbox one day. Sharon explained that she lived in South Africa, and her work covering a large swath of Africa kept her out in the field for weeks at a time. She had been in Sierra Leone, and had just read my messages.

Nothing would have happened without Sharon's help. She suggested I contact George Achibra, the man in Ghana who had assisted her in getting access to Mark and other boys for her story. George was a former schoolteacher in Kete Krachi, a town in northern Ghana, on Lake Volta, who now held an administrative position with the region's educational system. A few years earlier, he had founded a small nonprofit organization called Pacodep, short for Partners in Community Development. He had recently begun working to educate people in the villages around the lake where trafficked children were often brought to work, explaining the new anti-trafficking law.

I wrote George immediately, and got an e-mail back from him that same night. It was exactly what I had been hoping for. He was happy that I had contacted him, and said he had been curious whether the *New York Times* article had generated any interest among Americans. While I'd expected that many other people may have already found their way to him through Sharon, he said I was the first. He also said that he would do everything he could to get Mark off the lake. When I called him the next day, I liked him immediately. Struggling to understand each other at first through the time delay and his accented English, we eased into it, and George explained how this could work. Even with the new law, fishermen who had purchased children would hardly just hand one over; and without the required resources to enforce the law, there was very little fear of punishment. Therefore, George suggested we offer Mark's master something in exchange for his release. Not money, for fear he might use that to buy another boy, but things that might lessen the need for Mark's labor, like repairing his boats or buying new fishing nets.

"That sounds like a good plan," I said. "How much money would you need?"

"In American dollars," he said, after thinking about it for a few seconds, "about $350."

Three hundred and fifty dollars. He explained that in addition to the fishing equipment, the money would cover Mark's medical expenses, new clothing, and George's transportation to the village where Mark lived. George didn't want any money for his time.

"I'll wire you the money tomorrow," I said.

"Great," he said, his voice crackling into laughter. "But there's still one more problem. Where will Mark go?"

George explained his belief that children who had been sold by their parents should not simply be returned to them. He had seen how often children who'd found a way to return home—either by escaping, or with the help of charitable organizations—were just sold again. "The parents who sell their kids do not do this because they do not love their children. They do it because they cannot afford to feed them," he said. "Do not judge them. For many, it's an impossible choice between selling their children and surviving, or keeping them and starving. Unless that changes, the risk they will say yes when another man comes asking for the service of their son or daughter is too great. We need to find another option."

That night, after Van and Tatum were asleep, I told Randy about my conversation with George. By the time we were ready for bed, we had made a decision: We would spend thirty-six hundred dollars to rescue seven children, and find the money to support them for the rest of their lives. But I still needed to figure out where they might go afterward.

The next morning, I called my brother-in-law Mike to see if in his work as a minister he had come across an orphanage in Ghana where the kids might go after the rescue. I was astonished when he told me he had. The Village of Hope, about an hour outside Ghana's capital city of Accra, was largely funded by American donations. Mike had heard it was a wonderful program that had been established under a Ghanaian man named Fred Asare. The Village of Hope sounded like much more than the orphanages I had visited. The kids lived together in houses with a houseparent, and attended a school on the site. The education they received was considered so good that parents from surrounding villages often came to ask if they could pay to send their children there to study. Though Fred was constantly trying to raise money to expand the number of children he could provide a home for, and to educate, they were already above capacity with 116.

The next day, instead of going Christmas shopping with Penny as I had planned, I stayed home to call Fred at the Village of Hope at 9 AM his time. When he answered, I told him about Mark and the others and explained that while I understood that his program was already being stretched too thin, I was begging him to find room for seven more, and assured him that TAL would cover their expenses each month. I was accustomed to being disappointed when I asked people for help, and I braced myself for him to tell me that there was nothing they could do. But after quietly listening to my long spiel, he laughed loudly. "Pam," he said, "we are in the kids-getting business. Bring them on!"

Four days before Christmas, and about seven weeks after the article about Mark had appeared in the *Times,* George arrived at Mark's village with a list of seven names. I know arriving at that final list had required George to make some excruciating decisions. How do you choose which seven children to save when you must leave so many others behind?

George and his team had spent hours deliberating and finally settled on the group: In addition to Mark, they would take his two siblings, Kofi and Hagar. George had grown attached to John Arthur, a twelve-year-old who had been sold twice by his parents. Sarah was the only other girl who worked in this village other than Hagar, and it was a tragic reality that girls in forced labor situations were always at risk of being sexually abused. Richard and Kojo lived on one of the islands in the lake, and George worried that they had been especially mistreated.

After George had the seven children in the van and began the eleven-hour trek to the Village of Hope, he called me on his cell phone. "Pam," he said, as I heard the children's laughter and singing through the static. "You wouldn't believe the transformation. It's immediate. I thought they had forgotten how to smile."

———

A few days before Christmas, Crista called me from Texas, where she was in her first year of college. "I know that you're dying to go to Ghana, Mom," she said. She was right. As soon as I had heard the rescue was going to happen, I couldn't stop thinking about how much I wanted to go and meet these children—who, in our home, were becoming known as the Magnificent Seven. The photographs George had sent of them were hung on the fridge above Tatum's drawings and over my desk. I had called the Village of Hope to try to speak to Mark and the others, but we couldn't communicate. Even though English is the country's official language, they all spoke in different tribal dialects.

"You should go," Crista said. "But take me with you."

Now, one airline ticket from Missouri to Accra costs about fifteen hundred dollars, and of course there was a time I couldn't have considered buying even one. But at this point, it was kind of a no-brainer. After our move into the smaller house, and the fact that we were (finally) very close to living without any debt, we could find the money. After all, opportunities like this were exactly why we had made the decision in the first place.

And once again, what would I ever do without my husband? Randy agreed to stay home and take care of Van and Tatum. I spent the next week running around like crazy: organizing a last-minute visa, trying to figure out where to get a vaccination for yellow fever, and picking up bags of Laffy Taffy, suckers, bubblegum, and at least twelve different brands of anti-diarrhea medicine.

On January 3, 2007, Penny dropped Crista and me off at the airport. As I hugged her good-bye, I felt so excited I could barely stand it. With each stop—first in Chicago, then in London, before heading to Accra—my excitement grew. I've always loved the feeling of being inside a plane: the sense of stillness, of being removed from everything. I loved sharing that with Crista, her head resting against my shoulder. As the lights in the plane dimmed and the second movie started, I took her in my arms and breathed in the smell of her shampoo. She stirred a little and, before falling asleep, seemed to sense what I was thinking. "We've come so far, haven't we, Mom?" she asked, kissing my shoulder. "And I don't just mean to Africa."

———

We landed in Accra more than twenty-four hours after leaving Missouri. It was evening, and it was hot. When we stepped onto the glowing tarmac, the temperature hovered close to ninety degrees, and the air felt like the inside of a sauna. Outside the small terminal, honking minivans and small cars—many with tape covering the windshields, or doors held closed with rope—tried to push through the throngs of people. Across the street, piles of garbage smoldered on a grassy hill, sending white clouds of acrid smoke into the air. People around me hugged other arriving passengers, speaking in a language that sounded ancient and guttural.

George spotted us in the crowd and ran over to sweep Crista and me up in a huge embrace. "Hello, Pamela!" he boomed, using a name nobody except him ever calls me. "Hi, little Cristy! Welcome!" It was good to finally meet him after the hours we had spent talking on the phone and e-mailing. He was tall and lean, with an athletic build and an enormous smile. He grabbed our bags and led us to where a pickup truck waited. "You came at a good time," he said as I wiped the sweat from my forehead. "We're in the middle of a cold spell."

We inched along the one two-lane paved road that runs through the city. This year marked the fiftieth anniversary since Ghana became the first sub-Saharan African nation to gain independence from Britain, which the nation's residents take very seriously; it's a huge source of pride. The red, gold, and green flag hung from every light post and was painted onto many buildings. George told us that there were major events planned in celebration throughout the year.

Despite the fact that Accra is the nation's largest city, there was nothing Western about the place. Most of the buildings lining the street looked more like they belonged at an army base than a nation's capital. The shops resembled sheds, made of tin or wood. In the dust in front of them, the shop owners had laid out hand-carved rocking chairs, refrigerators, bolts of bright fabric, and mattresses for sale. Hand-painted on cement walls was the odd request: DO NOT URINATE HERE. Men and women ran along with the traffic, pounding on our closed windows to try to get us to buy the goods balanced in bowls and trays on their heads: candy, bottled water, small cakes wrapped in cellophane, and, oddly, American flags. One woman was even carrying on her head a cage filled with live chickens.

The public transportation system in Ghana is a fleet of minivans that appear to have been plucked from a junkyard. Many were missing their side and back windows, and were packed with more people than you would think possible. Mothers with young children and tiny babies crammed together, their arms and heads poking out the windows; in some vans, people were sitting on the roof, struggling to hold on to something as the vehicles jerked forward. People in the van next to us stared at us, and I saw ourselves as they saw us: strapped into our seat belts, enjoying the air-conditioning and the comfort of the van. The luckiest people in the city.

George filled us in on the seven children. They had settled well into their new lives at the Village of Hope. Initially, they stayed among themselves, but they were adjusting now, making new friends. They lived with two houseparents named Roland and Gladys, as well as twenty-five other children. In the afternoons, the comfortable dining room at which they shared their meals was transformed into a classroom where a woman named Matilda taught the six youngest. John Arthur, who was twelve and the oldest of the seven, had been placed in the kindergarten class, and Matilda was teaching the others the very basics, working to prepare them for kindergarten. Most of them had never held a pencil before.

About an hour later, we drove through the tiny village of Gomoa-Fetteh, turning down a grassy path toward the Village of Hope. Two men holding rifles waved us through the gates, and we drove past several small white houses with big cement porches. Fred was there to greet us. A strong, quiet man in his late thirties, he showed us where we'd spend the week: a comfortable guesthouse on the property that housed the volunteers from around the world who came to work at the Village of Hope. It had a main kitchen and living room, and private bedrooms with bunk beds. We even had our own cook, a friendly woman named Leticia, who would prepare three meals a day for us using bottled water. For all of this, we paid a fee of fifteen dollars per day.

When Crista and I woke up the next morning, the schoolday had already begun. We walked across the dusty lawn to the children's house. Matilda was in the middle of a lesson, reciting English words to the children, who repeated them after her in quiet, obedient voices.

"Jump. Jumped. Walk. Walked."

Not wanting to interrupt, we stood silently on the porch and just watched. Kofi, Kojo, Richard, Hagar, and Sarah sat among a few other children—likely new arrivals to the orphanage. It was impossible to see them there and not instinctively remember how I had first perceived them in the photos George had e-mailed to me before the rescue: their distended bellies, overdeveloped muscles, and fearful eyes. The kids I saw here, sitting around a large wooden table covered in paper scribbled with the alphabet, on chairs with big cushions, wearing their powder-blue-and-white uniforms—they were simply different people now.

Finally, Kofi looked up and saw Crista and me. I had e-mailed George several photos of our family, and I wondered if he had shared them with the children. Obviously, he had. Kofi threw down his pencil, hopped from his chair, and ran out to us. I thought he was going to knock me over with the force of his hug. He grabbed my hand and led us inside, where we were nearly tackled by the others.

"Mama Pam! Mama Pam!" they yelled, pushing one another out of the way to get closer to us, until they were all hanging from our waists and arms like wind chimes. "Sister Crista!" Each of them handed me a picture they had drawn. "To Mama Pam," Sarah's read. "I love you so much." Matilda clapped in excitement, and when the kids finally let go of us and we embraced Matilda hello, she told her students it was time to settle down and resume the lesson. Crista and I took seats at the table and watched in utter amazement. Every time one of them answered Matilda's question correctly, the others clapped twice in quick succession. Then they'd look at me, proud and shy.

Though I was happy to meet all of them, I was especially curious to see Mark. Matilda told me that he had come down with malaria, and when I found him he was still lying in his bed, wrapped in his blankets. Unable to eat for two days, he was running a very high fever and had trouble lifting himself out of his bed. Though it was sad to see him as sick as he was, it made me even happier to be there. The Village of Hope truly seemed to be a wonderful and happy environment, but at that moment, the one thing Mark needed most was a mother. I picked him up and carried him across the yard to the guesthouse. There Crista and I bathed him with a cold washcloth, trying to reduce his fever. Then we set him in one of the empty beds and covered him with the blankets a friend had given me to leave at the Village of Hope. He slept for hours. Every time he woke up, Crista or I was there with salty crackers and a cold Sprite.

After two days of this, I started to think it would be years before he woke up. His tiny body still bore many scars: marks on his forehead from where he had been beaten, the bottom of his feet torn to shreds, toe fungus from hours in the swampy water. He felt skeletal. Eventually his fever broke, but his lips became covered in painful sores, which one of the teachers explained was the final stage of malaria. By the next day, the illness had passed. When I went to Gladys's house to check on him, he was eating breakfast with the others. "You look great," I said, giving him a hug. "I think you can go back to classes now."

He frowned. "Maybe tomorrow," he said, as Gladys translated. "I think I'll feel better after a few more bottles of Sprite."

While every one of the seven children amazed me, I was

most taken with John Arthur. He was warm and friendly, but extremely driven and serious. One day, Crista and I were taking a walk through the grounds when two young boys spotted us and called us into their classroom. The teacher had left to take a student to the clinic, fearing he was also coming down with malaria, and the kids had been left on their own. One grabbed my camera and started taking photos of the others, and the room erupted into a party. The boys started drumming on their desks, and in front the girls joined in, swaying in the rhythmic movements of a graceful African dance. Afterward, they broke out into a chorus of "If you're happy and you know it clap your hands!" It was fun, but chaotic, and about fifteen minutes into it, I spotted John sitting quietly at a desk in the back. I hadn't noticed him there, silent and focused. I walked over to him and saw that he was practicing the alphabet in careful script on lined paper.

"Hi, John," I said.

"Hello, Mama Pam," he said. Then he pointed back down at his paper, apparently to tell me that he needed to work.

Later that day, after his classes were finished, he stopped by the guesthouse to say hello to me. I was sitting on the porch talking with Leticia, and John took a seat next to us. "I'm sorry I was studying when you visited our class today," he said, with Leticia's help translating. "I did not want to be rude."

I assured him it was okay, and asked him to tell me more about his life before coming to the Village of Hope. He sat down on the step beside me and, keeping his eyes on the boys playing soccer across the lawn, told me everything.

———

As one of the oldest slave children in Sofoline, the village where he and others had worked, a lot was expected of John. Like the other boys, he spent his mornings and afternoons fishing. But in the evenings, while the other kids rested, he was made to walk the five miles to Kete Krachi and stand outside the hospital, selling doughnuts his master's wife had baked to earn extra income. One day, exhausted from a long day on the canoe, he sat down in front of the hospital and fell asleep. When he woke up, he saw that his doughnuts and money had been stolen.

"I knew the beating I'd get for this," he told me, with little emotion. "And I was very afraid." Reduced to tears, he was noticed by a nurse leaving the hospital. After he told her what had happened, she walked him down the street to the police station. George, whose house is next to the police station, saw John speaking to the police, and, noticing that he was dressed in nothing other than dingy underpants and a flimsy T-shirt, understood immediately that this child had been trafficked. George went over and introduced himself. He asked the police what they were going to do to help John, but despite the fact the law required them to take action, they didn't seem very interested in his story.

George took John home for dinner and afterward, walked him back to Sofoline. With a firm hand on John's shoulder, he explained to the master, a large, forbidding man in his thirties named Kwadwo Takyi, that what he was doing was illegal, and the police had been notified. Takyi laughed. "We treat him well," he said. "If he tells you otherwise, he's lying."

George had no choice but to leave John there. He and his wife, Anna, had three kids that were grown and living on their own, and had since taken in three others whose families needed help. They could not afford to take in John. But he told Kwadwo Takyi that he'd be back to check on John frequently.

A few weeks later, John was back at the hospital selling his doughnuts. This time, a man approached and demanded John hand over the pastries. He wasn't willing to pay. When John went home with an empty tray and half the money he should have earned, Kwadwo Takyi was done being patient with him. He made John stretch across a bench and called another boy—John's best friend—to come over. He handed the boy a branch and told him to beat John with it. When the boy refused, Kwadwo Takyi got upset. "You're all useless," he said. Taking back the branch, he beat John until he was bloody and scarred. I remembered reading about such a beating in *The New York Times,* and I now realized that the child in question was John. That night, after everyone was asleep, John escaped. Running the whole way toward Kete Krachi, he didn't stop until he recognized the house where George lived.

When George opened his door, he found John standing there, his face streaked with tears, his back covered in blood, wearing nothing but underpants. George brought John inside, let him take a shower, and gave him his son's clothes to wear. They walked together back to the police station. There George showed the officers the wounds on John's back.

John stayed with George for several days. Realizing that the police either could not or would not do anything, George went back to Sofoline himself. "You're going to give me the information on how to find John's parents, or I'm coming back with the police," he told Takyi.

A few weeks later, George returned John to his parents' house. While John was hoping that meant he could go to school, his family needed his help, and he was put to work beside his mother, cleaning the tilapia and mudfish the fishermen in his village caught. It wasn't school, but at least he was freed from slavery. Or so he thought.

The next year, his parents divorced. Soon after his father left, a man arrived at his mother's doorstep. He had come to get John, he said, explaining that John's father had agreed to sell him again, this time to work as a fishermen on the ocean rather than Lake Volta. John was crushed, thinking his fishing days, and life under a master, were over. He worked on the ocean for another year.

Then one day, two months earlier, he was mending nets on the shore. He saw a tall man running toward him on the beach, and it took a minute for it to sink in: It was George. Though John didn't know this at the time, George had spent a week looking for him. He had heard that John had been sold again, and after he had gotten my call, George decided that he would do whatever it took to find him. It had not been easy. He traveled by bus to John's mother's village, but she did not know where her son was. He then went to where John's father lived, but he didn't know, either. All he knew was that he was working somewhere on the sea. With John's photo in hand, George roamed from village to village, asking people if they knew this twelve-year-old boy. Finally, thinking he had no choice but to give up, he spotted a lone figure down the beach, sitting in a canoe. He knew it was John.

"I can't explain it," John told me, "but I always knew he'd come back for me."

George took John back to his mother's village, but this time to ask her permission to bring John to the Village of Hope, where he'd be safe and could go to school. John's mother signed custody of him over to George, and a few days later she escorted him by bus to the Village of Hope.

"Are you happy here?" I asked him when he was finished speaking.

"I'm very happy here," he said. "It's even more than I prayed for."

"Would you rather be here or with your mother?"

"Here," he said, without hesitating. "I love my mother, but I am too much of a burden for her." He paused. "Are you going to get more kids like me?" he asked. "Will you get them off the lake?"

It's not that the thought hadn't occurred to me. Of course

I wanted to get more kids like John and Mark and Kofi and Hagar off the lake. But where would they go? There were thousands of children working on that lake, and they could not all come live at the Village of Hope.

Before I could explain this to John, he spoke again. "I hope you do. It's such a scary place and it's a miracle I even survived."

The week went by too quickly. In the mornings, Crista and I helped the kids get ready for school; each evening, we shared their meals with them at Gladys's big dining table: fried potatoes and chicken, yams, peanut butter stew. Nearly every meal included fufu: a thick paste made from pounded corn and potatoes that had the consistency of Play-Doh. It took me a while to realize you can't chew fufu. Rather, you have to let it slide down your throat like an oyster.

After their classes were finished, every child was given an afternoon chore. Boys and girls with machetes chopped firewood in the large open lawn. Others pounded the fufu with thick sticks, stirred big pots of beans that cooked over an open fire next to the houses, or washed clothes by hand in buckets of water. When they were done, the children were required to wash. They would fill their buckets at the nearby well that Fred had established and then walk to the large outdoor platform, divided into two sections for boys and girls. Everything was done outside, and it was one of the things that I loved most about the country. The people seemed to live so close to the earth, much like the Vietnamese, and I thought how much fun it would be to be more like them in this way—to have Van and Tatum help me prepare dinner outside, rather than having to pull them away from the flickering blue light of the Cartoon Network every evening.

After the children finished their chores, we gathered with them each day in the shade of one of the porches. I could see that Sarah was the shyest among the group, and Fred told me it had taken her a while to trust that she was safe here. On Christmas Day, which came a few days after the seven children had arrived at the Village of Hope, the staff prepared a special meal. When they finished, Sarah went from plate to plate, emptying any remaining scraps of food into a plastic bag. Gladys watched her and asked why she was doing that. "I want to make sure I have something to eat tomorrow," she said.

She and Hagar were not biologically related, but they seemed like sisters and, in fact, it was obvious that the seven children had formed a little family for themselves. Even at twelve, John was somewhat of a father figure to the younger ones, scolding them for misbehaving or consoling them if they were hurt or frustrated. Sarah and Hagar had made friends with many of the other girls, and, holding hands, they would lead Crista and me on walks through the school, showing us the tree under which they studied in the afternoons, and their dresses and skirts folded neatly on shelves in their bedroom. We would walk with them to the well before their baths. It was such a simple thing: a hole dug into the ground with a hand pump. But it was critical to the health of these children. Ghana is one of several nations where it's possible to contract a disease called Guinea worm from drinking contaminated water. It's an awful illness in which a tiny flea enters the body, maturing in the intestines into a worm that can grow to be three feet long. Eventually, the worm will crawl to the surface of the skin and cause a painful blister to form. When the skin finally breaks, the worm emerges, and the "treatment" includes wrapping the worm around a stick to try to slowly dislodge it from the body. This can take several weeks, depending on how large the Guinea worm has grown. Anyone in Ghana without access to safe drinking water is at great risk of contracting the disease.

When the morning came for Crista and me to pack our bags and head to the airport, neither of us felt ready. We said our good-byes and, as we walked to Fred's van, Crista looked back at Gladys's house. "You know," she said, setting her luggage on the ground, "I'm going to go say good-bye to them one more time."

On the plane ride back home I was both worn out and exhilarated, but what I felt more than anything was sheer privilege. Not only because I was returning home to my healthy family and the conveniences of life in America, but because it had been such an honor to have played a role in helping bring those kids to safety. I couldn't imagine any of them still working on that lake, under those conditions, and thinking about it made me wish, again, that I had been able to get seven hundred kids, and not seven. Although I didn't like to think in terms of numbers, but of children, of people. Mark, Kofi, Kojo, Richard, John, Hagar, and Sarah. The truly magnificent seven.

As I drifted off to sleep, our plane heading to London and then back to Missouri, the only image in my mind was Mark's eyes. The haunted look that had led me to this moment no longer existed. Where the plea for help had been, I had found something far more powerful. I found hope.

Chapter Ten

January 2007. Dear Jantsen, You are more alive than ever. I want to move mountains to help these children. All children deserve the chance to fulfill their dreams and destiny. I look at these seven, and every Touch A Life child, and think of them as an extension of you. Your life ended way too early but you still live through them. Love, Mom

Back home, I couldn't get John Arthur's words out of my head. *Are you going to get more kids off the lake?* Many evenings in Ghana, after the children had gone to sleep, George and I stayed up late talking. He told me it had long been a dream of his to build a boarding school similar to the Village of Hope up north in Kete Krachi for children rescued from the lake. He feared that the people he was trying to convince to free trafficked children would come to believe that his team was not bringing the kids to safety, but trafficking them themselves. It was therefore important to have a place in the region that others could come and visit, and see that the rescued children were being well cared for and educated. He even showed me building plans he had drawn up, careful depictions of the schoolhouse and cottages where the kids would live. He had named his project the Village of Life, and said he needed thirty thousand dollars to complete the first phase. This included the costs of building a cottage for twenty children, the salary for a houseparent, a well, and infrastructure, including electricity and roads.

When I brought up the idea at our next board of directors meeting, we all agreed that we would find the money to help George build the Village of Life. The decision meant so much to me—the idea of rescuing even one more child from working on the lake was enough to keep me awake with excitement for weeks. But of course, that's not to say it wasn't also extraordinarily daunting. We had never taken on a project of this scale. Although George would manage the project, we were ultimately responsible for all aspects of construction—in a developing nation, on another continent—as well as of ensuring that the kids who were brought to live there had everything they needed for the remainder of their lives.

When I told people that we had decided to wire thirty thousand dollars to George, many of them thought that I had lost my mind. That much money, to a man in Africa with whom I'd spent only one week? Could I trust him? I believed that I could, although, of course, it's impossible to know for sure. My instincts—which I had become much better at paying attention to—told me that George was the right person to help with this project, and if I turned out to be wrong (which I never did) well, that was a risk I was willing to take.

George found the perfect tract of land for the Village of Life a few weeks later. In most regions of Ghana, the village chief controls the land, and acquiring a piece of it can be a tricky deal. Because land cannot legally be bought or sold, money does not change hands, at least in theory. Rather, the village chief says that in exchange for permission to build on a piece of property, the family may offer him "drink money." The new landowner agrees, and when the deal is struck, he returns to the chief's home with something like a bottle of schnapps, and ten thousand dollars.

George explained that the land they had been offered by the village chief was not what they had originally requested. Rather, after learning about what George and his team wanted the land for, the chief offered them a much better option: several acres closer to town, high on a hill, with beautiful views of Lake Volta.

Well, this I had to see for myself. A few weeks later, and just two months after my first visit, I returned to Ghana. This time I was accompanied by Aimee Molloy, a journalist who wanted to come along to learn more about the child slaves on Lake Volta. When we arrived in Accra in early March, it was as hot as when I'd left. We went outside and into the blistering sun. Fred Asare of the Village of Hope had come to the airport to meet us, and when I spotted him in the crowd, I was so happy to see him that I wanted to run and embrace him in a big hug. But I restrained myself. Fred, though kind and generous, is thoroughly professional, exuding a sense of authority that sort of says, *You know what? Let's not hug.*

He grabbed our bags and led us to a van, where a driver waited. Once we got out of Accra and onto the dirt road toward Gomoa-Fetteh, Fred updated us on the seven children. In just two months, John Arthur had made great progress in learning English and had already advanced to the third grade, where he was considered one of the best students in his class. Mark had been put into the normal kindergarten class, and Matilda was still teaching the others, but now at a first-grade level. It was such good news, and as we bumped along the pockmarked road toward the orphanage, I couldn't wait to see them.

When we arrived at the Village of Hope, Mark was at the guesthouse waiting for us. He ran over to hug me as soon as I got out of the van. I almost didn't recognize him, despite the fact that his photograph still smiled at me from the fridge door every morning as I opened it to get milk for Van and Tatum's cereal. His once frail body looked plump and healthy, his skin glowed, and the scars from where he had been beaten had healed and disappeared.

I couldn't wait to see John Arthur. After hearing from Fred about how well he had done, I wanted to see for myself. Because he was in the third grade now, his class ran longer than those of the younger students, so I waited until it was dismissed before finding him. I spotted him walking across the dusty lawn. There is just something about this boy. He walks with an air of confidence that I've never seen in any other twelve-year-old, and has a face that could grace the pages of any magazine. When he saw me walking toward him, he ran into my arms.

"I knew you were coming back today, and I couldn't wait," he said in nearly flawless English. He then reached into the back pocket of his sky-blue shorts and pulled out a piece of paper. It was my name over a drawing of two hands holding what looked to be . . . an egg? Okay, maybe I wasn't as thin as I would have liked, but I wouldn't go so far as to say I looked like an egg. I asked him to explain.

"You carried us all as carefully as an egg, so we wouldn't be broken anymore," he said to me, smiling bashfully. "Thank you. Thank you for my life."

———

On our third afternoon there, Aimee and I decided that after dinner, we'd walk into the town of Gomoa-Fetteh and look around. We had been warned by some of the more, shall we say, reasonable Americans who were also staying at the Village of Hope at the time—people who had come to volunteer at the onsite medical clinic—that it wasn't safe for two women to walk through the village alone after dark. But we didn't care. We wanted to see the town, see how the people lived, and experience more of the culture. Okay, fine, we wanted a beer. Alcohol was strictly forbidden at the Village of Hope, and it wasn't like we could go to the corner store and pick up a six-pack anyway. While I knew at the time that I was possibly risking all the good karma I may have built to this point by what I was doing—lying to people to sneak out of a Christian orphanage that frowns upon alcohol to go have a beer—I was desperate. The electricity had gone out the last two nights, which meant we didn't even have a fan in our room and I swear it was like two thousand degrees in there.

So after a dinner of rice and beans, we headed out, past the security guards (who, I never understood why, wore pink knit caps as if they were waiting to get picked up to go skiing), and walked toward town. Now, should you ever find yourself in West Africa, allow me to impart a few bits of useful advice: Take your malaria pills, don't drink the water, and watch out for guys with strings around their waist, as they may try to urinate on you.

We had been told that the string was a local custom meant to identify people with mental illness, and one man in Gomoa-Fetteh, whose name was Kashee, had earned a reputation for peeing on people. As we entered the town, about a mile outside the Village of Hope, we saw him approaching. It was easy to see the string. It was all that he was wearing.

"Okay," Aimee said, linking her arm with mine. "Don't do your thing, Pam. Don't stop and talk and ask him about his life story. Just look ahead and try to blend into the scenery."

Aimee and I had only recently met, but ours was one of those immediate connections. Our first meeting took place a few weeks earlier at a small café in Manhattan, and an hour later we were sitting in my hotel room, shoes off, drinking coffee and revealing the intimate details of our lives. A few weeks later, we decided to travel to Ghana together. It was in the airport that our connection deepened: My luggage had gotten lost and for the last three days, I had been wearing her underwear. Well, because I liked Aimee, and thought I should be extra nice to her because I was wearing her underwear, I chose not to point out that her suggestion that we try to blend into the scenery was the single most ridiculous one I had ever heard. While that may have been a good idea in theory, it was made a little difficult by the reality of our situation: two white women walking alone down a dirt road in a remote village in Africa long after the sun had set. To make matters worse, a crowd of children had gathered behind us, kicking up dust and shouting into the darkness: *"Obroni! Obroni!"* White man! White man! They weren't trying to be rude, the way this might have seemed had it occurred back home; it's just that this village was so remote, it was likely we were the first white people these children had ever seen. Seriously, even the goats and chickens in the road seemed to register surprise.

I decided to take Aimee's advice anyway, and when Kashee stood in front of us, blocking our path, I simply looked away and tried to make out my surroundings in the darkness. Most of the houses had no electricity, and besides a small number of solitary fluorescent bulbs that hung from string on a few porches, the main source of light was the sticks on fire held by some of the young boys who ran behind us. Groups of women sat on the ground or on thick wooden benches along the road. Some of them smiled at us and waved but most looked at us with disinterest and went about their business: breast-feeding their children, washing their clothes in the bucket at their feet, or kneading the cornmeal and water that would be their family's meal the next morning. Children passed us carrying on their heads large buckets of water that they had likely gotten from the ocean or the well that had been dug at the Village of Hope, which people from the village were welcome to use.

"Are you sure you know where this place is?" Aimee asked, the doubt growing in her voice as she moved aside to allow a sickly goat to pass.

"Of course," I said. Crista and I had walked through the village one afternoon during our last trip, and had stopped for a Coke at a hotel bar around here. Somewhere. We passed a shack where men sat on stools sipping sodas and beer, and another with a sign that read MEDICINE SHOP. I stopped to peek inside. There were narrow shelves lined with dusty bottles of things I could not identify. It smelled of the earth.

Finally, about another half mile down the road, I saw the sign: a big yellow arrow pointing down a dirt path. Till's Beach Hotel. The little restaurant area at Till's is, I believe, the world's most perfect. It's right on the Atlantic Ocean, on a part that remains largely undiscovered by tourists, not that West Africa gets too many of those. It's wholly outdoors, with no walls—just a huge slanted thatched roof held up by large posts that people here call Summer Hats. The restaurant was empty except one table. Seven large, burly-looking white men sat around a table laden with large platters of steaming lobsters and bottles of bourbon and vodka. They smoked cigarettes and laughed loudly, taking long drinks right from the bottle. Aimee and I each ordered an African beer, and they glanced in our direction. "CIA," I said, sure of it. One of the men then waved to us and spoke in what sounded like Russian. "Okay, maybe former KGB," Aimee said as the waiter handed us two bottles of beer, dripping with ice.

As much as I would actually enjoy a conversation with seven former Russian spies at a bar in West Africa, Aimee and I decided to take our drinks down the grassy hill to the beach. Every single star in the sky seemed as if it were on fire, and the beach was empty. The only sound was the surf. I took off my sandals, and we walked down to the shore. The ocean felt like bathwater, and both of us waded in, getting wet from the waves, which soaked our shorts. Finally, we gave in to the ocean and dove in.

As we lay in the shallow water, the waves washing over us, I stared at the sky. "I'm not sure I've ever seen a darkness like this," Aimee said, breaking the silence.

I nodded in quiet agreement, my head sinking into the soft sand, and the water covering my ears so all that I could hear was the rhythm of the earth in my head.

"How do you feel right now, Pam Cope?" she asked.

This question had become somewhat of a joke between us. I had been telling her a lot about my life and about Jantsen and our work in Vietnam, and she'd often stop me and ask how I felt about something. I usually made fun of her when she asked me this question, telling her to stop trying to analyze everything, but this time I gave it some real thought.

I thought about the seven kids, who were sound asleep right now, and how safe and secure they were. I thought about how much I loved Randy, whom I hadn't spoken to since I'd left the United States three days earlier. He was probably wondering what we were doing while getting Van and Tatum ready for school. Crista was probably doing homework in her dorm room. I thought about how eager I was to help build the Village of Life, and bring home possibly hundreds of other slave children. I thought about the fact that here I was, lying in the Gulf of Guinea well past midnight, with the taste of salt on my lips and the water cascading over my chest and face.

And for perhaps the first time in my life, I knew *exactly* how I felt.

"I feel totally . . . content," I said.

The next day, we woke up before sunrise to get ready for the daylong trip to Kete Krachi and Lake Volta. We were planning on spending most of our days on the lake, talking to children who had been sold into slavery. My friend Dave Lettow, who is a photographer, had arrived the night before. He had volunteered to come along to document the interviews and the first stages of building the Village of Life. George was in Accra, attending a conference, and had arranged a car and driver for us. When I went outside to meet the driver, a large man with more gold chains than I'd ever seen, he was standing with George's nephew Kofi, a strong, handsome man in his early twenties. Kofi shook my hand and explained that he'd be going with us to Kete Krachi. He was just coming along for company, he said, and to make sure we were safe. When we arrived in Kete Krachi, he'd hop a bus for the daylong journey back to Accra, where he was attending college. This shows how seriously Ghanaians take the idea of hospitality. That's like visiting someone in San Francisco and expecting them to drive you to the airport in Seattle—*eleven hours away.*

The sun was rising as we drove out of the gates of the orphanage, then through the quiet streets of Gomoa-Fetteh. For the first three hours, the drive was easy and smooth, but then the pavement came to an abrupt end, turning into a dirt-and-gravel path with no markings and covered in potholes. Back home, nobody would have driven faster than maybe thirty miles an hour on a road like this, but our driver was either fearless or insane. He took the SUV at nearly ninety. In the backseat, Dave, Aimee, and I held on to each other for our lives. Several times, the SUV bounced so hard over a huge crater in the road that our heads knocked against the ceiling. "Sorry," the driver would mutter, pressing the accelerator even harder.

222 @ PAM COPE

We drove through tiny villages that made those I'd seen in Vietnam and Cambodia feel like Cleveland. Children, most of them wearing nothing, sat with their mothers on the dirt in front of mud houses. There was no electricity and no running water. The places where people lived could barely be described as huts. Women walked along the side of the road, carrying heavy logs tied up in rope atop their heads. We passed huge, creaky buses jam-packed with people, big bowls of smoked fish fastened to the top.

One thing to understand about Ghanaian culture: When you suggest something to somebody—as in *You should try the chicken,* or *You should buy that pair of shoes*—you'd better well mean it, because it's considered a commitment on your end. I had learned this the hard way during my first trip, after telling everyone I met who expressed an interest in America—*well, you should come to America.* Little did I know then that saying that meant I could expect to buy their ticket, pick them up at the airport, and grow old with them in my home. I vowed not to make the same mistake this trip, but I was beginning to understand there were many nuances of this. That morning, we had left the Village of Hope before breakfast and hadn't eaten a thing all day. Knowing we couldn't stop at a drive-through along the way, I had packed a big bag of granola bars and other snacks for the trip. Before Aimee, Dave, or I took any for ourselves, I reached the bag across the front seat. "Have some snacks," I said to the driver.

He took it, pulled out a package of trail mix, and then shoved the bag under his seat. We looked at one another. A few minutes later, he reached down between his feet and grabbed another snack for himself.

"Get it back!" Aimee whispered. But I knew that would have been considered very rude, and it was too late. The food was now his.

About seven hours into the drive, we arrived at a village called Dumbai, which is right on Lake Volta where the ferry crosses to meet the road to Kete Krachi. The driver pulled the truck onto the rocky beach, and we saw the ferry just across the way. A young man approached the SUV and spoke to Kofi, who nodded, then turned to explain to us that the ferry wouldn't return to our side of the lake for another two hours. *Two hours?* That was too long to keep the SUV running for the air-conditioning. We had no choice but to turn off the engine, open the doors, and simply wait.

It was market day in Dumbai, and the beach was crowded with hundreds of people who had come from many of the surrounding villages to sell their wares and buy fish and produce. All along the beach, women, dressed in long, colorful dresses and head scarves, sat on blankets next to bowls brimming with potatoes, smoked fish, tubes of toothpaste, and fruit. Children walked around selling bags of water and cakes. Kofi bought a skewer of a strange-looking meat and tofu, while the driver dug into the last of our bag of snacks. We were hungry, but we passed up the food available for sale, too afraid to eat something we couldn't identify.

The heat outside was intense. Aimee, Dave, and I climbed out of the truck to stretch our legs and check out the market, but we never did make it there because of the total weirdness that ensued. People looked at us and stopped dead in their tracks. We were the only white people around and, as Kofi explained, among the first white people most of the villagers had ever seen. Slowly, a group of people, mostly children, cautiously made their way over to the SUV. They just stood there, transfixed, staring at us under the merciless sun, in what seemed to be a mixture of disbelief, amusement, and fear.

I tried saying hello, but nobody spoke English, so instead we smiled and waved. Adults began to join the children, and soon the crowd surrounding our SUV had grown to over a hundred. Just staring at us, in complete silence. For the first few minutes, it was a little awkward. After that, it was totally awkward. Some of the women brought their babies over so they could get a closer look at us, prompting most of the infants to break out into desperate, terrified wails.

After about thirty minutes of us all standing there staring at one another, I realized how badly I had to go to the bathroom. "Do you think there is a public restroom around here?" I asked Kofi. A bizarre look crossed his face before he asked one of the villagers surrounding the truck, who pointed up a nearby hill, toward a row of wooden shacks.

"Come on," I said to Aimee. "You're coming with me for this."

Now, you'll have to excuse me a little bit, but a word about . . . well, going to the bathroom. In a few more days, I would have no problem with the idea of dropping my shorts and squatting anywhere, preferably behind a tree if I could find one, but I wasn't there yet. I was still trying to be polite. Aimee and I walked through the heat up the hill, past a group of six pigs sloshing around in a dirty puddle, past women breast-feeding their children, and up to the public restroom. With Aimee behind me, I opened the door to one of the stalls. Inside, a large metal pot sat in the mud, overflowing with a steaming mound of human excrement. It slowly began to make sense to me. This was where the villagers came to do *this,* as few of the houses likely had any indoor plumbing. When it came to urination, that was a different story. The men would go absolutely anywhere, right there, in a crowd of people, in the middle of a conversation. Sometimes, I would even see women in their long dresses simply spread their legs and relieve themselves as they walked, barely missing a step.

"No freaking way," I heard Aimee say behind me.

But I really had to go. I held my breath and stepped into the shack. It was horrible. I won't even try to describe the smell. I just held my breath and tried to be as quick as I could, pushing aside the thoughts of germs and disease that were fighting their way into my head. I probably wasn't inside the stall for longer than one minute, but it felt like forever. Aimee was waiting for me down near the water.

"How was it?" she asked. I tried to tell her that it was fine and that, unlike her, I was a brave traveler unafraid of doing whatever the situation called for. But as I opened my mouth to speak, the smell of the outhouse filled my nostrils and I gagged. I thought I was going to throw up, but I didn't. I just kept gagging.

Aimee grabbed my arm. "Are you okay?"

Every time I tried to speak, I gagged.

"I think I have Guinea worm," I finally said.

Well, apparently Aimee found this very funny, and she started laughing so hard she could barely breathe. Which made me laugh. There we were, two new friends, standing on the shore of this lake, feeling out of place, with me trying my hardest to "fit in" to the culture, and laughing so hard we were kind of snorting. For the next few minutes, I stood on the beach, alternating between fits of laughter and bouts of gagging so intense my eyes filled with water.

"Oh my gosh," she said, rubbing my back and laughing hysterically. "I've never seen anyone enjoy gagging this much."

"I think I need to go lie down in the truck," I was finally able to say.

Dave was down at the water taking photographs, and I lay down across the backseat and tried to get the stench out of my nose. Outside, Aimee began to teach the children a dance her nephews and nieces liked, which they called the Chicken Dance. A group of young boys came with buckets. They turned them upside down to make drums. A young girl peeked her head into the truck and took my hand. She led me to where her friends stood. It was their turn to teach us: showing us how to move our legs and arms in the graceful movements of a local African dance. We did our best, but our performance was so awful, the children fell onto the sand in a puddle of giggles. Finally, a bell sounded, and I looked up and saw that the ferry had finally made its way back to our side of the beach.

The breeze on the ferry helped to blow my nausea away a little, thankfully, because we still had another two hours before we arrived in Kete Krachi. Finally, we passed into Katanga, a small village on top of a mountain. To this point, most of the terrain we drove through was dry and savanna-like, but here it was all jungle green and lush, and we rolled down the windows to take in the cool air. As we rounded a bumpy corner, we passed a group of four men gathered along the side of the road, their clothes ripped to shreds and covered in blood. While it never would have even occurred to me to stop the car and see what they were up to, Kofi yelled something to the driver, who slammed on the brakes and pulled the SUV along the edge of the road in a screeching halt. "Come on," Kofi said to us, opening his door and jumping out.

We followed him back to where the men stood, and Kofi hugged one of them before introducing us. This was Paramount Chief Mprah, the supreme leader of the Krachi district. He took each of our hands into his sweaty palms. "It is truly my honor to meet you," he said. "We are very excited about the Village of Life. I am here to help you in whatever way I can." He then apologized for the way he looked. "We are out doing a little hunting today to stock up on our food." Behind him, lying on a bloody piece of newspaper, was the large, severed head of a wild boar, and next to that, steaming in a metal bowl, a pile of legs and ribs. *For crying out loud,* I thought to myself. *Is this going to be one long gagfest?*

It was nearly 6 PM when we arrived at George's house, stinky, sticky, and famished. Compared with most other houses in the town, George's was considered luxurious. It was one-story and very simple, but there was indoor plumbing, and three bedrooms. We walked up the grassy driveway to the front yard, where four women were busy cooking under the shade of a large mango tree. A pot of bubbling stew boiled over a fire pit carved into the grass next to a small pile of charcoal, which they made here by burning wood until it was black and crisp. George's daughter Erica, who was twenty-two, was studying catering at a college in Accra but had come home to cook for us during our stay in Kete Krachi. She welcomed us and brought us inside, where George's wife, Anna, was waiting for us. Anna, a beautiful and heavyset woman in her fifties, shyly said hello and took our bags. She led Aimee and me to a small, comfortable room with two beds and explained the importance of keeping the screen door closed to keep out the mosquitoes. On the lawn outside our room, a cluster of chickens and roosters squawked.

Erica had prepared a huge, celebratory dinner to mark our arrival. After we unpacked, Albert Mensah arrived. A small man with a huge smile, he worked a full-time job as a translator and volunteered with Pacodep. Because George was going to be in Accra for most of our visit, Albert was going to accompany us on the lake and serve as our guide. Over a lovely dinner of rice and chicken, which we ate by candlelight at a plastic table on the front lawn, Albert told us he had rented a motorboat for us called the *Krachi Queen,* along with two boat hands to help us. We would leave very early the following day because the children we hoped to speak with usually began work before sunrise and it would take us nearly two hours to get to the middle of the lake, where most of the fishing was done.

Sitting on that lawn that evening, swatting away mosquitoes and breathing in the warm March air, I felt just as I had that day in Vietnam, holding the crying infant in the orphanage. *I can't believe I'm here,* I thought. There was no other place that I would rather have been.

———

Despite the fact that it was late and we were all tired, I asked Albert if we could go that night to see the land they had purchased for the Village of Life. He walked into town and returned in a taxi, or, at least a car with four wheels, a sputtering engine, and doors held shut with rope. A few miles from town, the car turned down a stony path, covered in piles of garbage. Before the Pacodep team purchased the land, it was, for all intents and purposes, the dump of Kete Krachi. There was no public system of garbage collection, and the town residents carried their trash here to burn it. Piles of paper, food scraps, and cans still smoldered, emitting an acrid smell, and we wound around them up a hill.

We got out of the taxi at the top of the hill, where hundreds of cement blocks lay in perfect rows. Workers had made these bricks by hand, combining the cement, mud, and water in a large wheelbarrow and casting the mixture in a mold. They would be used to build the first cottage of the Village of Life. Standing on top of the hill, I could see all of Kete Krachi stretching out to the lake. It was a beautiful site. There were ancient, leafy trees behind us, and Albert explained that none would be bulldozed during construction; they wanted the Village of Life to feel like a green, shaded garden. He walked around, pointing out where everything was going to be built: *Here is where the first building will go. Here is where the vegetable garden will be. Here is where we will keep the goats and cows. Here is where the children will play.*

As I walked with him, I could not believe that this was becoming a reality. I had seen photographs of this land, which George had e-mailed to me, but standing here, smelling the African air and the earth at my feet, felt like a dream come true. I pictured Randy and me and our children spending weeks here together, getting to know the kids who would come to find a home on this land. Van and Tatum would love it. Van would learn to do soccer tricks with a mango the way that Mark had, and Tatum would paint with watercolors, tracing the distant waters of Lake Volta and shading them in until they were perfectly turquoise.

―――――

If there's one thing the beaches of Lake Volta have no shortage of, it's garbage. When we arrived on the shore the next morning at seven o'clock, the sun looked as if it were being pulled from the water by a chain of foggy arms. We walked down the sandy hill toward the water, having to step over the garbage. Piles of it reached down the rocky beach, and black plastic bags clung to large boulders that appeared to be clawing their way out from under the sand. I saw figures in the distance, men waiting to catch a ride on someone's boat to one of the smaller islands. Others slept on the sand, their faces covered with towels or shirts to block the sunlight. Down the beach, several dozen men stood naked in the surf, scrubbing themselves with blocks of white soap and rinsing off by diving into the dark water. Near them, children filled large buckets and bowls with lake water, hoisted them to their heads, and headed back up the hill toward town. That was likely their cooking water, or what they would use to wash. I wondered if they would also drink that water. Kete Krachi is one of the few places in Ghana that has a filtered public water system. But, I realized, in order to access that water you had to have indoor plumbing. Although George did, it was likely that many here did not.

The *Krachi Queen* was there waiting for us, bobbing in the shallow surf. We hiked up our pants and waded through the water to climb the creaky ladder. It was a medium-size boat with absolutely no frills. There was a rusty outboard motor, and the wooden floor looked about to crumble under the weight of one wrong step. Two benches—with room for eight perhaps—had been hastily nailed to the floor along each side. Across the top, a white-and-pink canopy provided mercy from the sun, a critical necessity during the long days we had planned, in temperatures that would reach well above ninety degrees.

Bright and Mohammed—the two men Albert had hired to ferry us around the lake over the next few days—were already on board. Bright, who was twenty-three, was large and affable and had a smile to match his name. Mohammed looked far younger than his twenty-one years. He was small and spry, with a body molded almost completely of muscle.

Dave, Aimee, Albert, and I walked gingerly to take a seat as Mohammed climbed to the front of the boat and Bright took his place at the back. Bright pulled a string on the motor; after several attempts, it sputtered to life, sending a dark cloud of diesel smoke into the boat. I let the mist from the lake cool my face as we headed out to the deep waters.

Lake Volta is a truly eerie place. One of the largest artificial lakes in the world, it covers more than three thousand square miles. On a map, it looks like a swelling heart on the eastern edge of the country, from which extend a complicated, wandering series of veins and capillaries—and in many ways, that's a useful analogy. The lake was created in 1965 when the White and Black Volta rivers were dammed at a town called Akosombo in order to generate hydroelectric power for the nation; the dam was considered a sign of progress and the driving force behind the future economic prosperity for the newly liberated country. But there were also downsides. Erecting the dam meant the flooding of the Volta River basin, or nearly 4 percent of the nation's total land area, and led to the displacement of more than eighty thousand people in seven hundred villages. While much of this area had once been used for farming, large swaths of tropical forests were also submerged, and the lake today bears clear proof of this. It is full of trees.

All around us, treetops emerged from the water: knotty, branchless trunks of thick ancient wood, standing like totem poles. Some areas were so crowded with trees that the only way Bright could navigate through them was to shut off the motor and use a long bamboo pole to push off from the lake bottom. Mohammed helped by using his hands to shove off from stumps the boat floated near.

The trees cast an eerie glow not only on the scenery, but on the significance of the whole experience—this area had once nurtured life before it was taken in the name of progress, and then progress led to the creation of this thriving slave trade. I couldn't help but think that while the lake was a great step forward for the people of Ghana, it was also, at the same time, a tremendous step back.

We sailed for about two hours before Albert stood up and motioned for Bright to slow the boat. In the dark water before us, dozens of plastic containers bobbed up and down, marking the place where the fishermen had set their nets the day before. In the near distance, I began to make out silhouettes of canoes filled with three or four figures. We journeyed a few more minutes before Bright shut off the motor and Albert yelled hello in the direction of a nearby canoe. Inside of it were three people. The oldest looked to be about twenty years old and Albert threw him a rope, which he grabbed and used to pull his canoe toward the *Krachi Queen* until our boats were close enough to touch.

I thought I had prepared myself for this moment, but I felt the breath catch in my throat when I saw just how young the other two boys were. One looked to be nine years old, and the other could not have been older than five. The younger one sat in back, balancing a large paddle and small bucket on the edge of the boat, his foot dangling in the pitch-black water. He was completely naked, and when I looked at him and smiled, he turned away and tried to cover himself with his free hand, which was tiny and pruned. His one visible foot revealed toenails that were dark with fungus. His feet and knees were covered in thick calluses. The rest of his body looked to belong to a much older boy. His shoulders and arms were chiseled, and his chest swelled like that of a man accustomed to heavy lifting.

Albert spoke to them in the local dialect, explaining who we were. He said that he worked in Kete Krachi with an organization that was trying to understand the situation on the lake, and wanted to talk to boys who didn't go to school because they were fishing. While he spoke, none of the boys stopped working. The two oldest used a thin, sharp knife to cut away fish that had gotten tangled in the nets, which were crowded in a pile at their feet. Their work was practiced and methodical. In easy movements, they cut the fish loose and then tossed them into a squirming, moving pile between them. The youngest boy sat perfectly erect, his eyes alternating between the bucket he used to scoop up the water filling the canoe, and some spot in the distance. His face and eyes revealed nothing.

The oldest boy explained that they were all cousins and lived together on a nearby island, working under their parents. None of them knew how old they were, which surprised me. I wondered if they celebrated birthdays, and I remembered the last birthday party I had attended. I could not even remember the kid's name, but it was for a friend of Van's. I went to at least ten like these a summer: the huge cake, the balloons, a table stacked with gifts.

The boy described their typical day. They woke up at 4 AM and walked down to the lake in the dark. By 5 AM, they had paddled out to where they laid their nets the night before, and worked for four hours lifting them into the boat. Because the nets often became tangled in the tree stumps under the water, the boy said, patting the water with his hand to make his point, they took turns diving under to free them. Today it was the young boy's turn, and that was why he was not wearing any clothes. Shirts and shorts only got heavy in the water and made the work harder. After the nets had been collected, they paddled back to shore and spent the remainder of the afternoon on the beach, mending the nets that had gotten ripped and tangled, with thick thread and makeshift needles. Afterward they returned to the lake and relaid the nets, so that by morning they could start the process over again. They usually ate just once, in the evening, and were never given a day off, even if they were sick.

He recounted the details with no emotion, as if this experience were the most normal thing in the world. It reminded me of the way Jantsen had once described baseball practice, or the way Tatum would announce that, finally, she had decided that spelling was her favorite subject. Aimee asked them how they felt about the work they did, and for the first time, the older boy smiled. It wasn't a joyous smile, but one that suggested that this may, in fact, have been the stupidest question he'd ever heard.

"This is the life we know," he said. "Our parents need our help, and we must work. But too many people are fishing the lake now, and the catches are getting smaller and smaller. Perhaps our parents will reconsider and we won't have to do this forever. Perhaps we will be able to go to school. Especially," he said, pointing at the naked boy in the back, "this one."

Albert shook the older boy's hand and thanked him for talking to us. He turned to us and explained that we should probably keep going. Because these boys lived with their parents, there was nothing we could do for them. Albert and George were very careful about that. Despite the fact that these boys' lives were no less difficult than those of trafficked children, the Pacodep team had no intention of taking children away from their own parents. "We are not in the business of kidnapping children," George had once explained to me.

"I'm sorry," Albert said to us now. "I know this is not easy, but we must move away."

Bright walked to the back to restart the motor, and I pulled out the bag of candy we had packed that morning. I offered the kids some Swedish fish. The naked boy in the back reached up to take some. It was, of course, such a meager and useless gift—and seriously, did I have to pick *fish* as the candy—but it was all we could do. As we pulled away, I watched the three boys silently rip open their bags and toss the colorful wrappers into the lake as they studied the jellied candy. The naked boy saw me watching and he lifted his hand to offer a timid wave.

It didn't take us long to come across another canoe, this one with two people: a man in his twenties and a boy who looked to be about seven. The younger one was shirtless and wore light blue shorts that were too big for him, hanging below his knees. He was so small, he had to stretch his body down, his back arching, so that his paddle would touch the water, and he rowed in broad, vigorous strokes. Like the others, he was extremely muscular and his belly was distended, a sign of malnutrition. There were bald patches on his head, and his hair was a mess of matted curls that had been bleached a light auburn by the sun.

Albert called out to them to come closer. As they did, he explained to us that it was sometimes possible to identify trafficked children simply by the length of their hair. Because it was so hot in Ghana, most of the children, even the girls, have their heads shaved as a means of staying cool. But trafficked children who were not treated as well will have longer hair, a simple sign of neglect.

Once again, Albert addressed the older boy, a twenty-five-year-old named Atu. He was frank and amiable and explained that he worked for his father; the younger boy, Kofi, was bought by his father to work on the lake.

"My father went to the parents of the boy and offered him money, but I do not know how much," Atu said. "I do not know how long he has to work for us, but he lives with us in our village."

Kofi stared silently in the back of the boat, and I asked Albert if we could speak directly to him. Because he looked so vacant, I was surprised when he began to speak and continued for a while without stopping, his voice as sweet as syrup.

"My name is Kofi and I am seven years old. My job is to sit and control the canoe and bail out water," he said. "I also pull fish from the nets. There are twenty kids like me that the Master has bought. We live with them, but we are not part of the family. We are people the Master paid money for. I have not seen my parents since I came here two years ago."

"Do you wish you were home with them?" Albert asked.

At this, Atu moved closer to Kofi, stepping over the nets at his feet. The gesture seemed to scare Kofi, and he stopped talking, withdrawing farther into himself. Albert continued with the questions. Can you swim? Are you afraid out here on the lake? Stealing furtive glances at Atu, Kofi said nothing.

I leaned over to be closer to Kofi. "It's okay," I said, as Albert translated. "It's safe to talk to us."

236

"No, it's not," Kofi said, refusing to look at anybody.

"Tell me what you don't like about working here," Albert said.

"I do like working here. Very much."

We had lost him.

"Did you know how to swim?"

"Yes," he said, scooping a handful of dirty lake water into his cupped hand, which he then drank. The gesture turned my stomach. "But there were others who did not, and they went down and never came up."

"How many boys have you seen that happen to?"

Atu stood up in the canoe and started to speak quickly to Albert in Fanti, a local dialect. Albert waited until he was finished and then explained to us that we should probably leave, as it was possible that Kofi could be punished for speaking to us and there wasn't anything we could do to help him just then. Albert had gotten the information he needed: the village where Kofi lived and the name of his master. He would talk to George and the others about adding this village to the communities they visited to begin the slow process of educating the elders about the fact that child trafficking was illegal.

I felt sick to my stomach. Even though I understood the process this work entailed for Albert and the others, it did not make it any easier to meet a boy like Kofi, and then simply walk away. I leaned over the boat and offered him some candy.

"Good-bye," I said to him. "Hopefully I will see you again."

Kofi looked at me with so much sadness. Then he spoke to Albert.

"Maybe someday somebody will get me off of this lake," he said, nearly pleading. "I think about who that would be, but I do not know. Sometimes I think my mother will come back and get me, but I do not know if that will happen. But I would be good in school if I could go, and I would become an even better footballer."

———

It was just 10 AM, but I already felt exhausted. I took a bag of purified water that Albert had packed for us and bit into the plastic. The water spilled into my mouth. It was thick and warm, and tasted faintly of salt and minerals. I lay down on the bench and tried to block the sun from my face. About an hour later, Bright shut off the motor, and I saw that we were approaching one of the tiny islands in the lake. This was Old Nkomi and we were here for two reasons. It was the village where Richard had lived, and I wanted to learn more about what his life had been like before the rescue. Also, Albert wanted us to meet a woman who lived here named Howa Bellame. She had sold two of her sons, who currently worked with a master on another island. After word had spread of the work that Pacodep was doing, Howa had contacted George and Albert to ask for their help in getting her sons back.

Pulling our pant legs up, we climbed down the ladder and walked through the water to shore. A group of young boys sat in a canoe on the sand mending nets, and when they saw us, they stopped working for a moment and waved. The sand eventually gave way to grass, and we hiked along a narrow rocky path that had been worn by thousands of trips between the water and the village. Along the way, goats and chickens ran circles in front of us; to our left, in a parched parcel of mud and sand, a large square had been marked by stones. Albert explained it was the village soccer field.

Up the hill, about five minutes from shore, we entered into what appeared to be the village center. I was struck by how remote it was. We had passed some extremely primitive villages on the drive from Accra to Kete Krachi, but this was a whole other level of isolation. The houses were a collection of huts, and it felt straight out of *National Geographic*. Some were made of mud, with thatched roofs and an opening that was covered in a piece of fabric. Others were not structures at all, but simply grass roofs held up, impossibly, by eight large branches. The roofs sagged and looked too flimsy to withstand a sturdy breeze. There was no electricity at all, and no running water. A plump woman stood naked behind a short mud wall. Her hair and body were covered in soapy bubbles, which she rinsed away by pouring a bucket of water over her head. I did not want to embarrass her, standing naked as she was, but when our eyes met, she did not even look away.

"*Akwabba,*" she said. You are welcome here.

About a dozen people milled about, surrounded by roosters, chickens, and feeble-looking dogs. Four women, all of whom wore long dresses and had tiny infants wrapped to their backs by a large piece of fabric, worked under the shade of the thatched structures cleaning fish, or washing clothes in foam-covered buckets at their feet. The smell of smoking fish was nearly overpowering, coming from one of the many mud ovens built among the dry ground.

As they saw us, the women yelled out to us: *Akwabba!* They instructed some of the children, many of whom were wearing nothing at all, to prepare a meeting place for us, and the kids ran to gather wooden benches and plastic chairs. They lifted them over their heads and carried them to a shady spot under a thatched roof. We thanked them and took a seat. Behind us, laundry dried on a clothesline and the sickliest-looking kitten stumbled over to us, falling in a weak pile at my feet.

We were clearly a curiosity in this village. Three men came over and took a seat on one of the benches. Albert was off making a phone call—it never failed to amaze me that in these villages that had no running water and no electricity, cell phones still worked—and we sat awkwardly staring at one another. One of the men, who was wearing a linen pantsuit in a bright green-and-white African design, tried to speak to us. He knew a little English and told us that he was a fisherman; the other two with him were farmers. Subsistence farming is still a way of life in much of Ghana, and beyond some of the houses I saw fields planted with yams and other vegetables. Keeping those fields irrigated must be such hard work, I thought.

Aimee slowly explained that we were here to ask questions about some of the trafficked children. I partially expected the men to respond with embarrassment or shame—the way a thief might react when openly asked about his practice of breaking the law—but the fisherman did not seem to mind at all. Rather, he genially explained that he had purchased two boys from their parents, but a few years ago, when they turned twenty years old, he released them. They went on to build their own canoes and nets, and then bought a few boys of their own.

I tried to imagine Richard living here, and asked the fisherman if he remembered him. He smiled. "Richard! What a good, strong worker." *Yes,* I thought. *For an eight-year-old.* He pointed at a woman nearby, who sat on a short stool bathing an infant. "That is the wife of his master," the man said. "And that is where he slept." He pointed at a tiny mud hut near where the woman worked. I stood up and walked over to it.

"May I?" I asked. She nodded and waved her hand.

It was dark inside the hut, and empty except for a few wire baskets used to carry fish. The smell was strong and distinct: a mixture of earth and sweat and drying tilapia, piles of which were laid out on paper and towels throughout the tiny village. I looked at those piles and wondered how much they would sell for, what kind of prosperity or comfort they provided for the people in this village. How many piles of fish had it cost to purchase Richard?

Albert had rejoined the group, and as I took my seat he introduced us to the woman next to him, who looked to be in her forties. She had perfect creamy skin, the color of caramel, and wore a green-and-yellow dress. It was too big for her, and revealed two thick dirty bra straps underneath. Her hair was tied back with a black-and-white scarf, and she wore big silver hoop earrings. A small boy in a pink T-shirt and light blue underpants ran up to her side and pressed himself against her back, peering at us over his mother's shoulder. I said hello to him, and he grabbed his mother's neck and buried himself shyly in her lap.

Howa Bellame had come to this village a few months earlier from Kumasi, a large town about two hours away. She had lived there her whole life, and had married a local man with whom she had three sons. Last year, her husband suffered a heart attack and died at the age of forty-one. "It was devastating to lose him," she said quietly. "I didn't know how I would care for my three young boys. Or how we would survive."

After her husband's death, she had to withstand the widowhood rites that are still practiced in many villages of Ghana. According to this old tradition, once a woman loses her husband, she is forced to go through a one-week cleansing ritual. Howa was kept indoors in a dark room for the week, and was prohibited from seeing her husband's corpse. She could eat only when it was quiet, and should someone make a noise while she took food—a child crying, say, or a drum beating—her meal was taken away. At the end of the week, the village chief sent one of the elders to her house to "cleanse" her, meaning that her vagina was rinsed with fluid containing Ghanaian pepper, a practice that often led to a serious infection. Afterward, she could only wash with cold water, and no soap.

The worst part of this tradition, however, was what happened at the end of the seven days. Though Howa said she did not have to perform this part of the ritual, many women are made to sleep with an unknown man, with whom they must have unprotected sexual intercourse as a sign that they are now available to the other men. It goes without saying that the chances of contracting AIDS from this are frighteningly high. According to George, who works with tribal chiefs to stop this dreadful tradition, it was very common for a Krachi widow who had to undergo these widowhood rites to die shortly after her husband, leaving many children orphaned.

At the end of the ritual, Howa explained, she could never find enough food for the children to eat. A man named Isaac, who was in Kumasi visiting his parents, saw how she suffered and offered to take her two oldest sons to Kete Krachi. He lived there with his wife and children, and told Howa he would take them into his home and enroll them in school. Such gestures are not uncommon in Ghana. Howa did not want to give up her boys, but she knew they could not survive on their own and she was grateful for Isaac's help. She agreed.

A few months later, after she had gotten back on her feet by doing odd jobs in her village, she decided to travel to Kete Krachi to visit her two sons and see how they were faring in school. When she arrived in town, she met a woman she knew and asked where she might find Isaac's house. The woman told her that he had left Kete Krachi for one of the remote islands in Lake Volta, and had taken her sons with him; they now worked on his canoes, fishing. Howa was very upset to learn that Isaac had deceived her and went to the shore to beg a ride to the island on a fisherman's boat. There she met Isaac. He told her that her sons were out working, and that it was their way of earning the food and shelter he had been providing them with for the last few months.

"No," she said. "You are not going to mislead me like this. I am taking my children back."

She waited until the boys returned from the lake, and when they saw their mother and their little brother, they ran up the shore into her arms. By evening, they were all together in Old Nkomi, where she knew some of the villagers. They agreed to let her stay there and offered her and her sons a sleeping space in one of the tiny huts.

A few weeks later, as Howa tried to figure out a way of getting back to Kumasi, she fell ill. "I think there was something wrong with my heart," she told us, "and I went to see a doctor in Kete Krachi. He told me I needed to take medicine for my heart." But she had no way to pay for the medicine, and so she did the unthinkable. She went back to Isaac.

"Okay," she said. "You can take the two boys, but you have to pay me money for their work." They negotiated a deal. For about twenty dollars a year, he would keep her two oldest boys for six years.

That had been a few months earlier. In the ensuing time, Howa said, she had come to fully regret her decision to sell her sons. She felt better now and wanted them back home with her, and when she heard about the work George, Albert, and the others were doing, she had gone to Kete Krachi to speak with them. If she could earn the money to buy back her sons, she asked, could they help her? They had agreed to do what they could, and were working with Isaac to set up an exchange.

While Howa spoke, her son fell asleep across her lap, and she absentmindedly scraped scabs off his back with her fingernails. When she finished her story, she took us to the hut where she lived. It was similar to the one Richard had shared with other boys: tiny, about the size of a large closet. There was only enough room for a makeshift bed—a wooden slatted mat balanced on mud bricks, covered with a dirty white sheet. There was a small wooden table against one wall, leaving little room to walk. It was covered in a piece of light blue fabric, an empty glass bottle, and a red toothbrush. On the floor—which was mud and dust—sat a pair of flip-flops and a few candles. There were no windows, and the door was covered with fabric. Even though it was a very bright and sunny day, it was nearly pitch black inside, and smelled overwhelmingly of sweat.

A tall man walked into the dark room. He nodded hello to us and said something to Howa's son, which sent him running out of the house into the sunlight. Howa took a seat on the bed and explained that this was her boyfriend. He also fished the lake. Immediately I felt my heart sink. She had a boyfriend? Her story was so sad and desperate that the idea of romance being part of her life felt so, well, odd. It was quiet for a minute, and then Aimee asked a few easy questions—what was his name, how old was he—before she got to the one on everyone's mind: Did Howa want more children?

She laughed and shook her head. But even so, she did not use birth control. She was aware of a contraceptive shot that women could get in Kete Krachi, but she was afraid to try it because there were rumors it could make you very sick. This was something that we would hear many times when talking to women in these small villages.

"I know I have to be careful," she said. "But it's hard, especially because my boyfriend wants me to have more children." She then explained that it was difficult to be intimate because she and her boyfriend shared this bed with her son. They would wait for him to fall asleep before having sex.

These moments were among my most challenging. No matter how much time and effort I had spent battling my inclination to judge people, I couldn't help but wonder how this woman could claim on one hand that she regretted her decision to sell her sons, and then put herself in a situation where she could easily get pregnant again. And, I thought, how did we know she was telling the truth about why she wanted her sons back?

Was it because she missed them, or because her boyfriend had decided they would be put to better use working with him on his own canoes?

We were back on the *Krachi Queen* by 1 PM. The sun had left its stinging mark on my arms and neck, and my feet itched in my sandals from wading through the dirty water to the boat. Albert told us it was time to head back to town. I wanted a distraction from everything, so I moved to the back of the boat to strike up a conversation with Bright. In good English, he told me that he had been working on this boat for several months. Although he had attended school up to the fifth level, he had to stop because his parents could not afford it any longer.

When we got to shore at Kete Krachi, the beach was deserted except for a few children bathing in the lake. We walked through the water and up the hill toward town. The street was crowded with people shopping at many of the small stands, and the shopkeepers yelled out to us in greeting. A group of children came running over and gathered behind us, yelling the now familiar *Obroni! Obroni!* We passed in front of a small café, with a small hand-painted sign in front that read SPYGLASS. Its walls were painted a bright red and yellow, and it had a thatched roof with a few ceiling fans to circulate the air. Inside were about six creaky wooden tables and plastic chairs. It was empty except for a table with three men, who were laughing loudly and sipping on bottles of beer.

I looked at Aimee. "I think it's time for some balance," I said.

Albert, Bright, and Mohammed joined us. Within a few minutes, we were settled into a table under one of the fans, each with an icy cold bottle of Starr beer. Albert thanked us for our work that day. "I know this may be difficult for you," he said, sensing our exhaustion. He explained that the next day would be much busier. "I want you to meet as many trafficked children as possible. We will leave tomorrow at 5 AM, and we've hired the boat for the whole day. I also want to take you to a village where we've been working to release some children. The masters there are known to abuse their boys very badly."

Dave, who had been quiet for most of the day, sat forward in his chair. "I have to ask you something, Albert," he said, appearing to choose his words carefully. "I know that you guys are committed to these negotiations. But the whole time I was out on that boat today, I had to fight an urge to grab every single one of those kids and take them into our boat and bring them here to safety. I'm having a hard time understanding why everyone is so gentle about this. This is wrong. These kids are slaves. They are miserable and we can do something more immediate. Every day that goes by during your negotiations is another day that these kids have to experience this hell. Don't you ever just want to grab a gun, or whatever you need, and tell them enough is enough?"

Albert quietly sipped his drink. "I understand what you are saying, David," he said. "I understand the desire to do this with more brute force. But we have to keep in mind that our goal is to get every child off the lake. Were we to charge into these villages making threats and demanding that the children be released to us immediately, we might be able to free some of the kids, but it would ultimately hurt our efforts." He explained that there were a few main concerns. One was that if they threatened to bring in the police—which was itself an empty threat, given the lack of police resources—it was possible that some of the masters who depended on trafficked children might simply up and move to another village, or settle another island. That needed to be avoided at all costs, because it would undo months of careful work.

Another problem with adopting a more threatening approach was that people would start to see his team as hostile, and then stop telling the truth about which children were trafficked. He had already seen evidence of this. Masters were beginning to increasingly claim that kids Albert knew to be trafficked were their own children. Since Sharon LaFraniere came to report her story for the *Times,* word had begun to spread, and people were becoming less willing to speak honestly to Albert, especially when he was accompanied by white people. Should they assume a more threatening stance, the lies would increase.

"Trust me," Albert said, "we believe that we are doing what needs to be done, in the best way possible. And of course, until we have a place for these children to go, there are only so many we can save, with force or with peace."

———

The rooster in the yard had absolutely no mercy. It was awake by four o'clock the next morning, apparently hosting a small get-together with the chickens and dogs right underneath our bedroom window. I woke up startled and looked over at Aimee, who had a pillow covering her head. "You know that gun Dave was talking about using on the masters yesterday?" I said. "Let's get that and do some target practice on that rooster."

I took a quick shower to rinse off the sweat and joined the others on the front porch for a breakfast of bread, butter, cheese, and coffee. The sun had not yet risen, and the air was cool. Erica was brushing her teeth in the front yard, a large piece of pink cotton wrapped around her white nightgown to stave off the chill.

Albert arrived at George's around 5 AM and quickly drank the coffee Erica poured for him. After loading the back of his motorbike with bags of water and a basket of food Erica prepared, we walked into the darkness toward the lake. The town was sleepy and deserted. When we got to shore, the boat was there waiting for us . . . but unfortunately, there was no motor. Nor could we find Bright or Mohammed anywhere. Albert paced the shore on his cell phone, trying to figure out what had happened. After an hour, as the sun appeared over the horizon, Bright and Mohammed arrived, pulling the motor behind them on a creaky wagon. They hit a small boulder, which sent the wagon to its side. Together, they hoisted the motor off the sand and back into the wagon with a loud bang. I tried not to think about what would happen should that tortured motor suddenly stop working in the middle of the lake.

"Okay," Albert said with a smile. "Let's get to work."

We took our seats on the *Krachi Queen*. Within two hours, we began to spot the canoes bobbing in the distant waters. Bright shut off the motor, and a boy in a nearby boat stood and waved his arms at us. He wore long pants and an adult-size zip-up jacket. The man beside him was wearing the opposite extreme: nothing except bright yellow underpants. On each end, two very young boys balanced with their paddles.

After pulling alongside and exchanging greetings, Albert addressed the youngest boy. His name was Kwasi, and he looked to be about seven. He was wearing a long-sleeved thermal shirt, printed with a cartoon character, and red sweatpants. The crotch had large holes in it, which someone had sewn together with thick beige thread. His hair was long and cast a shadow onto his eyes.

The man in the yellow underpants, who was probably in his early thirties, did not want to talk to us. He told Albert that they were too busy working, and they needed to be left alone. Albert asked him about Kwasi.

"He's my son," he said. As they talked, Kwasi looked back and forth between them and said nothing. The conversation with Albert and the older man became heated. Their voices grew louder and as Albert spoke, he pointed at Kwasi and looked sternly at the man. Bright came over to translate for us. He told us that Albert was accusing the man of lying about the child. "He's arguing that there is no resemblance between the two of them," Bright said. "He is telling him to stop lying."

But the man in the yellow underwear insisted. "I have seven children and he is my youngest," he said.

Finally, Albert gave up. "Forget it," he said with frustration. "We are wasting time on him." He turned back to look at the man. "He knows he's breaking the law, and that there will be a price to pay."

The next canoe we came across held two young boys and one adult, who told us a similar story. He said the two young ones were his nephews and that they had been in school, but the school had closed recently and now the kids worked while the village elders tried to find teachers to reestablish another. Albert tried to direct his questions to the boy in the middle, who was perhaps ten years old and wore nothing but white underpants, but every time he did, the older man answered first. As he sat there, staring into the water, the young boy's body shivered in the cold. His underpants and hair were soaking wet, and he wrapped his thin arms around himself to keep warm. It was heartbreaking to look at him. I tried to hand him some candy, but he wouldn't accept it. He wouldn't even lift his eyes to look at it.

The older man would not stop interjecting. "I'm telling you," he said, "he is my nephew." Albert moved closer to the man, speaking to him more gently, taking, it seemed, a friendlier approach to the situation. He smiled widely and rested his hand on the man's shoulder; he didn't stop to translate for us. We were happy to get the man out of the conversation, and I realized perhaps that Albert had purposefully drawn the man aside to give us privacy with the boy. I motioned to Bright to come closer.

"Help us translate," I said. "Ask him his name."

Bright asked, but there was no answer. "Can you tell us how old you are?" I asked. Bright spoke gently to the boy but still, nothing. Aimee reached down under the bench and took a long-sleeved white shirt that we had brought with us. She held it out to the shivering boy, offering it to him. For the first time, he lifted his head, but he did not seem to understand the gesture.

"Go ahead," Bright said. "Take it and put it on."

He looked confused, as if the idea that somebody would offer him this basic comfort was wholly implausible. But instantly, something seemed to change in his eyes. He timidly reached up his hand, his fingers shriveled with moisture, and took the shirt. At first, he simply held it and looked at it. Then he lifted the shirt over his head and pulled his knees to his chest, tucking them tightly under the soft white cotton. He hid his face in his shoulder, still shivering despite the shirt. Then he reached up and touched my hand, which was resting on the side of the boat.

After a few minutes, Albert once again said it was time to move on. "He's not going to give us any information we want," he said. None of us wanted to leave, yet there was nothing left to do.

"Did you find out the village where he lives?" I asked.

"He told me, but I don't believe him," Albert said. "I will go there next week and will look for myself."

Bright walked to restart the motor, and the young boy on the end of the canoe grabbed his paddle and pushed off from our boat. Only then did the shivering boy let go of my hand. When our hands parted, he waved good-bye.

We never saw him again.

Our next stop, which we reached around noon, was Alavanyor, the island village that had the Pacodep team most concerned. During one of their visits, they had met a teenager named Kwasi Tweranim, who bore a huge scar on his head from where his master had beaten him with a paddle. Team members were focusing their efforts here, trying to convince the village elders to release some of the trafficked children.

"Our meetings have become somewhat contentious," Albert explained as we hiked up a rocky hill. That certainly was not apparent from the reception we received. When we entered the village, the adults called out to us in friendly greeting, and a young girl escorted us to benches that had been set in the shade of a large tree. Near us, clouds of smoke from the smoking fish filled the air with an earthy and pungent aroma.

Before long, the village chief appeared, shook hands with each of us and hugged Albert as if they were old friends. He wore maroon cotton pants, a yellow mesh tank top, and blue sandals on his feet, and took a seat on a plastic chair across from us. He had two wives, one of whom dozed on a bench under a nearby tree, and eleven children between them. He did not use trafficked children himself, but the oldest of his children worked with him on the lake.

After Albert inquired about the health of the chief's family, smiling amiably the whole time, he turned serious. By this time, six other men had gathered around us, some of them taking the available seats; others stood, not saying a word but paying close attention to us and the conversation. "You know why we are here," Albert said, addressing the crowd. "We have spent long hours speaking to each other about how important it is that these children go to school. There are too many trafficked children living in this village." He introduced me, explaining that we were working together to build the Village of Life so that the children would have a safe place to go, plenty of food, and the opportunity to receive a good education. The men met my eyes, and some of them smiled and nodded.

"You smile at her," Albert said, not missing a beat, "but what are you doing to address the problem? It is an embarrassment to the nation of Ghana that American newspapers have written about this problem. You stand there smiling, while at the same time you are the cause of the problem."

Some of the men shifted uncomfortably in their seats, and I noticed two of them stealing glances at each other. That was also when I noticed a number of machetes lying on the ground at the men's feet. *Did they purposefully place those there?* I wondered, realizing how precarious a situation we may have put ourselves in. I looked at Dave, thankful in that moment to have a former navy SEAL along, and saw that he, too, was taking notice of the machetes. He slowly sat forward in his chair, clasping his hands between his knees. Looking at him—a large man with piercing blue eyes and a shaven head—even I was momentarily intimidated.

"Here is our offer," Albert continued. "We will start with four children. You agree to release them to us, and we will come back for them when the Village of Life is complete." His words hung in the air. Everyone waited for the village chief to respond.

And waited.

He and Albert stared at each other over the machetes. Nobody moved. Finally, the chief spoke. "What, then, is the offer? What will you provide us if we release these children?"

With that, Albert stood and took a stack of rolled-up paper from his back pocket. "Here is what I offer you," he said, and began to read the first few paragraphs of the anti-trafficking law. After a few moments, he stopped reading. "It's simple. You stop breaking the law, and there will be no need for the police to come."

The chief wiped sweat from his brow with the bottom of his shirt and then turned his head to look toward the man who had the twelve trafficked children, who was leaning against the tree. An unspoken agreement passed between them. The village chief looked as if he was going to speak, but he did not. Instead, he slowly shook his head. No.

And with that, our strange summit came to an abrupt end. The chief stood and came over to me, extending his hand. "Thank you," he said, and then turned and walked away.

Back on the boat, we gathered together. Erica had prepared a bowl of smoked tuna and tomatoes for us, and a small bunch of sweet green bananas. We unwrapped the bowl and each grabbed a fork. "Now what?" I asked. Albert took a sip of water and spit over the side of the boat.

"We will keep going back," he said, "and we will pray in the meantime that they do the right thing." He shook his head. "But I have to admit, I do not feel hopeful."

"And if they do not release any children?" Dave asked.

"I don't know. We will report them to the police, but everyone there knew that this was an empty threat."

———

After lunch, we headed back out to the deeper waters of the lake, to speak with more children. We passed a canoe in the distance filled with four children. The two in the middle had their shirts pulled over their heads to protect themselves from the blazing sun. "They are probably heading home," Albert said. "Let's not stop them. They need their rest."

I looked at Bright and realized that he had not been his usual friendly and affable self all day. "What's wrong?" I asked, offering him a bag of water. "Is the heat getting to you?"

He smiled. "No, Pamela," he said. "I am fine."

"Okay, good," I said. "We don't need you nodding asleep back here and falling off the boat."

Bright laughed. "I am not sleepy," he said. "Just sad."

"What's wrong?"

He looked into the distance. "I have been working on this boat for several months, and many times I have accompanied George and Albert on these trips. But today, I feel particularly sad about what is happening on this lake. Look at these boys. What is their future? What is the answer?"

I rested my hand on Bright's arm. "I understand," I said. While I had never questioned the importance of building the Village of Life, being here on the lake made me absolutely sure of it. Yes, it was daunting to see the reality of this situation, and the challenges of this work. And maybe it would take an entire lifetime to get every child off the lake.

But I shook away the growing sense of doubt. So what? So this is what I will spend my lifetime doing. Maybe I'd stumble along the way—actually, I was *sure* I'd stumble along the way—but trying was better than nothing.

I heard Albert yell to Bright to stop the boat. I didn't know if I had it in me to meet another child whose future seemed hopeless. But then I sat up and saw the young boy in the blue tank top, his eyes as big as saucers.

Chapter Eleven

March 2007. Dear Jantsen, I can't believe I am in the middle of nowhere, Africa. The sacred thread of grief has led me far. Where, though, has the time gone? With each passing day I realize it is one day closer to seeing you. I no longer think of the years I endure without you but the richness and fullness you have brought to this world, in your presence and in your absence. My dear precious son, you are not forgotten. I love you, Mom

His name was Teteh, and he didn't know his own age. He was whip-thin and filthy, with a mess of matted hair on his head. Unlike many of the other boys we had met, Teteh had attended school for one year before his mother told him he had to stop and go to work. This was a few years ago, although he didn't remember how long exactly. All he remembered was that a few days after he stopped going to school, a man came to get him—a different man from the one who had come for his brother a year earlier. He was brought to a village called Atigangome Kope on one of the grassy islands that dotted the lake. Though Teteh looked for his brother every day, hoping to spot him in one of the other boats he passed, he never did see him again.

Teteh, who was probably ten years old, was with two other boys, both of whom worked for their father, Teteh's master. The second, about the same age as Teteh, had long, stick-thin legs and large, crooked teeth; he wore royal blue underpants and a light blue sweatshirt that was so dirty, it looked brown. The oldest boy in the canoe, Ima, was in a bright yellow tank top and shorts.

Teteh told us that there were many trafficked children in Atigangome Kope. He shared a tiny hut with five others, sleeping on the dirt floor. When he first arrived there, he didn't know how to swim. He often cried in the beginning when he was told to jump into the water and untangle the nets from whatever they had been caught on, but he got stronger and had taught himself to close his eyes, hold his breath, and pull as hard as he could.

Since leaving his parents' house, his days had been filled by the same endless routine: wake before sunrise, hike to the beach, paddle to the nets, return to shore to mend the nets, and go back out again by evening. He usually ate twice a day but sometimes, if he misbehaved, or there was a small catch that day, only once. Sometimes, he said, he was caned for these things.

"I am often hungry," he said, "but we all are. We eat as much as we are given."

Like the others, he had seen boys—some of them his friends—drown.

"How many?" Albert asked.

"I don't know. Many."

He told us his story with no emotion and not once during the hour we spent talking to him did he break even a faint smile; nor did he ever stop working—constantly moving his yellow bucket in and out, bailing out water. Meanwhile, Ima sat on the bow of the canoe, using a large knife to cut paper, which he then stuck into some of the holes in the bottom. What an inane system this was. Two children spending hours with paper and a bucket to keep this boat from sinking.

Teteh missed his parents, both of whom were farmers. He said he thought about them every day, and he felt sorry for whatever he did to anger them.

"What do you mean?" Albert asked.

"I think they must have sent me here to punish me," he said. "I do not know what I did wrong, but I fought with my sister a lot, and maybe that is why my parents had to sell me. When I am sleeping at night, I see my mother in my dreams and I apologize to her. Then she comes and says that I can go to school. That is all I want to do, go to school."

"Is there anything you get to do that you do like?" I asked.

"I like to play football," he quietly said, picking at a scab on his foot. "My friends and I sometimes play together when the work is done, if we are not too hungry or tired."

As he talked, I could not take my eyes off the middle boy in the blue sweatshirt. He sat silently, staring vacantly at Teteh as he cut fish from the nets. Despite the fact he lived with his parents, his life was clearly no better than Teteh's.

Albert excused himself from the conversation and ushered us to the other side of the boat, away from the canoe. "I know the village where Teteh lives. It is one of the communities where we have been working," he said. "I think that it might be possible for us to go to his village today and talk to his master."

"You mean, to ask for his release right now?" I said.

"Yes." He paused. "Are you interested in trying?"

Were we *interested*? I don't think I'd ever been quite so interested in anything in my life.

"Yes," I said. "We're interested."

"I don't want any of us to get our hopes up," Albert said, "but we can at least try."

He turned back to the boat, where the boys were sharing the Swedish fish we had given them. "Listen," he said, addressing Teteh. "We are going to go to your village and talk to your master. Would you like to come with us?"

Hearing him say this made my heart fall to my knees. What if the master said no, or wasn't there? There were probably a hundred reasons that we might not be able to take him with us. Were we filling him with false hope? But then I looked at Teteh's face and knew we had to trust this. His huge eyes grew bigger, and he tried to fight back his tears. "Please," he nearly whispered, "please take me with you. I will be good at school and work hard if you give me the chance."

Pulling away from the canoe, we sat down on the benches of the *Krachi Queen*. Albert handed us each a bag of water, and we sat in silence, sipping the salty liquid and praying the master would be there. I looked back toward the canoe. Teteh was standing, and waving good-bye to us, a huge smile on his face this time.

The boy in the blue sweatshirt was also watching us. I met his eyes and waved but he simply turned his head and looked out at the horizon.

We arrived at Atigangome Kope by 3 PM. Groups of young boys sat in canoes on the shore, mending the nets. Many of them were naked, their hair long, wild, and bleached orange by the sun. Albert knew this village well, and people passing us on the path to the village, carrying buckets of lake water, stopped to greet him. About forty adults lived here, and perhaps five times as many children. Those too young to work were everywhere: tied to their mothers' backs, sleeping under a tree, chasing one another around the mud ovens. Some of the older children grabbed plastic chairs and placed them under a tiny thatched awning next to a wooden bench where four goats slept. The children shooed the goats away, and one extended his arm in an invitation to sit.

A man came over and he and Albert hugged, greeting each other in English. This man, who had inherited the post of village assemblyman, was tall and strikingly handsome. About forty years old, he wore a light blue linen shirt with an open collar, white shorts, and Adidas flip-flops. A heavyset woman in a long flowered dress and large hoop earrings came over to us with a cooler. She offered us each a bag of purified water. I knew it was risky to drink this—some companies were known to sell dirty water that had not, in fact, been purified—but it would have been rude to decline the gesture of hospitality, and each of us took a bag and ripped into the plastic with our teeth. A group of children came and gathered around, and I handed them suckers from my bag. They looked at them without understanding what they were, slipping them onto their tongues without taking off the wrapper. I took a sucker and showed them how to do it, and when they tasted the sweetness of the candy, they shrieked in joy, offering one another tastes.

The assemblyman explained that he had been trying to establish a school here in the village. He pointed to an area to our left where stones had been laid out in a circle in the sand and dust. This was also where the villagers gathered on Sunday for church services—most Ghanaians practice Christianity—and some of the women had been working with the children when they completed their work on the lake. But most of the women who assumed these teaching posts had not been educated themselves; few of them were able to read or write, or knew more than a few words in English. Even the assemblyman, who was the most respected member of this community, had left school in the fifth grade to become a fisherman. "We were very poor and I needed to help my parents," he said as his daughter walked over to stand between his legs, carrying a doll with no head. "I have been fishing since then, and I will probably fish forever."

He told us that there were many trafficked children in his village, although he did not know exactly how many, adding that he was very concerned about this practice of buying and selling children. If he was concerned about it, I wondered, why did he allow people in his village to buy them and bring them here? He did, after all, have the authority to stop it. He seemed to sense the question in my face. "I have been trying to explain to the masters that there is now a law in our country that prohibits people from buying children," he said. Seeing how remote these villages were, I understood how most people had no way of even knowing about the law. It's not as if they had television, or read newspapers. In one village we visited, a woman we spoke to told us that she had never heard of the United States and had no knowledge of current events, like the terrorist attacks of September 11, 2001. Their only exposure to the world outside these primitive villages was a trip to the one of the bigger markets in Kete Krachi or Dumbai every few months. "It is a slow process," the assemblyman said, "and the people who do know about the law are reluctant to adhere to it."

I asked him about Teteh. "Yes," the assemblyman said, "I think I know who he is, although there are a few boys in this village who are called Teteh." That was not unusual, as it is the custom in Ghana for children to be named for the day on which they were born. Albert then slowly, and carefully, explained why we had come.

"These people are very concerned about the situation with the children who work on the lake," he said gently, leaning closer to the assemblyman. "They, and I, are here to see if we can take Teteh with us to Kete Krachi and enroll him in school. We want to help him. We want to give Teteh a future."

The assemblyman said nothing, as he intertwined his fingers with his daughter's. Behind him, a rooster crowed loudly.

Finally he spoke.

"I think that is a good idea."

I looked at Aimee. *Did he just agree to release Teteh?* Aimee nodded at me, sensing my question. *I think so.*

"But," the assemblyman continued, "his master is not around, so it's not possible today."

"This is no problem," Albert responded. "We will talk to his master's wife. She must be here." He was so skilled in these situations, speaking delicately while never backing down.

"Yes, she is. I do not know what she will say."

"No," Albert said. "But of course it never hurts to ask."

The assemblyman was quiet, and I could see the hesitation in his eyes. Finally, he slapped his hands on his knees. "The law is there now," he said with obvious reluctance. "There is nothing else to do."

He stood and told us to follow him. As we walked down a narrow, dusty path between some of the huts, we passed a young girl, standing by herself under the shade of a large palm plant. There was something about her that made me stop in my tracks. She was absolutely beautiful. Maybe ten years old, she had long, muscular limbs and shaved hair. She wore a dress with green and red flowers printed on the fabric. On her back, wound with a large orange-and-lime-green scarf, was a baby that looked to be a few weeks old. The baby was sound asleep and his head, unsupported in the fabric casing, leaned back at nearly a right angle, his arms slouched to the side. These babies could sleep anywhere.

"Hello," I said to her, reaching out to touch her shoulder. "What is your name?"

"Regina," she said, so softly I had to kneel down to hear her.

"Hi, Regina. I'm Pam." I pulled a sucker from my bag and handed it to her. She took it, but refused to draw her eyes away from the ground.

Nearby, under the shade of a thatched hut, the assemblyman's wife and another woman sat on stools cleaning fish, which spilled from several large metal bowls at their feet. They kept their gazes fixed on us as we walked by, and the assemblyman pointed to another hut. "The man who lived here died recently at seventy-five," he said. "But he had seven wives and at least forty children. And many of the trafficked children in our village are here because he bought them." The assemblyman directed us to a few benches that had been set out under the shade of a thatched awning. There two women sat crowded among several children. The assemblyman explained that they were both married to Teteh's master.

Georgina was in her early thirties and the other wife, Fatima, probably ten years older. Georgina was large with an open, friendly face and an easy laugh. She sat on a low bench, resting against the tire of a big, broken wagon behind her; she held a sleeping infant. She wore a piece of fabric tied around her like a towel, revealing the thick white straps of her bra underneath. Fatima looked forebidding. She was rail-thin and wiry—so thin, that I wondered if she might be sick. Like Georgina, she wore only a piece of fabric, in bright orange and navy blue. A yellow knit cap covered her hair, and her face was marked with tribal scars around her eyes, six narrow slits, like a cat. She kept her head cast down, her chin in her hands, refusing to make eye contact with any of us, picking at her toes.

Georgina did most of the talking. She had been born here on this island and rarely left it. She married her husband when she was nineteen years old, and when I asked her how many children her husband had, she laughed and looked around the crowd for help, because she didn't know. She rattled off the names of children, counting on her fingers. Finally, with the help of the assemblyman, they figured it out: twelve. I asked Georgina if she would like to have more children, and she laughed and said no. "I think this is enough." Even so, she didn't practice any type of birth control because she, too, had heard that it could make her sick. I asked her if I could hold her baby. She sent one of the older children inside the hut behind us, and he came out carrying a dirty rag, which she wrapped around the baby's bottom like a diaper. Then she placed the young boy gingerly in my arms.

She did not know how much her husband had paid for Teteh's service or how many years he had left on his contract. When Albert asked her if she considered Teteh like a son, she laughed again. "I don't know," she said. "I guess so." There was one way that she treated him as she did any of her own children: When he misbehaved, she had to correct him, often by caning him.

"How do you do it?" I asked.

Georgina pointed to the branches in the tree above us. "I grab one of those and hit him."

When she was done talking, Albert once again started from the beginning, explaining to Georgina and Fatima why we were here, and that we would like to take Teteh to Kete Krachi to attend school. But this time, he spoke to the women—and the dozen or so people who had crowded around us by now—not as if he were asking permission, but as if the decision to release him to us was final. He talked about the great opportunities that awaited Teteh and how he would be well cared for.

"Will you miss Teteh when he's gone?" I asked, trying to help us figure out if this was actually going to happen.

Fatima snickered and scowled at the ground. Georgina laughed. "I do not know if I will miss him," she said.

By this time, a group of at least ten boys had joined the crowd. Many of them were covered in filth and wore no shirts. They appeared to have just come off the lake, and some of them sat quietly in the shade, listening. Three boys seemed particularly interested. They looked to be about nine or ten. One of them wore only bright yellow underpants and orange flip-flops, and another a blue-and-yellow adult-size T-shirt that hung on him like a dress. The third was tall and very thin, and, surprisingly, he spoke some English. He tried speaking to us, but when it was clear we did not understand him, he gestured toward Aimee's notebook and pen, and wrote out his name, in careful penmanship: Ezekiel.

"How did you learn that?" I asked him.

"I went to a little school before I came here," he said. He then wrote out the names of the two boys beside him, Israel and Ebenezer.

The assemblyman asked to speak to Albert. They stepped away from the group and talked for a few minutes. Albert then came over to us. "What wonderful news this is," he said. "The kind assemblyman has agreed to release this boy here, Israel, in addition to Teteh."

What?

Albert pointed to the boy in the blue-and-yellow shirt and explained that Israel had been living in Atigangome Kope for seven years. His master had since left the island, and the rest of the village struggled to keep him fed and clothed. They simply didn't want him anymore.

Israel looked confused, and Albert placed his arm around the boy's shoulder, knelt on the ground, and explained what was happening. "You and Teteh are coming with us," he said. "Do you want to go to school?" Israel looked back toward Ezekiel and Ebenezer. He quietly nodded.

I was as confused as Israel. Were we simply going to take him right then? None of the adults seemed to care, or even to be paying much attention. Israel said that he had not seen his parents for at least five years, and he did not know how old he was. "Do you enjoy the work here?" Albert asked.

His eyes cast down, he simply shook his head. Then Ezekiel and Ebenezer came over to where Israel sat, and they talked in hushed tones. I could not understand them, but it seemed that Israel was explaining what was happening. I made out the word *school*. Ezekiel reached over and rested his hand on Israel's leg, and at this loving gesture, his eyes filled with tears.

"Why are you sad?" I asked him.

He whispered something, which the assemblyman translated. "These three are best friends. He is sad about leaving them behind. They are on the same soccer team, and Israel here is the captain."

Ebenezer and Ezekiel looked miserable. At that moment, I began to question if this was the right thing to do. Were we taking these kids away from the only home they'd ever had, from a family they had forged through their miserable, but shared, experience? And how could we just randomly pick and choose which kids to rescue, and which ones would be left behind? Would those who remain come to believe they simply were not worthy of coming, too? It was overwhelming, but immediately, I remembered the conversation I'd had with John Arthur. "Please," he had said, "go get more kids. Do whatever you can."

It took Albert nearly an hour to complete the paperwork—which they were careful to fill out to protect themselves from any claims that they were themselves child traffickers—and by the end of it, we were sweating so much in the heat and sun that our clothes were drenched. We wanted to get these kids and get out. The problem, however, was that Teteh was nowhere to be found. He was probably still out on the lake, and we needed to get going. The ride back to Kete Krachi was another two hours, and we had to get there before the sun set, as our boat had no lights.

Thirty minutes later, we had to make a hard decision. We decided that we would leave, and return to Atigangome Kope the next day. When Israel heard this, he asked if he could also wait until then to leave, so that he had one more night to spend with Ebenezer and Ezekiel. It felt like the right thing to do, although deep down I worried that we were taking a huge risk. So many things could happen. The boatmen could fail to arrive. The assemblyman could change his mind. The boys could be nowhere in sight when we returned. But we decided we couldn't wait any longer, and as we hiked back down the grassy path to the lake, I whispered a quiet prayer that everything would work out.

Back in Kete Krachi, we were tired and hungry but decided to keep what had become our daily ritual: stopping at the Spyglass for a Starr beer. None of us said too much, just staring into the darkness and swatting away the mosquitoes. I got up to use the restroom, which was nothing more than a drain in a cement floor, behind a stone wall. Compared with where we had been going these last few days—mostly behind trees, or in an open field on an island—this felt luxurious. I ran back to the table to Aimee.

"You have to go to the bathroom!" I said. "It's so nice and clean."

Aimee came back a few minutes later. "Pam," she said. "It's a drain in the floor and a wall. I think you've been in Ghana too long."

That night, I could not get to sleep. I lay there in the dark, listening to the orchestra of crickets and frogs in the yard beyond our window. I tried to picture in my mind the faces of

Teteh and Israel, and how, if everything worked out, the next evening they would be sitting on George's lawn, eating as much dinner as they wanted. But as I finally drifted off to sleep, it wasn't their faces in my mind. Instead, all I could see was the boy in the blue sweatshirt, the one we had left behind, and the emptiness in his eyes.

———

Despite a night of very fitful sleep, I woke up feeling charged, rejuvenated, and nervous as all get-out. Everyone was up by 5 AM, eager to get down to the boat and back to Atigangome Kope. We were at the lake an hour later, but when we arrived, the *Krachi Queen* was not in the water, and Bright and Mohammed were nowhere to be found. I lay down on the beach, covering my face with a towel, the sweat pooling in the sand under my neck. An hour later, there was still no boat. A young woman came by, selling orange soft drinks that she carried in a large pail on her head. Two children yelled out to us, "Hello, *Obroni*! What is your name?"

Finally, at 11 AM, Albert's cell phone rang. It was Bright. There had been a misunderstanding, and the company had rented the *Krachi Queen* out that day to another party. We had no choice but to abandon the plan. It was heartbreaking. Albert assured us that the boat would be there the next day, but I could think only about Teteh and Israel sitting on the shore, waiting for us to arrive, and believing we had abandoned them.

Walking back up the hill toward town, I tried to tell myself that there was nothing we could do, and the power was not in my hands. This, I was learning, was simply how Ghana worked. All we could hope for was that when we arrived the following day, the boat, the motor, and the men would be ready for us. The good news was that George was scheduled to return to Kete Krachi the next morning and would therefore be able to accompany us on the rescue. I heard the frustration in Albert's voice as he called Bright back to stress how important it was that everything be in order the next day. Bright promised.

When we got back to George's house, I decided the day should not go to waste, and asked Albert if we could go to Sofoline, the village where Mark, John, Kofi, Sarah, and Hagar had lived. We could get there by car, and Albert agreed, going back toward the beach to hire a taxi. It pulled up to George's house a few minutes later, and the car looked as if it had been used to fight a war. The back windshield was covered in duct tape; the front was a mess of cracks and holes. The driver warned us not to step on the floor in the back, through which we could see the pavement below. We tried to squeeze into the back, no easy task when you can't step on the floor, and the driver started the car, which filled the backseat with smoke and diesel fumes. "Don't worry," the driver said. "It's only about a thirty-minute ride."

The road to Sofoline was a dirt path cut through a large field. When we arrived, we were welcomed as we had been in the other villages. Although I had expected that this village would be less poor than the island villages—simply because its residents had more access to Kete Krachi and other towns and villages—many of the people, and the children especially, looked among the poorest we had seen. Their bellies bulged, and most ran around with no clothes. But, I thought, perhaps these kids were all enslaved and it was not that they were poorer, just more poorly cared for.

As we waited for the adults to join us, I asked Albert to show me the hut where Mark, John, and the others had slept. He pointed to a tiny mud structure next to the ovens, which were filled with smoking fish. Even though it was bright daylight, it was hard to see inside the hut, which had only a small opening cut into the wall for use as a door, with a tiny window covered in thin fabric. Inside, the smell of rotting fish was overpowering, and flies buzzed around buckets of discarded, unidentifiable fish parts. The floor was dust and dirt, and the ceiling was grass. I wondered if that ceiling could keep out the rain. It was tiny, maybe four feet by four feet, and I couldn't imagine how they all squeezed into this space. Although, after the excruciating work they endured each day, they probably could have slept standing up in the sun.

As I walked back to our meeting spot, I fell into step next to a muscular man who looked to be in his late thirties, wearing a purple short-sleeved T-shirt and white shorts. He held a young boy's hand, his own spitting image, and took a seat on one of the benches. He had the darkest eyes I'd ever seen, and his face bore pockmarks from some long-ago skin ailment. He and Albert exchanged a friendly greeting in their language before Albert introduced us. This was Kwadwo Takyi, the kids' former master. He sat quietly, looking at us sideways, unwilling, it seemed, to meet our eyes.

―――――――

Kwadwo Takyi never attended school. He couldn't read or write, and had never even held a pencil. When he was five years old, he was sent to work on his grandfather's canoe, where he fished alongside his own father. Eventually, when he was old enough, he bought two canoes of his own. Four years earlier, after getting married and having two children, and more mouths to feed, he decided that he needed help. He traveled to Aboadzi, a small rural village that he knew to be very poor, and put out the word that he was looking for children to help him in Sofoline in exchange for money. He got many offers, and from among the children, he chose John, Mark, Hagar, Kofi, and Sarah. For John, given his age, he paid four million cedis (the equivalent of about $430) for a four-year contract, and half of that for each of the other children.

His own children did not work on the lake but attended school in Kete Krachi, which they traveled to on foot every day, making the thirty-minute walk by themselves. "I do not want my children to have to work. I want them in school. It is harder now that I do not have any help because I lost my children," he said, referring to John, Kofi, Mark, Sarah, and Hagar. "But I will try to keep my children in school."

I decided to ask him the question that had been gnawing at me as he spoke. "If I wanted to buy your son here," I said, pointing to the young boy standing between his legs, nodding off to sleep, "would you let me? What if I wanted to offer you 120 million cedis." That, in Ghanaian terms, was a ridiculous amount of money, nearly thirteen thousand dollars, and more than most people would earn during a lifetime.

The master, however, did not even pause.

"No, of course I would not sell you my son. You could not buy or sell human beings."

"But isn't that what you did with the five kids who were rescued?" I asked.

"Of course not. What I did was a favor for the family. Their mothers could not afford to take care of them, so I agreed to bring them here, teach them a skill, and provide food for them. The money I gave to their families was a way to help them cope with their poverty. It was a gift."

"But did you negotiate the gift—the four million cedis you paid to John, for example?"

"Of course," he said, looking at me like I was an idiot.

"Well then, it does not seem like a gift. People do not negotiate gifts."

"You do not understand," he said. "What I did was a blessing for their families. These kids, their parents, they might have starved had I not saved them."

As he spoke, his brother joined us, sitting next to Takyi

on the bench. A young child, perhaps three years old, walked over to Takyi's brother and started to cry, wanting to be picked up. The man tried to quiet the child, who wouldn't stop. He then grabbed a handful of dirt and stones and threw it in the child's face.

On the drive here, I had tried to prepare myself for how I would feel to meet this man. I had seen, obviously, the conditions under which so many people in Ghana live, especially in these tiny villages. I had seen how hard they struggled to eat and to provide not only for their kids, but for themselves. I had seen withering piles of fish on the sand and come to know that the desperation here was so acute, those piles were worth more than a child's dignity. I had seen that, and I had thought that I had come to understand the factors that made this system—this slave trade—not only possible, but necessary.

But as soon as Albert mentioned the word *master* in the same sentence as Mark and John and the others, the sympathy went away immediately, and all I felt was pure hatred. I thought about the story John told us: how he had been made to work so hard and given little to eat, not only because there wasn't enough but because, he thought, he had done something to "deserve" his hunger. And how he had been made to lie down on a bench by this man sitting before me, and beaten with a stick. And how the shadow in Mark's eyes captured in that *New York Times* photo had been cast from the experiences he suffered at this man's direction. I didn't care that he was poor, or that he may have been in the same situation when he was Mark's age, or that he may have believed that he was helping the families whose children he enslaved. I didn't have any sympathy at all. All I had was a nagging desire to walk over to him and beat the crap out of him.

Luckily, Aimee chose that very instant to stand up, which sent one end of the bench into the air and me to the ground, distracting me from my thoughts. Everyone stood up, trying to help me and right the bench and wipe the dust and dirt from my elbows and knees. "I'm sorry," Kwadwo Takyi said in English, meeting my eyes and extending a hand to lift me to my feet.

I took it, and I stood.

———

I woke up in the middle of the night, unsure of where I was. The electricity was out but there was a cool breeze coming in through the screen windows, and I was happy to not wake up, for once, drenched in sweat. Branches from the trees outside our bedroom knocked against the house, and loud claps of thunder bounced around the room. I reached for my watch on the floor beside my bed. It was 2 AM. We had to wake up in three hours for breakfast, because we wanted to be prepared to leave immediately upon George's arrival at 7 AM. Unable to go back to sleep, I grabbed my journal from my bag and wrote a letter to Jantsen.

I slept maybe one more hour before the rooster crowed, announcing that our night had officially come to an end. Outside on the porch, Erica had our breakfast set out, and Albert was there, drinking his tea. The rain had stopped, thankfully, but it was windy and the air was cool, maybe sixty degrees. Men passed by on the road in front of the house, bundled up in jackets. This was probably as cold as it ever got in Ghana, and I realized the kids on the lake must be freezing.

As we waited for George to arrive, Aimee, Dave, and I packed up our clothes. I couldn't believe how quickly the time had passed and that we had to leave the next day to head back to the Village of Hope before flying home. At 9 AM, George called from the road. He had been driving through the night, and the travel had been particularly difficult with the storm, which flooded some of the roads. "Do not worry," he said cheerily through the static. "I will be there."

When he arrived thirty minutes later, we were thrilled to see him. He climbed the driveway with his son George Junior, who had come home from Accra to help that day. "Hello!" George called out, grabbing each of us for a tight hug. "You are at your own home now. You are so welcome!" My worries that something would go wrong today subsided a little. That is the power that George has. Just being in his presence, it's difficult not to feel hopeful.

While he was in Accra, he had printed out a few e-mails he'd received from people who had learned about his work rescuing kids off the lake. Sipping the last of our coffee, we passed the e-mails among us. There were some from schoolchildren in Mississippi asking how they could help, and one from a single mom in New Jersey. One was even from a woman in Kuwait, saying she represented thirty people who wanted to do whatever they could to help rescue more children. Every message was so touching and hopeful, and exactly what we needed at that moment. The energy flowing among us on that porch could have lit all of Kete Krachi, which would have been helpful, as the electricity was still out.

After we gathered what we'd be taking with us—bags of water, candy and snacks for the kids—and George led us in prayer under the mango tree, near where Erica was busy preparing the banku that would be the children's dinner that evening, we set out toward the lake.

It was already 10 AM when we arrived, much later than we had expected, and I could feel the anxiety brewing, especially among us impatient Americans. But at least the sky was clear of last night's storm, and the sun was beginning to burn off the cold air, bringing with it a humid, steaming haze.

I quickly tried to take stock of the situation. I saw Bright and Mohammed. Good. I saw the *Krachi Queen* bobbing in the distance. Good. I did not see the motor. Damn it. Where was the motor? My heart sank. It was going to be a process, I quietly told myself, willing the patience that often eluded me.

Albert was already yelling into his cell phone, and pointing wildly toward the *Krachi Queen,* as if the person on the other end could see that there was, in fact, no motor. Aimee, Dave, and I took a seat on the sand. Finally, about half an hour later, we saw little Mohammed running down the hill toward the beach. On his back—and he had to weigh all of about 120 pounds—was a large diesel motor. He ran hunched over, his arms trying to balance the motor, and his spindly legs looked about to buckle. When he got to the water's edge, he dumped it on the sand with a loud, painful groan.

We all nearly ran down the beach to the water, and Bright steered us toward Atigangome Kope. I looked across the lake and was once again struck by how eerie it felt, as if we had arrived in a forgotten place, one that couldn't possibly exist within the same universe as Neosho, Missouri. What were Van and Tatum doing that moment? I wondered. Where was Crista? I missed them intensely.

As George told Aimee about his hopes for the Village of Life, I thought about the night after I read the *New York Times* article, when I had searched online for information about Lake Volta. Was that really only five months ago? In that time, so much had happened: these two trips here, the decision to build the Village of Life, meeting Teteh and Israel. It felt like a lifetime ago that I sat at my desk, sipping a Diet Coke and reading about this country, this lake, once seemingly distant and foreign.

We arrived in Atigangome Kope around 1 PM. The boys on the beach waved to us, their hands resting for a moment from their work mending nets. In the village, we took our place on the chairs where we had sat two days earlier, and the assembly-man's wife came over, again offering us bags of water from a cooler. Georgina carried her infant son and a bucket of soapy water. *Akwabba,* she said, and took a seat on a bench, plunging the baby into the suds.

I scanned the area, trying to locate either Teteh or Israel, but I didn't see them anywhere. George was engaged in a quiet conversation with the assemblyman, ending in English. "Let the children go. Let the children go." Finally, I saw Israel walk-ing through the dusty field toward where we were gathered. He wore the same blue-and-yellow shirt he'd had on when we first met him but he looked less scared, which eased my mind a bit. I called over to him and invited him to sit next to me on the bench. He walked over, shyly looking away, a thin smile stretched across his face. He lifted his skinny arm and pointed. There was Teteh, walking toward us, wearing a man-size short-sleeved buttondown shirt, its hem nearly dragging in the dirt. George came over and introduced himself to the boys, taking each of them into his large embrace. "Do you want to come with us and go to school?" he asked. Both boys quietly nodded.

"Good," he said. "Now go pack your bags."

George spoke to the people sitting with us and, in his charming way, explained that the decision to release the two boys to us was the right one. He told them that the team would take good care of them, that they would go to school, that their future was as bright as the sun. As the adults listened to George talk, I noticed Ebenezer and Ezekiel standing under a nearby tree, also listening to George and looking downright miserable. The look in their eyes was painful, it was obvious they were quietly begging to come with us. Ezekiel, the older boy, then came over and sat next to Aimee on the bench.

"Hello," she said. I saw Ezekiel lean toward her and whisper something.

Aimee looked at me. "Oh, Pam," she said. "He's asking to come with us."

What could we do? The assemblyman had told us that these boys lived with their parents. We simply could not take them. I tried to set aside everything and focus on George and get through this process. I tried not to think about Ezekiel or Ebenezer.

Luckily, something happened to divert my attention. The assemblyman walked over to us, holding the arm of Regina, the beautiful young girl we had passed two days earlier, the one who had the baby strapped to her back. She had piercing eyes, which she kept cast downward, and there was something about her that was both full of want, and totally vacant. The assemblyman came to stand before me.

"We'd like to offer you the girl," he said.

Offer me the girl?

"I'm sorry," I said. "I don't understand."

"We want you to take her with you, with Israel and Teteh," he said as Regina looked at me from under her long eyelashes. "She is very stubborn, and her master must beat her often. She is too much work for us now."

I got down on my knees in the dirt and gently lifted her chin with my hand. "Hi," I said. There was no response. "I'm Pam. Do you remember we met the other day?" Still, nothing.

"Her name is Regina," he said, then looked at her and asked her something, to which she quietly mumbled an answer. "She is twelve years old." He explained that she had been living in the village for three years, when her mother sold her to the master for two million cedis, or a little more than two hundred dollars, after falling ill and needing medicine. When her mother left her here in Atigangome Kope, she told

Regina she would raise the money to buy her back, but she never did return. The last time Regina saw her mother was three years ago, when she boarded a canoe down at the shore and waved good-bye.

"Regina," I said, lifting her face again to meet my eyes. "Do you want to come with us?"

The assemblyman translated the question and for the first time, her eyes registered emotion. It wasn't happiness, necessarily, but a flicker of relief. I stood up and called Aimee over. "You remember Regina," I said. "She's coming with us, too."

I saw the look on Aimee's face as she stole a glance toward George, who was talking quietly to Israel, and I understood. It was great news, but it was another child. Of course we wanted her, we wanted every one of those kids. But we were not the ones who were going to take them home and feed them for several months before the Village of Life was finished. Then I thought about what I had heard from the staff member at IOM when I had first e-mailed about rescuing Mark, and how he had used the term *cost-effective*. I would find the money . . . we all would. Somehow.

I stood up and kept my hand on Regina's shoulder. She then did the sweetest thing, taking my arms and wrapping them around her chest, pressing her back to my stomach and legs, my heart to her back. It was exactly how Van and Tatum often stood with me when they were feeling shy or vulnerable. She gripped my arm tightly and I rested my cheek on her head, her short hair scratchy against my skin.

Just then, the assemblyman came over with another child, this one a very young boy. He looked to be about four years old, and his stomach was bloated with malnutrition. He wore only a pair of bright yellow underpants and lime-green flip-flops, and his legs and arms were covered in calluses and filth. Seeing him, I thought instantly of Mark, and how he had looked in that photo. Kobi, as we were told this boy's name was, had the same terrified look.

"We want you to take this one, too," the assemblyman said, this time to George. "He is too young to work, and is not of use to us anymore."

I could not believe this. Kobi stood there, looking among us, picking at his fingernails. George knelt down beside him and rested his hand on Kobi's shoulder as the assemblyman explained that Kobi had been brought to the village after both of his parents died, and he had been sold by an uncle. "Hello, Kobi," George said, speaking to him in English. "You are going to come with us, and everything is going to be wonderful." Albert then took Kobi's hand and led him to a place where they could sit and, with the help of one of the adults, fill out the necessary paperwork. What was this moment like for Kobi? As far as he knew, we were just another group of strangers, there to offer money so that he would then be ours.

The whole thing felt confusing and surreal. Why was the assemblyman simply handing over these children? Was it because they had become a burden on the community? Or that they could not afford to feed them? Or was it the law, and their growing fears that should they not appear ready to abide by it, they might pay the penalty?

While this was happening, the situation with Ezekiel and Ebenezer was becoming harder to handle. They watched quietly as first Regina and then Kobi was brought to us. Then, silently holding each other's hands, they walked to the door of the hut they shared with Teteh and Israel to watch them pack to leave. Teteh came out from his hut carrying a black plastic bag that was tied into a knot on top. When I looked in the bag later, I saw that it held a very dirty T-shirt, a tiny notebook with nothing written in it, and a pen we had given him two days earlier: everything he owned.

Ebenezer and Ezekiel sat back down on the bench, slowly inching their way closer to us. Ebenezer's hand rested on Ezekiel's knee and again, Ezekiel whispered to Aimee. "Please," he said, "can't you take us, too?"

If they did live with their parents, I thought, would they be this adamant in their desire to come with us? We had to try something. I called George Junior over. "Take him somewhere," I said, "and try to figure out the story. We need to know if the assemblyman was telling the truth that they live with their parents."

George Junior didn't hesitate. He casually motioned for Ezekiel to come with him, and they walked to a grassy area behind the hut. He came back with a look of real concern on his face. "They say that they do not live with their parents, but were brought to work here several years ago. I believe they are telling the truth."

George was working with Albert to fill out the paperwork for Kobi and Regina, and I quietly approached them. "George," I said, "I think the assemblyman was not telling the truth about Ezekiel and Ebenezer. I know that we already have more children than you and Anna can manage, but we will find a way to make this work. I think that we have to do something to help these two boys."

George looked at his son, who nodded agreement, and then sprang into action. He walked over to the assemblyman. With a big smile on his face, George talked loudly and motioned toward the two boys. I asked Albert to translate. "He's telling him that he thinks those two boys have an eye infection and that we'd like to take them into town for medical treatment and then keep them and enroll them in school with the others."

This wasn't true, of course, because the boys did not appear to have an eye infection. It was simply George's way of telling the assemblyman that he did not believe him, and one of the reasons why he was able to get this work done. Every interaction, I was beginning to learn, was a gentle threat that did not appear threatening.

The assemblyman was quiet. He looked at George, then at the boys, who seemed to sink into each other on the bench. A flash of anger crossed the assemblyman's face, which made me very worried. It seemed unlikely that he'd agree to release them, and once we left, would this mean punishment for Ebenezer and Ezekiel?

Shockingly, he nodded. "Okay," he said, "they can go, too."

I thought I was going to leap up, take the assemblyman in my arms, and French kiss him, but I found restraint and followed George over to where they sat. "Do you want to come with us?" he asked.

The look on their faces was electric. They both stood up, their arms linked, and Ezekiel placed his hand on George's arm. They nodded wildly.

"Good," George said. "Now go pack your bags."

Ezekiel and Ebenezer grabbed each other, and one of them let out a joyous whoop. Israel came running over and took both of them into his embrace. I don't know if I'd ever seen any three young boys so happy. They rushed into the hut to pack.

By this time, nearly three hours had passed since we'd arrived in the village. The heat was becoming unbearable, and I was beginning to fear we'd never get out of there. All I wanted to do was to take the kids and get them on the boat before anyone could change their mind.

Someone had dressed Kobi in shorts and a T-shirt and he stood by himself under the tree, picking nervously at a scab on his wrist. As far as I knew, he still hadn't said a word to anyone. I walked over to him and put out my hand. He took it, looking at me with a lot of confusion.

And a look that said, *It's time to go.*

"Okay," I said to Aimee and Dave. "Let's get this show on the road. Why don't we start rounding up the children and head down to the boat?"

Everyone agreed. George Junior helped us gather Teteh, Israel, Regina, Ezekiel, Ebenezer, and Kobi, each carrying a small plastic bag. Most of the adults remained seated under the tree, and the moment felt wholly awkward.

"Do you think anyone wants to say anything to the children before they leave?" I asked George. He addressed the group in Fanti. When he was done speaking, the children lifted their hands and waved good-bye to the adults, but still nobody moved. I expected Georgina to say something to them, but she didn't. She sat quietly, rocking the infant in her arms. Finally, a man who looked to be in his seventies called Regina over to where he sat. She walked shyly over and he whispered softly to her, holding her wrist while he did. She stared at the ground and when he was finished, she nodded, took back her arm, and walked back to the group. Then she slipped her hand in mine.

And that was that.

We started the hike down to the boat. Regina never let go of my hand, and Teteh took my other one. George Junior swept Kobi into his arms, and Aimee had Israel. Down at the water, the boys we'd passed when we'd arrived were still sitting in the canoe, mending their nets. Israel and Teteh broke away from our group and went over to the boys. They motioned toward the *Krachi Queen,* and I could tell they were explaining that they were leaving with us. One of the older boys stood up from the boat and reached out his hand to Israel. They held hands for a minute before letting go.

Bright lifted each of the kids over the edge. Dave and I climbed in after them, and as I handed out the snacks and bags of water we had packed, I suddenly realized that Ebenezer and Ezekiel were not with us.

Where were they?

I looked back toward the village and then called out to Aimee, who was standing on the shore, "Where are the other two?"

"I don't know," she said with concern. "I'm hoping they're coming with George." As we waited, Dave and I took a seat on the bench, and Kobi came to stand before me. Then he hoisted himself onto my lap. I fed him some water from a cool bag, and after taking a long drink, he rested his head on my chest. Within minutes, he was sound asleep. Regina slid closer to Dave on the bench, and she laid her head against his shoulder.

Finally, I saw George walking down the path toward the beach. He was alone. Aimee went to meet him where the sand met the grass.

"Where are Ebenezer and Ezekiel?" she asked.

George was silent. "I'm sorry," he said. "They are not coming."

"What do you mean?"

"The assemblyman changed his mind. He said the boys are needed here, and that perhaps they can be released at a later date. But not today."

I was stunned. They had packed their bags. They had stood in the group and waved good-bye. We had told them they were coming.

"I don't understand," Aimee said. "Did you explain to them that they are not coming with us?"

"Yes," George said, his voice sad and low.

"And?"

"It's hard to talk about," he said, wiping sweat from his arms with a handkerchief. "They were devastated. Ezekiel threw himself on the ground and was sobbing. I could not comfort him." He paused. "We will do what we can to come back for them another day."

I watched in utter disbelief.

"I'm sorry," he said. "I understand."

George turned and started toward the boat. "Wait," Aimee said, when they had reached the water. "This just isn't right. What is this really about? How can we just let the assemblyman do this? We made a promise to those boys. We have to stand by it."

George was quiet for a few minutes. "Listen," he said. "I want those boys, too. But I do not want to show too much disrespect to the assemblyman. We need to work with him so that all the children in this village will be released to us. But we don't have enough space. We don't have the resources yet. We need to continue to work to get the Village of Life built quickly so that it won't be such a hardship to take more children."

Is that what it was about? Even if we had all the money in the world to pay for their food and clothing and school—which we didn't—George and Anna were making a huge sacrifice.

"I understand," she said. "I do. But it's hard to walk away from them. I'm sure we could get people to help. I'm sure that we can raise more money if that is what this is about."

George looked at me. I nodded, pleading with him as much as I could without saying anything. "Of course," he said. "We can do this. We can get those kids. I'm sorry."

With that, he turned toward some men who had followed him down to the beach. He went over to them and spoke for a few minutes. Then one of them turned and headed back toward the village.

None of us said a word, just waiting, our gazes fixed on the path. For several minutes, nothing happened. The only sound was the heavy sighs Kobi released in his sleep, and I could feel the sweat trickling down my neck and back. George paced back and forth on the shore, stopping only to look toward the village.

We all saw them at the same time: Sprinting down the hill, their arms swinging wildly, clutching their little black bags, Ebenezer and Ezekiel came charging toward us. Aimee walked toward them, and when they met, the boys ran into her arms with so much force, they almost knocked her down. She let go of them, and hand in hand they walked to the boat.

A few minutes later, Bright was steering the *Krachi Queen* toward home. George knelt before the children, saying something to them that brought toothy smiles to their faces. Ebenezer and Ezekiel were sitting on either side of me, their bodies squished tightly next to mine. I looked back toward shore one last time. There, sitting on a large boulder, was one boy, all alone. I stood up and walked toward the back of the boat to get a closer look.

It was the boy in the blue sweatshirt we had met the other day in Teteh's boat. I waved my hand, and while I know he saw me, he did not wave back. He simply got off the rock. Without turning to look back even once, he walked alone toward the village.

We had been sailing for twenty minutes when the sky turned very dark and the rain began to fall. We passed boys in canoes, rowing furiously to get to safety on one of the tiny islands, their boats being thrown around in the water. The *Krachi Queen*, much bigger and heavier than those canoes, rocked violently in the waves, and water spilled over the edge into the boat. A clap of thunder woke Kobi; startled, he climbed from where he had been sleeping and onto my lap.

The timing could not have been worse, because we had

arrived in a part of the lake crowded with hundreds of trees. Bright had to turn off the motor as Mohammed stood in the front, using his bamboo pole to try to push off the lake bottom and through the trees. But the pole was no match for the lake. A huge wave came and crashed the boat against a large trunk. The force of it knocked Teteh and Ebenezer to the floor, and they scrambled back to take a seat, holding tight to the side of the boat.

Another wave came quickly, and once again the *Krachi Queen* was thrown against a tree trunk. The bamboo pole Mohammed was holding was caught between the tree and the boat, and we heard a loud snapping noise before we watched the pole splinter into two pieces. They slipped from Mohammed's grip, and into the raging water. It was gone. He looked at Bright with a face full of worry.

George, Albert, Dave, and Mohammed scrambled to the side of the boat, using their hands to push away from the trees. The next time our boat was thrown against a tree, we heard a large crack. The *Krachi Queen* had been fractured. It was a long break, toward the back of the boat, and we quietly watched the water seeping in, wetting our shoes.

Aimee and I grabbed the kids, and I felt total panic rising in my chest. All I could think was, *Are you kidding me?* Without the bamboo pole, we had no way to maneuver through these trees. We were at nature's mercy. Was this really happening? After everything these kids had survived, were they going to die here in the middle of the lake, on their way to safety?

George yelled out orders to everyone, telling Albert to try to find something in which to wrap his cell phone to keep it dry, in case the boat sank. Bright and Mohammed used all of their strength to push us away from the trees. The kids held tight to one another, crowding together on the bench, their hands intertwined.

After Jantsen died, I thought I no longer feared death. There were, in fact, those times I had even longed for it, if only for the opportunity to see Jantsen again. But that moment, I was absolutely terrified. I felt ill equipped to protect these children and I prayed to God to keep us alive.

For the next twenty minutes, as Aimee and I sat on the floor of the boat holding the children in our arms, the others did their best to push away from the tree stumps. Kobi was the most scared, and he kept his head buried in my lap. Ezekiel, the oldest among the children, rubbed Kobi's back and whispered to him in a reassuring voice. I mustered my courage to do the same, smiling at Regina, who looked to me for a sign that we'd be okay. I didn't feel very convincing, however, because at that moment I didn't know if we'd be okay. The water was continuing to rise in the boat, and every time we got thrown against another tree, I braced myself and waited for the *Krachi Queen* to splinter in two and sink.

It was then that I saw the hawk.

I'm not sure why exactly, but ever since Jantsen died, whenever I'd see a hawk floating gracefully overhead, I had the feeling that he was near, watching over me. Maybe that's crazy, but I'm okay with that, because it brings me comfort. And sitting in the cold water pooling in the bottom of the boat and seeing the lightning reflecting in the children's fearful eyes, I watched the hawk, and knew that we were safe.

When, thirty minutes later, the shore of Kete Krachi finally came into sight, relief surged inside me. Mohammed steered the boat into the shallow waters of the beach, and we lifted the children off the *Krachi Queen*. I knew that if ever there was a moment to stop at the Spyglass for a celebration, as well as a cold beer, this was it. We took our usual table and ordered soft drinks for the kids. They drank their Cokes and orange soda from straws, passing the cold bottles back and forth, giving one another sips. When they finished, we ordered them each another.

On the walk up the hill toward George's house, the kids broke out in song. Kobi held tight to my hand, but the others ran ahead, skipping along the dirt, and kicking stones. Erica was waiting with a huge pot of banku. When she saw us coming, she ran down the driveway and hugged her father and brother tightly. Then she went to work, setting the pot on the ground between two benches. The kids took a seat and dug into the sticky dinner with their hands, dipping the mixture into a bowl of spicy liquid. Long after the older children were finished and had gone to clean up in a small outdoor shower in George's backyard, Kobi kept eating. And eating. When he was finally done, as full as he could be, he ran to find the others.

They stayed awake for hours, enchanted by the simple things: the lantern that lit the darkness, as the electricity was still out; a roll of toilet paper, which they ripped into pieces and passed among themselves. They took Aimee's camera and snapped photos of one another, laughing hysterically at their own images reflected in the camera's screen. Finally, it was time to sleep. George had transformed his previous office into a cozy sleeping area, laid with mats and pillows. Before turning off the light, we knelt there with them and said a prayer.

A prayer of so much gratitude.

―――――

We had to leave the next morning, but none of us was ready to go. The kids were awake by 5 AM, and when I went out to the porch thirty minutes later, dragging my luggage behind me, they put down the bread and cheese they were eating and came to give me a hug. They already looked like different people.

I've always hated good-byes, so after a quick round of hugs for George, Albert, Erica, Anna, and the children, Dave,

Aimee, and I climbed back into the truck and headed out on the daylong trip south. We were mostly quiet on the drive back. I wished that we'd had more time with the kids, but I knew they were in good hands. Anna was going to take them shopping that day for new clothes and shoes. They were well fed and safe. And best of all, for the first day in many years they were not heading out on the lake. They were no longer slaves. Simply children.

We arrived back at the Village of Hope around midnight. When we woke the next morning—Saturday—the kids did not have classes, so I took my coffee out to the porch. Mark was waiting for me. "Ma Pam!" he yelled, running onto my lap. I breathed in his smell: soap and powder.

"How are you?" I asked.

"Fine, thank you. And how are you?" he replied in accented English. And then he stated the reason he had been waiting for me with such anticipation. "You bring me football boots?" he asked, giggling. I laughed and hugged him tightly.

"Maybe today I will see if I can find something."

Aimee came and joined us until Leticia called out that breakfast was ready. Mark sat with us at the dining table, and I offered him a plate of eggs. He shook his head.

"Thank you," he said. "But I am not hungry."

He was not hungry. I don't know if I'd ever heard anything as wonderful in my life.

After breakfast, the other kids arrived at our guesthouse. We sat on the floor of the porch, the kids sipping soft drinks and eating cookies and painting with watercolors I had brought. I asked John Arthur to come inside with me, and I opened Aimee's laptop. I flipped through the photos we had taken of Teteh, Israel, Regina, Ebenezer, Ezekiel, and Kobi.

"I am very happy for them," he said, tears filling his eyes, an unlikely thing for this otherwise stoic young man.

"You're going to write a story about them?" he asked, wiping his eyes.

"Yes," I said. "And you, too."

"When people learn about us, and all of the boys still on the lake, will they do something to help get them?" he asked.

"I don't know," I said. "I hope so."

"Yes," he replied. "I hope so, too."

———

We had one more stop before heading home, and the next morning, before leaving for the airport, we hired a driver to take us to the ocean. The Elmina Castle stands on the western coast of Ghana, about two hours from the Village of Hope. It is a mammoth fortress, and driving up to it, it seems like a mirage of grandiosity amid the total squalor of the surrounding town. Built in 1482 by the Portuguese, it was originally used as a trading post for gold; after the gold trade proved to be immensely profitable for the Portuguese, other European nations began to pay attention. A struggle for control of the castle ensued, and in 1637, after two previously unsuccessful attempts, the Dutch captured Elmina Castle. They remained in control for the next 274 years, until it was ceded to Britain in 1872. By this time, the castle had been transformed into a trading post for what was proving most profitable: slaves.

By the eighteenth century, more than thirty thousand Africans sold into slavery were brought to Elmina Castle. They were captured from all over sub-Saharan Africa and made to march here from thousands of miles away. More than half of the captives did not survive the arduous journey. Those who did were imprisoned here for as long as it took for a ship to arrive, and, in exchange for guns, knives, linens, silk, and beads, the men and women were marched onto the ship and sailed to the Americas to begin—and end—their lives in slavery.

Walking around the huge fortress, which has since been renovated into a museum by the Ghanaian government, is a miserable experience. A tour guide led us through a series of tiny rooms where the captives were kept. They were dug underground and were tiny and dark, with no windows. The prisoners were locked inside, two hundred to a small room, with no space to even lie down. Already weakened from the journey across the desert, they were beaten and starved, ensuring they'd offer no resistance when their time came to be walked through the Door of No Return in chains to a waiting ship. Many people died here of starvation and disease. The rooms had no bathrooms, and people were forced to stand in their own urine and excrement. They were rarely if ever allowed to bathe. The floors of these dungeons are now several inches higher than when the castle was built, after centuries of buildup of filth and excrement. When the tour guide shut the door to demonstrate what it had felt like for them, the panic rose in my chest. I felt like we had been buried alive.

On the upper levels of the castle, the Europeans lived in luxury suites of grand rooms, each with a balcony overlooking a large open courtyard below. Here the captive women were often brought to stand in the sun for hours. In the evening, the officers would laze on their balcony and choose a woman from below. She was then led through a trapdoor to a basement room, where she would be raped. Those who refused to peacefully comply were brought back to the courtyard and chained to a metal hook in the ground, scorching in the hot sun until they either acquiesced or died.

When our tour was over, I walked out to one of the huge terraces that overlooked the town of Elmina. People bathed in the dirty river below, and children carried buckets of river water up a rocky cliff, back toward town. Before me, the ocean stretched out to the horizon, where it was impossible to tell where the water ended and the sky began. I stood there for a while, walking around in the quiet, the breeze from the ocean at my back. I stopped before a plaque fastened to the wall.

IN EVERLASTING MEMORY OF THE ANGUISH OF OUR ANCESTORS. MAY THOSE WHO DIED REST IN PEACE. MAY THOSE WHO RETURNED FIND THEIR ROOTS. MAY HUMANITY NEVER AGAIN PERPETRATE SUCH INJUSTICE AGAINST HUMANITY. WE THE LIVING VOW TO UPHOLD THIS.

I let the words of the final line seep inside of me, and then looked out across the ocean. There, in the distance, were a dozen canoes. Inside one, three young boys hoisted up a net, brimming and swollen with fish. A few minutes later, one pulled off his shirt and pants. He then closed his eyes, held his breath, and dove into the black waters alone.

GRACE

Epilogue

I was recently asked to speak at Crista's college about my work in Ghana. I've hardly gotten any more comfortable speaking in front of a group than that first time, when Penny and I lugged that slide projector to a small luncheon for a handful of women in Neosho. But somehow I muster the courage I need, and afterward I try not to think about how many *ummms* and *you know, liiiiikes* I manage to utter in every speech, as if I'm sixteen.

When I was preparing for this talk, I looked through the dozens of scrapbooks I've put together from all of my travels to try to find the one photograph that most accurately represents the story that I wanted to tell. There are many of Mark, with his shiny skin and huge smile, painting with watercolors. There's John Arthur, with his J.Crew good looks, playing soccer; Sarah and Hagar, preparing dinner for their housemates at the Village of Hope; and little Kobi, who looks almost nothing like the young boy I first met when the assemblyman handed him over to us.

But I didn't choose any of these. Instead, I chose one of

that young boy I met in Atigangome Kope—the one who wore the dirty blue sweatshirt and, from atop a pile of rocks on the shore, watched as the *Krachi Queen* sailed away with his friends. The one we left behind, whose name we didn't even think to get. I don't know what's happened to him, but I think about him often. My guess is that right now, as I write this, he's freezing cold in a canoe, scooping out water or pulling up nets, wondering when he'll eat again. And wondering, perhaps, why he wasn't chosen to come with us.

Nobody has an accurate count, but by some estimates, as many as seven thousand children remain enslaved in Ghana. That may seem like an insurmountable number, but it's not. We just have to keep working, to do what we can, even if that means taking it one child at a time. I truly believe that every positive action sets into motion a series of events, some of which may be beyond anything we might imagine. I did what I did because a *New York Times* reporter named Sharon LaFraniere and a photographer named João Silva thought this issue was worth exploring. Did Sharon imagine when she wrote about Mark that eight weeks later, he'd be eating ice cream at a boarding school in Accra? And so many others have already taken action, such as a particularly inspiring group of fourteen-year-old girls from Long Island, New York. After reading about the problem, they came together to ask the right question: How do we save *one child* from slavery in Ghana? The girls decided to start an organization called One Is Greater Than None, and they made bracelets and necklaces, packaged with information to educate people about the trafficking situation in Ghana, and sold them from wooden tables set up outside the local shopping mall. Within a few months, they had raised enough money to save their first child. Since then, they have rescued seven more and are now working on sponsoring a rescue mission of twenty-five children. I'm so proud of what they've done. I've also seen how seemingly small gestures can make a big difference. After meeting Bright on the *Krachi Queen*, my friend Dave, who came with us to take photographs, donated three hundred dollars to Touch A Life to send Bright back to school. He's now doing great as a student and I have no doubt he'll go on to accomplish wonderful things.

We have ourselves made a lot of progress even during the writing of this book. Kobi, Regina, Ebenezer, Ezekiel, Teteh, and Israel are all doing great. George rented a small house across the street from his own, and the children were moved there to live with a houseparent we hired. It didn't take long to discover that Ezekiel, Ebenezer, and Kobi were incredibly gifted children, and after a few weeks Fred agreed to bring them to the Village of Hope, where they could get the best education possible. The others later joined them there as well. Mark and Kobi, the two youngest, are best buddies, and like brothers; John Arthur and Ezekiel, the two oldest, are always there to help out the others when needed. We still support them, as we will for the remainder of their lives, sending Fred about ninety dollars per child each month to cover the costs of their room, board, tuition, and a portion of the houseparent's salary. We've also donated an additional fifty thousand dollars to Village of Hope to support the construction of a new cottage.

It also quickly became obvious to me that I couldn't keep up with the work in Ghana on my own—there's something about spending twenty minutes studying a blueprint, only to realize it's upside down, that can do that to a person. Thankfully, in fall 2007, our friend Bud Reed came on board as our first employee. Because he was getting Social Security, he didn't require a typical salary, and Randy and I decided that we'd personally pay for his position. We did this for two reasons: After downsizing our house, we had the money; also, it's important to us that people who donate money to Touch A Life know their money goes directly toward helping the kids. Unfortuntately, a few months later, Randy unexpectedly lost his job, and we could no longer afford to keep Bud on staff. But as I've learned, that's the way it goes, and we continue to plug on.

Bud's first order of business as a Touch A Life employee was to go to Africa for a month, which he did in August 2007, to help manage the construction of the Village of Life, which is under way. The first cottage will house twenty children and two houseparents and is scheduled to be completed in the summer of 2008 within just weeks of this writing. We have decided, on George's advice, that the Village of Life will primarily be used as a safe house and vocational training school for older boys rescued off the lake. George and George Junior will work with the locals, asking them to donate their time to educate and teach a trade of interest to the young men. In addition to learning a skill, the boys who live at the Village of Life will work with George and the other members of Pacodep to educate the residents of the local villages about the anti-trafficking law, and help bring more kids to safety.

The project has been exhilarating and very challenging. The first phase of construction was initially estimated to cost about thirty thousand dollars. When it's finished, it will have cost us close to one hundred thousand. We had underestimated the costs of the infrastructure, including bringing electricity to the site, and drilling a well. George Junior, his wife, Rebecca, and their daughter have agreed to live full-time at the Village of Life. They recently called to tell me they are preparing to plant yams and cabbage in the next few weeks in the garden spot they have plowed. They have already built bee boxes to raise honey and have a plan to use a river that is within walking distance for cage fishing.

This past August, Randy and I took Van and Tatum with us to Ghana. Our friend Mai Lai, who started the Children's

Art Village, an arts organization in Los Angeles, organizes an annual week-long arts camp at the Village of Hope. We decided that at nine years old, our kids were ready for their first big trip. Van and Tatum had the time of their lives, and they forged friendships with the rescued children and others that I believe will last a lifetime. I barely saw them during that trip—Van was usually playing basketball or soccer with Kojo, and Richard, and the other boys his age; Tatum was hand-in-hand with Sarah, Hagar, and Regina. They came up with secret handshakes and taught each other songs. Watching them all together—during the afternoon jam sessions when the kids learned to play the flute, or as I sat under a mango tree with Mark on my lap, listening to local musicians play the drums—I was overwhelmed with joy.

My favorite moment of that week occurred on our first day there. Van was walking away with a group of boys and I wanted to get his attention. He was so involved with his new friends that my son—the only Asian boy around—didn't hear me calling for him. Hagar offered to get him and went running in his direction. Tatum yelled after her. "Hagar," she shouted, "he's the one wearing the red shirt." It was so beautiful, and I was filled with such a sense of pride that at nine years old, my daughter was completely unaware of skin color.

At the end of the trip, neither Van or Tatum wanted to leave. Van begged us to stay just six more days. While he was packing his bags to go, he came into our room and asked if he could give Ishmael, his new best friend who lives at the Village of Hope, his St. Louis Cardinals T-shirt. This was no small thing for my son, one of the biggest Cardinals fans I know. I told him it was a good idea and when I went to find him later, the T-shirt was on top of a pile of his other favorite shirts and shorts. He wanted to leave them all behind.

We've also expanded our work in Vietnam, and currently

have 224 children under our care. Of these, seventy-five live full-time in one of six shelters we now operate; the others are in an empowerment program, through which we assist them with school tuition, day care, a feeding program, and vocational training for older students. In Cambodia, my friend Marie has turned her program, Place of Rescue, into a home for sixteen families suffering from AIDS. More than a hundred children live in her orphanage, and eleven elderly women in the "Granny House." She's done this largely on her own, and with her great staff; I certainly would never take any credit for that.

It hasn't all been easy, of course, and I had one of my most challenging experiences in Cambodia this past fall. Aimee and I traveled to Phnom Penh in October to visit Marie and learn more about the realities of the child trafficking industry in Cambodia. While we were there, we visited a former brothel for teenage prostitutes in the Svay Pak district. Walking through the tiny cell-like rooms where the young girls had serviced their clients was a truly harrowing experience. On the second floor, a cement room had been painted in shades of pink. This was where the brothel owners had filmed very young girls for child pornography purposes. Are there even words to express the horror that someone would buy such a video?

We also spent one afternoon with two young women who had been sold by their parents to work in the sex industry. They were scared to speak with us initially and refused to give us their names. One was twenty-one and the other claimed to be eighteen, although she didn't look a day older than fifteen. Both of them had been working as prostitutes for several years, and the night before we met, they each had been with ten different men. For each client, they were paid the equivalent of about three dollars, half of which they had to give to the brothel owner. The rest they sent home to their families.

These young women were so scared and emotionally spent,

and the years of trauma they had endured in their work showed on their faces. The older girl was also addicted to heroin—which is not unusual. Many brothel owners purposefully hook their employees on drugs as a way of keeping them dependent on the work. Hearing the stories of their lives was heartbreaking. The girls could not always convince their clients to wear a condom, and both were too scared to get tested for HIV. They cried openly when discussing how degraded and ashamed they felt every morning, yet when we offered to take them immediately to a safe house for prostitutes, they both refused. The older one didn't want to go because she knew she couldn't get drugs there; she panicked at the idea of it. The younger said her family would starve were it not for the money she sent home each week.

Watching the two of them walk out of our hotel room, their eyes swollen and their tiny frames hunched over with exhaustion, was definitely one of the more difficult experiences I've had since beginning my work with Touch A Life.

I understand the impulse to simply judge these girls as "Asian prostitutes" beyond help, but that's not who they were to me. They were scared, broken girls who could not see any hope. I sometimes imagine how different my life would be had I not fought my desire to judge—if I had looked at Mai on that plane trip simply as an Asian woman who couldn't possibly have anything in common with me, or at George simply as a black man from an impoverished village whom I could never trust wiring money to, or even at the whole of Africa as a continent and a culture I had absolutely no reason to try to understand. Had I done that, I now know, I certainly wouldn't have been the only one to lose out on so much. So would have Van and Tatum. And Haven. And Tuan. And Mark, Kofi, Sarah, Hagar, John Arthur, Kojo, Ezekiel, Ebenezer, Regina, Kobi, Teteh, and Israel. So would have each of the more than thirty adopted kids who come to my pool parties—and all their moms and dads and aunts and uncles. To not judge people based on our differences, but to see the things we share—well, that to me is real grace.

I never thought that Jantsen's death would lead me to grace, and it is my hope that nobody ever has to go through what I went through to arrive there. Even writing this book feels like another step away from Jantsen. I do take comfort in the idea that even one more person will get to know a little about him, but the fact that I can write about his death without crawling to my bed and staying there, curled up in my grief for weeks, shows how far I've come. Of course, in many ways I am happy to be free from that type of grief, but it's a reminder of the distance, and there's still a lot of pain in that.

I often think about my brother-in-law Mike's words that evening on a Florida beach a few weeks after Jantsen died: Your life will definitely be sad, but it's also possible that it will be richer and fuller than ever before. I had found his words almost too hard to believe at the time, but I know now that it's in the moments when we are stripped of everything we identify with that we're forced to consider who we *really* are. It wasn't just my son that I lost; it was my ego, and my fears, and the labels I had allowed myself to be defined by: hairdresser, stay-at-home mom, wife. Yes, I am and was all of those things, but I made the mistake of believing that that was *all* I was. Only when I was forced to abandon those labels, and the limitations I put on myself, was I able to discover a sense of peace and purpose I never thought possible.

Of course, that's not to say that I still don't have many "issues," as Crista would say. I still struggle with the challenges of raising two young children and managing my work with Touch A Life. I definitely still struggle with my desire to please people too much, and there are moments where I fight the more superficial urges that plagued me before Jantsen died. I'm on Jenny Craig right now, for crying out loud—what better sign that I still give in to the pressures of the more superficial side of American culture? But Crista got married last month, to her lovely fiancé Zach, and I did manage to fit into that perfect dress I found.

And I'm still making a lot of mistakes. Recently, I got a call from a woman who had made a donation to Touch A Life in memory of someone she loved. I appreciated it very much, of course, but had forgotten to send her a thank-you letter to acknowledge the donation. She was very angry, and rightly so, and when I heard the pain and anger in her voice when she called to tell me about it, I understood. I hung up, and I felt crushed, and it stayed with me for days. There was once a time when feeling that way—like I had screwed up, and failed this woman—would have made me give up: to throw up my hands and decide that I'm not smart enough to run this nonprofit, and I don't know what I'm doing, and maybe it's finally time to just focus on the laundry and Van and Tatum and all the responsibilities of parenting two nine-year-olds.

But then, a few days later, I received a letter from Tommy Drinnen, who works at the Village of Hope. He was writing to tell me about a young girl named Salamatu. She's in second grade and had come to the Village of Hope after being orphaned. As Tommy explained, she is the type of girl who can hide no emotion. Every time something good happens to her, she jumps up and down with excitement. Well, she had received some stickers in the mail as a gift from an American couple, and she was so excited that she ran around the grounds clapping and showing everyone her gift. She wanted to write the couple a thank-you letter, and after she did, she took every single sticker that she had received and plastered them on the paper. She gave away her entire gift.

As I think about my life, and everything I've faced since los-ing Jantsen, I've come to understand that maybe Salamatu can teach us all a lesson. Maybe the answer to grief, or to feeling lost, is to do what she did: to give recklessly and passionately, to the point where people have to say, "You're crazy! That is enough! Stop giving!" And yet we go on, and we give some more. I firmly believe that in those acts of giving—when you have given away your very last sticker—you become open to receiving life's most tremendous blessings.

I don't think it's a coincidence that I received Tommy's letter just when I was beginning to doubt myself. I recently experienced another coincidence like this. For twelve years I have been wearing Obsession, the perfume by Calvin Klein. I never even tried anything else, I loved it so much, and it sort of became part of me. I was Obsession. But a few weeks before New Year's I found myself thinking that maybe it was time for a new perfume. I didn't mention this to anyone, but on New Year's Day, Randy handed me a package. It was perfume called Euphoria.

I think I'm ready to be open to that.

———

PS: If you want to learn more about Touch A Life, please visit our Web site at www.touchalifekids.org.

Afterword

March 2011

A few days ago, I was rushing to get Van and Tatum fed and out the door for school, when I heard the chime of a new e-mail arriving on my cell phone. It was a message from Randy, writing from Ghana.

I waited until the kids were out the door before pouring myself a fresh cup of coffee and opening the e-mail. "It's so wonderful to be here," my husband wrote. He'd left three days earlier. A rare break at work had given him a few free days, and he had decided that he wanted to spend them in Ghana, visiting the children at the Village of Hope before heading up north to Kete Krachi and the Village of Life, the residential facility for forty-five children on the shores of Lake Volta, which we completed in 2009. "I'm sitting on the porch in front of Jantsen's House at the Village of Life, watching a group of boys play soccer. These kids amaze me. They're all doing so well, and it's times like these that I question how I can return to corporate life, when this is all I want to be doing."

I felt a pang of jealousy that I wasn't there with him, but I could hardly complain. In the two years since *Jantsen's Gift* was published, I have been back to Ghana ten times, unable to stay away for too long. I often travel with others—mostly people who have been touched by what they've learned about our work in Ghana, and want to go see for themselves what this is all about. During each visit, I spend as much time as I can with the children at the Village of Hope. The Magnificent Seven are, well, even more magnificent now, and it's been such a pleasure, and a real treasure, to watch them transform into young men and women. Ebenezer, Ezekiel, Teteh, Israel, Regina, and Kobi are also now at the Village of Hope. Each of them speaks fluent English and it's a rare week that goes by that I won't get a text message or call from one of the children, having convinced their houseparent to let them use their phone to call me, just to tell Ma Pam hello.

Of course, as is typical with our work with Touch A Life, the hope I feel after reading Randy's e-mail is replaced far too soon with the familiar, nagging sense of urgency. Because two days after receiving that e-mail, I receive another, this one far more disheartening. "I just returned from the lake, and feel exhausted and spent. We found a very young boy today—he couldn't have been older than four—hiding under the nets in one of the boats. He was naked and terrified and as soon as his master banked the boat, he ran off screaming. George thinks that they are beginning to tell the trafficked children that the white people are coming to take them away and kill them. It's very disturbing. I'm heading back to the hotel. The electricity has been out every night. Tell the kids hello and know how much I love you guys."

Attached to the e-mail was a photo that Randy had somehow captured of the boy. His large, red-rimmed eyes poked out from under the gauzy fishing net, which he had wrapped around himself. All day, the image stayed with me, and haunted me the way the first photo I saw of Mark had. Despite the number of times I've been to Lake Volta, I have never gotten used to seeing the thousands of children who remain enslaved. But images like this, and the trips I take, also drive me to work harder, and that evening, as I drove to speak to a group of college students about my work with Touch A Life, I reminded myself that I am doing everything I can.

In the last two years, we've gone on to rescue seventy-five more children, bringing the total number of children we've helped rescue from slavery in Ghana to eighty-seven. This allows the Village of Life to serve as a safe house for additional kids that we are now working to rescue.

Our newest kids—who range in age from five to twenty—are now an important part of our growing family. They all amaze me and it truly floors me to watch how quickly they transform from terrified, neglected children to happy, healthy little souls— how little they need to be happy. It has become a goal of ours to give them whatever they need to succeed: the best education, the very best medical care, and the best staff of people who will love them and help them remember how special they are.

My favorite trip the past two years was the one I took in November. During a previous visit, some medical personnel who travelled with me had evaluated the children, and discovered that eleven of the boys were suffering from hernias that had gone untreated and were making their lives miserable. One young boy named Moses, whom we rescued in 2009, was so affected by the hernia that it looked as if he had a large stick jutting out of his stomach. Each surgery went great, and afterwards, the children recovered under the loving care of their houseparents. Moses was so proud afterward that he walked around Village of Life lifting his shirt, showing everyone his new, flat stomach.

Two of my friends, Lisa Bloecher and Stacey Young, decided they would accompany me on this trip. Before we left, they had received donations of personalized, handmade quilts for all the TAL kids, embroidered with each child's name. When we passed the blankets out, it was unbelievable to witness how much they appreciated the simple idea that they now had their very own bedding. Each night, as I walked through the dorms, bidding the children good night, I relished watching them crawl under the quilts.

Seeing how much the boys had gained from their hernia surgeries, I decided during my next trip to Ghana that I would take all of the older girls to their first gynecologist appointment. The doctor we saw is German, and his waiting room was full of foreign women. I noticed that at first, the girls were shy—intimidated, even—to be surrounded by these older, well-dressed white women. But then, slowly, that began to change. The girls sat quietly, taking in their surroundings, and then they began to mimic what the women around them were doing: properly flipping through the magazines, buying bottled water from the machine, and quietly engaging with each other in conversation. It was priceless.

We stayed for a night in a hotel and when our day was finished, I took the elevator upstairs with Sara and Hagar and walked them to their room.

"Remember to be dressed and ready to go tomorrow morning by eight," I said.

They both looked at each other and then Hagar spoke. "Ma Pam, what are our chores at this house?"

"You don't have chores," I told them. "You are guests here."

They both smiled. "We can sleep until 6:30!" Hagar said. It is moments like this when I am reminded about the many things I still take for granted, and how often I can forget how sheltered and small their world still is. It makes me want to give them everything I can, to help them understand that there is a big world out there and they are smart enough, and equipped enough, to explore and embrace as much of it as they want. These kids have been told their whole lives that they are worthless children—slaves—and it is going to take time and a steady stream of love to convince them how amazingly special they are. That's a job I will never tire of doing.

Many days I wish that were my *only* job, but there are many other things on our plate. We continue to struggle with the problem of where to place the children we rescue from the lake. The lack of a permanent placement remains the most significant obstacle that keeps us from being able to rescue more children. To help address this, we are in the process of purchasing ten acres of land on the Gulf of Guinea, not too far from the Village of Hope, where we will build a residential facility for one hundred children. The children—all former slaves—will live together in houses large enough for sixteen children and a set of houseparents. They will attend school at the Village of Hope and come home to this facility, where there will be an art center, a music room, and a computer lab. And, of course, plenty of land to run around and ride bicycles.

———

When we were thinking about titles for this book, we struggled at first, trying to find the right idea to best capture the story. Little did I know at the time how a propos the title we chose would be. Just as I feel that Jantsen's memorial fund—and his life—has been a gift to so many children around the world, this book has been such a tremendous gift to me. So many people were moved to donate to Touch A Life and to our work in Vietnam and Ghana, and it is largely because of the checks we've received from readers that we have been able to continue our work and bring seventy-five additional children to safety in the last two years. Every time a check arrives with a note saying how much they loved the book, I am filled with a tremendous sense of gratitude I still can't describe.

These last few years, I've had the privilege of traveling to many places across the country that I'd never visited before, invited to speak about my life. It's been such a pleasure, and a true gift, to meet people who have been touched by my story—whether in person, or through the letters and e-mails I've received.

I've also found that people have gotten something else from my story—something that I was not expecting. So many people have told me that after reading *Jantsen's Gift*, they finally felt they had the courage to do what they needed to follow their dreams. I have heard stories about those who have quit their jobs to pursue the career they've always wanted, or the business idea that kept poking them for years, or that they have finally found the courage to take the trip they've long dreamed of taking. I love hearing how this story has helped people take a careful look at their life, and abandon elements of themselves that may have never really fit them, or were simply their way of trying to appear to be something that never felt genuine.

I've also had the opportunity to meet so many people who have lost children and who have, through this book, been able to see a way out of the grief, at least for a few moments at a time. The best part is when people ask me about Jantsen. It's now been nearly twelve years since he died, and every time I hear a stranger mention his name to me, I get to have the experience of speaking about him again. Too often, when people die—especially when they die too young—we are afraid to speak of them. But I love to speak about Jantsen every chance I get. I still, of course, struggle with my grief sometimes. My friend Ron, who lost his son Connor in February 2009, said it this way to me once: I feel like the train we are on has two rails;

the left is sadness (deep, deep sadness) and the right is wonderful memories. The left is anguish, the right hope. The left anger, the right trust. The left sorrow, the right peace. Neither rail invalidates the other. Neither excludes the other. We travel them both, side by side. This is our life as grieving parents.

Ron's wife, Nan, accompanied me on one of my trips to Ghana, during a time when she was experiencing tremendous grief. I was so grateful to have been able to bring her along with me, and to be there with her during some of her darkest times. I watched as the kids surrounded her every morning and competed for her attention. And I watched, too, as she began to find herself again in the presence of these children. It wasn't until I got home that I realized that I had been able to offer Nan what Carol had offered me after Jantsen died: a trip to a foreign country and a newfound love for life. Nan repeatedly thanks me for saving her life. But I did not save her life. The Touch A Life kids did, just like they are saving mine every day.

As for me, I turn forty-nine in a few weeks, and to be honest, I cannot wait for this next decade of life. In December 2008, Randy took a new job and we moved to Dallas. The weather here is so much milder than Missouri, and I love the energy that comes with living near a big city. Randy and I continue to give each other as much grace as possible, and that seems to work for us. He no longer needs to mow the lawn because we have a yard the size of a bathtub. His choice of freedom is to just hop on his Harley and take off for the day.

And I find that I go less often these days to the gold wingback chair. Instead, I am able to find God, and a sense of grace, in broader ways. Each morning, Randy and I take our dog Truman on a walk, and in the quiet of the mornings, I feel a sense of peace that grounds me. Since writing the book, I have lost my nephew Dallas, who was just twenty-eight when he died, and also my dad. The last decade of my dad's life was spent caring for my nephew, who battled a rare bone disease. I know it knocked the wind out of both my parents when Jantsen died, but Dallas's long battle with a painful disease really took a toll on them. When my dad died, the only thing that was left to clean up after his life was a limited amount of clothes in his closet and a messy workshop that my mom was never allowed to touch. He left my mother well-cared for. They were debt free, lived in a modest, comfortable home that he always maintained, and cultivated close friendships with a long list of faithful friends. He did not value "stuff," just relationships. And through his death, I have been reminded once again that a simple life is the best one.

It was very hard for me in the days and weeks after Dallas and my dad died, but in those days—and on other days when I just cannot find the energy or excitement for life—I remind myself that I am here on earth for a limited time, and my role is to love and cultivate relationships with others in simple, easy acts of love and kindness.

I often find myself thinking about Jantsen, and where he'd be if he were still alive. He'd be twenty-seven now. A college graduate, probably. Married, perhaps. Possibly even a father. It is difficult in these moments, thinking about how much we've all lost. But then, instead, I remind myself to think about all the people who have been touched by his life, by how much he has contributed to this world. I would have been proud of him, whatever path he may have chosen. But I also know that I'm incredibly proud of him still—by how many lives he has touched, and by what great things his life has brought about. I was reminded of this just this past November, as I was sitting alone with Mark in his room, getting him ready for bed. He asked for one more story and before climbing onto my lap, he grabbed *The Cat In the Hat* from the pile. Then he read the story to me, in perfect English. Holding him that night, I sat in the near darkness, soaking in the miracle of it all: the chance to hold this little boy, to hear him read aloud to me, to hear him giggle at the words, and to know that he is safe.

That is, truly, Jantsen's gift. And what a wonderful gift it has been.

Reading Group Guide
Discussion Questions

1. When Pam was in her twenties and thirties, she'd accepted certain labels about herself, and believed she could be content "if only..." What was holding Pam back and what are some of the labels and *if only*'s that hold you back?

2. After Jantsen's death, Pam begins to explore different cultural beliefs surrounding death and to question American Christian traditions she had previously taken for granted. With what does Pam take issue and why? Do you agree with her? Why or why not?

3. One way Pam deals with her anger and grief after Jantsen's death is by "screaming" at God. Pam is a spiritual person, but she admits that before Jantsen's death she "hadn't the faintest idea of who God was." What does she mean and how does Pam's relationship with God and religion change over the course of the book?

4. Pam was forced to confront a lot of fears about travelling when she decided to go to Vietnam. But in confronting these fears, she was eventually able to accomplish great things. What are your fears, and have they ever held you back?

5. When Pam discovers she is seated next to Mia Lang on the plane to Vietnam, she remembers a quote she once read: "A coincidence is a small miracle in which God chooses to remain anonymous." Do you agree that Pam's seat on the airplane is a "small miracle"? Have you ever had a similar experience to Pam, where a seemingly insignificant coincidence changed the course of your life?

6. Pam was very honest throughout the book about the grief she experienced and how it impacted her. How did Pam's marriage to Randy change after Jantsen's death? And how did Jantsen's death affect Pam's relationship with her adopted daughter, Crista? Why do you think tragedy strengthens some relationships and tests others?

7. Toward the middle of the book, Pam is ambivalent about going on a trip to Cambodia because she doesn't want to be a "horrible, neglectful mother" to Van. However, she ultimately concluded that "being a good mom meant showing my children that the world was bigger than our family." Do you think Pam made the right decision? What do you think it means to be a good mother?

8. When Pam first begins fundraising for Touch A Life, people ask her why she chooses to help children in other countries before helping American children. How does Pam answer this question? Do you agree with her reasoning?

9. While trying to obtain Tuan's medical visa, Pam jokes that she has become the "crazy lady from Missouri." Time and again, Pam refuses to give up on her goals, even when the situation appears hopeless. How much of Pam's success can be attributed to her persistence alone? Can persistence

help us achieve anything we set our minds to, or is it only part of the equation?

10. Toward the end of the book, Pam quotes John Ruskin: "Every increased possession loads us with a new weariness." Pam finds much truth in this statement. Why? Do you agree that material possessions can often be a burden?

11. When Pam first reads about Mark Kwadwo in the *New York Times*, she feels compelled to help him immediately. Why does Mark's story move Pam to act? Have you ever felt a similar urge? How did you respond?

12. Pam writes, "I never thought that Jantsen's death would lead me to grace, and it is my hope that nobody ever has to go through what I went through to get there." Do you think people must experience tragedy or loss before they are truly willing to examine their lives or take drastic steps to change their lives?

13. At the end of the book, Pam muses, "Maybe the answer to grief, or to feeling lost, is to give recklessly and passionately." What does Pam mean? Do you agree that giving may be the best way to overcome grief or loss?